The Successful Craftsman

BY THE SAME AUTHOR:

Old Ways of Working Wood
The Picture-Skin Story
The Art of Blacksmithing
Only the Names Remain

The Successful Craftsman

Making Your Craft Your Business

By Alex W. Bealer

With Illustrations by the Author

BARRE PUBLISHING

Barre, Massachusetts
Distributed by Crown Publishers, Inc.
New York

Photographs: Evon Streetman: pages 16, 32, 48, 128, 142, 156, 186, 214, 256; Fred H. Lines: pages 38, 54, 68, 76, 86, 92, 100, 106, 116, 136, 234, 244.

Printed in the United States of America
Library of Congress Catalog Card Number: 73–81741
Published simultaneously in Canada by General Publishing Company Limited.
Inquiries should be addressed to Crown Publishers, Inc., 419 Park Avenue South, New York, N.Y. 10016.
First Edition

TO THE MEMORY OF SALLY ADAMS

Who did as much as anyone I know intelligently to lead, direct, and sometimes to push her fellow craftsmen to higher standards of quality and design. She contributed much to the growing renaissance of the crafts.

Contents

Introduction

THIS is not a book about how to do crafts. It is about what to do with them; what is required to make any of the crafts treated herein a way of life, a source of livelihood, a serious profession in this day of automated technology and mass production. This book is designed to be a practical guide on such ghastly subjects as costs and capitalization, prices and merchandising, and where to buy and where to sell. Perhaps its major purpose is to provide some direction to aspiring craftsmen as to how they may survive, and ultimately how the crafts may survive as a living, relevant, important part of American life.

There is no doubt that in the 1970s the United States is experiencing a revival of the crafts. Such a revival is happening here, perhaps, because we had gotten farther away from the everyday need of craftsmanship than the less progressive, less industrialized societies in Europe, Asia, and Latin America. After all, the American way of life has been based on mass production, mass selling, and mass distribution for many generations. It has brought us material riches and the comforts thereof, the resources for education and jobs, and plenty of food on a national basis most of the time. It has earned us the envy of most other nations, but it has also given us the strength to help keep the world in some sort of order. Our position has not been all bad.

But our lot, between 1840, roughly the beginning of the industrial revolution in this country, and World War II, when many new scientific and industrial concepts were developed, has brought a rather natural reaction against the impersonality of machine-made, mass-produced items to wear and use and look at. This reaction has given great impetus to the revival of craftsmanship. We want things that reflect our individual personalities, things that can only be produced one at a time with hand labor. Only the crafts can fulfill this need.

Fortunately, the crafts never wholly died out in America. In certain areas of our country, such as Southern Appalachia, craftsmanship survived as a way of life until the 1940s. In addition we have had the opportunity to see and buy and enjoy the craftsmanship of Europe and Mexico and Africa during our periods of progress. And there have always been, despite machines, a few fine craftsmen in the population centers of our country who continued to make fine ironwork and furniture and pottery to sell to the more affluent among us. These people and the skills and attitudes they preserved have been the bridge between the pre-1840 age of craftsmanship and the revival of interest in the crafts which we are experiencing in the 1970s.

Perhaps we should really consider craft activity today as a rebirth, a renaissance, rather than a revival, however, for our modern craftsmen simply cannot re-create the old. We have gone too far for that.

The crafts have positive values to contribute to the world of the late twentieth century. These contributions will not be made, however, unless the new craftsmen face the realities of their age. They must realize, for instance, that the machine and mass production, against which they compete to some degree, are not going to disappear. Production time, as set by the machine, is an immutable factor in the pricing and selling of goods, and without sales the craftsman cannot expect to survive as an independent artist and crafts cannot be reborn.

The new craftsmen must realize, too, that it is not sheer labor that makes craftsmanship valuable to the world, but its qualities of intellect, art, and inspiration. Design, made palpable by techniques forever denied a machine, is the basic factor, and part of the social value of craft design lies in the fact that it demonstrates the remarkable versatility of the human body and mind; the ability to make each object unique; the compatibility of handmade objects and individual personalities; and the comfort that such objects give to people.

Such a goal ideally calls for crafts that are entirely made by hand from raw material to finished object. Few modern craftsmen can afford the time for complete hand processing, however. Potters might, for many very successful ceramicists prefer a kick wheel to an electrically driven wheel, but after the pot is made most modern potters use gas or oil to fire the kilns and certainly these fuels must be bought. Weavers must weave by hand and a few spin their own yarns by hand, but when a weaver considers charging for the time needed to spin, in addition to the painstaking hours needed for the actual weaving, the price of the objects gets so high that the market becomes terribly limited, thus limiting the number of weavers needed to satisfy it.

The point is this: the modern craftsman may compromise on his equipment in regard to hand work so long as his design and actual hand work retain and add to the standards which make handcraftsmanship desirable and unique.

Certainly the furniture maker must buy his boards from mills rather than cut his trees and pit-saw his lumber by hand. He needs a bench saw in his shop to rip his boards into proper widths in 1/10 the time this task requires with a hand saw. When new tools are developed which give the craftsman more time to apply to the artistic aspects of his work, he should acquire the tools. Such compromise will in no way affect the quality of his work but only allow him to produce more good work in a lifetime.

The modern blacksmith must use an electric blower instead of a bellows, regardless of how comforting the use of a bellows may be. He should acquire a trip hammer to allow him to do much more work in a single heat to save time and increase production, regardless of the irreducible minimum time needed to heat his iron.

The modern craftsman cannot take this era back to the age of pure handcraftsmanship because he lives in an age of machines. He may normally use machines to help him conserve the basic values of craftsmanship and project them into the future. Machines will help him enjoy a good life and a good living and will contribute much to the society of his modern age. In most of the crafts, he won't be able to without some machinery.

Let it be emphasized, though, that in his training the modern craftsman in any field should gain as much experience as possible in learning the entire processing of an item using only hand tools.

Such training will help him appreciate how machinery may help him, and will develop in him certain standards that will keep his work honest.

Actually, the good craftsman of any age has always needed the proper attitude. Attitude is really much more important than technique, for the technique is wasted if the attitude is wrong. And the craftsman must develop the same attitudes toward precision, proportion, form and color and rhythm, the same basic contrasts and harmony as a fine painter or musician or sculptor demonstrates. He may become content with his work but he should never be wholly satisfied. He must look upon his craft not as individual pieces but as a lifetime's body of work. And he should continually try to improve. Hubris is the ruination of good craftsmanship and good men. Arrogance is anathema.

And helping, teaching, those who show a genuine desire to learn can sometimes be the best training a craftsman can acquire.

There are suggestions in this book on sources of training for each of the crafts treated herein (see Appendix, p. 271). But the modern craftsman should be cautioned about becoming too specialized. He should really learn as much as time and interest allow about all crafts. For the crafts are siblings of a sort, and none is entirely isolated from the others. The blacksmith can likely learn something from the embroiderer, and the glassblower from the candlemaker.

While this book should give a measure of direction to those who wish to make a living in the crafts, it is also hoped that it will be of value to those who like to produce good craftsmanship for its innate pleasure, or who wish to make things on a part-time basis for sale. For selling something one has made is often more satisfying than the money involved, although the money may buttress the satisfaction.

In the 1970s, social attitudes are changing in the United States and in other parts of the world. The more prosperous European nations seem to be putting the crafts aside in order to reach the rather sterile social state which has driven Americans back to the crafts. In a few years the United States may well have to make its own crafts or not have them at all, but we seem to be preparing for this eventuality.

Perhaps we can do something with it, more than the older, stabler nations of the world. For ours is a most heterogeneous society. We have inherited traditional designs and craft techniques from all these older societies and mixed them up together. The result may be a stronger sense of craft art than the world has seen since the Crusades. And the serious readers of this and other books may be the ones who make the renaissance of crafts real and lasting and beautiful for us all.

It is a matter of sharing one's talents, and that, too, is beautiful.

1
Textiles

CHAPTER I

The Weaver

THE weaver in twentieth-century America is far more than a lonely cotter toiling over his loom by candlelight to make a precarious living selling his goods by the yard to a nearby merchant. Certainly the toil is still there, perhaps to a greater degree than ever before, but it is a most satisfying toil, and many of the traditional techniques have been retained and applied to creating modern design. Now the traditional handwoven patterns have largely disappeared, for textile factories can duplicate these for clothing, bed coverings, and all the many uses of cloth far more inexpensively than the hand weaver. So the weaver, traditional and ancient as is his craft, has become an artist more than most craftsmen have. As a consequence he has far more problems in selling his production at a price which pays him adequately for his time at the loom. On the other hand, the pressure of being an artist, of having to come up with original designs, has greatly stimulated the imagination of the weaving community and resulted in much unusual and distinctive art.

There are still some weavers in Europe and America who maintain the traditions of the trade by continuing to produce handwoven fabrics for clothing, such as Harris tweed, and for expensive draperies and upholstery. These fine fabrics have a distinction forever denied machine-made fabrics, but they are quite expensive and can almost be duplicated by machines at far less cost.

In the United States the weaver's alternative is to offer unique pieces of work, both functional and decorative. One product of the hand loom, for instance, might be a set of unique table mats. Another, harking back to early America, might be wool coverlets and bedspreads. Some weavers produce handwoven ponchos, capes, or pouches, while others make belts or rugs. Many, however, responding to the acceptance of weaving as an art, produce an infinite variety of wall hangings whose function is solely decorative, and demonstrate that the medium of warp and weft can result in colorful, abstract wall decorations with textures quite beyond the capability of paint, pastel, or sculptural materials and sometimes with the dimensional qualities of sculpture. Wall hangings, however, have rather limited acceptance and, while growing as architectural items, still have not developed a definable market, such as that for paintings, among homeowners, art collectors, and aficionados.

It seems, to a large extent because of the cost of labor, that smaller, simpler, woven items sell best, especially articles of clothing, bed coverings, or seat coverings for furniture.

Almost every craft school offers extensive training in weaving of every type. Indeed, because weavers do not generally fare as well as other craftsmen in selling their production, many have fallen back on teaching as a means of supplementing income from sales or commissions. Many outstanding weavers and weaving teachers have been awarded grants and fellowships for research into the equipment and techniques of ancient and primitive weaving all over the world; their main objective is often to correlate technique and design to stimulate the creation of imaginative modern design on the loom.

The weaving teachers in craft schools and universities generally are most stimulating. They offer the basic techniques of weaving, often teaching the ancient techniques of carding and spinning as well as the methods of setting up the loom and creating patterns in the fabric. Most weaving courses, especially within universities, offer workshops on the use of different types of looms, primitive and advanced, plus instruction in tapestry, basket making, and other specialties of the field. In addition, modern weaving courses utilize imaginative new effects through the inclusion of natural materials such as grasses, leaves, and seashells.

Virtually all courses of instruction in weaving make available to students the types and sizes of looms, spinning wheels, carders, dye pots, and other equipment necessary to the weaver's art. Instructors are knowledgeable and well qualified to advise aspiring weavers of the sources and prices of the equipment best suited to individual skills and interests.

The American Crafts Council will send upon request and for a small sum a list of schools and universities which offer courses in weaving.

When instruction is completed and shop is planned, the weaver should choose the equipment best suited to his temperament and capital. There are several very good loom manufacturers in the United States and even more in Europe, most of whom offer looms of different function and complexity. A small table loom which is capable of producing quite complicated designs up to about 24 inches wide will cost around $150. Table looms may usually be folded for storage in a closet and are ideal for working in a small space.

Many weavers, however, object to spending capital on small looms when a larger floor loom may be acquired that will greatly increase the variety of design and is far more versatile in every way than a table loom. Narrow looms are considered better for narrow work, however, because a narrow band of warp on a wide loom will sometimes bend the beam, making it impossible to maintain equal tautness for each warp thread as the finished work is wound up. Larger standing looms cost from $225 to $600, depending on width and the number of harnesses.

There are several factors in deciding the type of loom with which to initiate a career in weaving. First of all, the question may be decided by available capital. If one is determined to weave and cannot afford equipment larger than a table loom, then he should acquire the table loom and produce within its limitations until enough capital is accumulated to buy a larger type.

Space is also a factor. Weaving does not require the space of a blacksmith's, potter's, or glassblower's shop, but the weaving room should certainly not be unduly cramped. If the weaving room is spacious enough a large loom will be quite suitable so long as it does not crowd the space. It is well to remember that one might want room for storing yarns and other materials, or for displaying the products of the loom or, in some cases, for a spinning wheel, warping board, and other equipment favored by the individual weaver.

Also, the specialty of the weaver should be considered. Belts, for instance, may be woven on a 40-inch, 8-treadle loom, but they may also be woven on a narrow, uncomplicated belt loom which may easily be stored in a closet when not in use. Therefore, it would be foolish for a weaver to buy a large, expensive loom if he can find a market only for belts or prefers designing and weaving belts above all other types of production.

Other equipment might be required by some weavers. Some delight in spinning their own yarn from wool, cotton, or flax and must have a suitable spinning wheel for this restful activity.

The spinner also needs at least one pair of carders or a small, efficient modern carding machine, all of which are available from a number of sources listed in the back of this chapter, and a bench or chair on which to sit while carding wool, cotton, or flax. A basket, the traditional container, a sack, or even a large discarded cardboard carton is needed to hold the raw material before it is carded and another might be useful for holding the carded material until it is spun. A pair of carders cost $6, a carding machine, $30.

After spinning, the finished yarn must be wound on a large vertical or horizontal skein winder which may be bought for under $30

Homemade warping tree

from a commercial source listed in the appendix of this chapter or from a home craftsman. Skein winders are not complicated in design or construction. Any weaver, whether he spins his own yarn or not, will need a large warping board or tree on which to wind and measure the warp before setting up the loom. These may be bought or made at home. A warping board may be made from 1- by 2-inch pine boards, fitted carefully together as shown in the sketch. Cost of material should be no more than $7.50 at most lumber stores.

Weavers of modern bent who specialize in wall hangings, belts, and other items of contemporary design will need a supply of heavy needles and several pairs of heavy and light scissors, all of which are available from department or notion or sewing stores. Needles cost about 39¢ a package; scissors range from $1.50 to $8 a pair.

Other essential equipment needed by weavers is shuttles in three different forms for different uses. A rug shuttle, used with heavy yarn for weaving heavy fabrics and rugs, is no more than two thin boards from 8 to 18 inches long joined transversely by three small dowels. Rug shuttles are usually available by mail order from the suppliers listed in the appendix to this chapter for from $2.50 to $4. Sometimes they may be bought at craft centers.

Stick shuttles, for weaving narrow pieces and for table looms, may be homemade from any piece of thin board about 2 inches wide. They are also sold at craft centers and may be ordered from weaving supply houses by mail for about 65¢ to $1 each.

Boat shuttles are the most generally used type. They come in several sizes, each with a bobbin, on which the yarn is wound, which is inserted in the shuttle. This type of shuttle may be found at the same supply sources as other weaving equipment. It sells, complete with bobbin, for from $3.50 to $8 each. Additional bobbins may be purchased for about 25¢ each.

A bobbin winder, either hand- or electrically operated, considerably speeds the job of correctly winding yarn on the bobbin. This tool sells for about $7 for a hand-operated winder; for about $35 for an electrically operated winder from suppliers listed at the back of this chapter.

And for winding the warp on the warping board, a spool rack is a great aid. As the sketch shows, this is a vertical frame, on

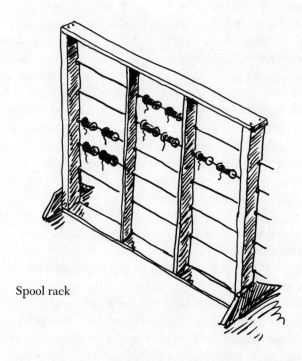

Spool rack

standards, with thin rods held horizontally in holes or notches cut
into the upright members of the frame. Spools are held on the rod,
to be unwound easily as the warp is wound. Spool racks may be
homemade from about $10 worth of wood and rods, which may be
purchased at retail lumber dealers. They may be bought ready-
made from weaving supply houses for from $30 to $40, depending
on size.

Loom benches, high enough for the weaver to comfortably
operate the loom, particularly for table and foot looms, fit a variety of forms and may be homemade or readymade. Homemade
benches, similar to the sketch, may be constructed from about $6
worth of lumber from a retail lumber store. Readymade benches,
available from regular weaving supply houses, may be ordered at
a price of about $25.

Loom bench

The ideal place in which to weave is a separate weaving studio much like the sheds found on the feudal landholdings of the jarls (or chieftains) in ancient Scandinavia. The size of a detached studio should depend on the variety of activity being done and the number of weavers using it. One weaver with several looms for different purposes will need as large a shed as that for several weavers with one loom apiece. Cost of building or renting such a studio must be investigated through local builders or real estate firms.

A separate studio, however nice, is not usually practical when judged purely from the standpoint of capital expenditure. A regular frame building, weather-boarded outside and finished inside with water and electrical connections, can hardly be built in the 1970s without an expenditure of a couple of thousand dollars for material and an additional two or three thousand for labor. Small steel buildings suitable for studios may be bought and built for perhaps a thousand dollars, but again the installation of electricity and water can easily run the cost up another couple of thousand. Depending on locality, adequate space can be rented in a store or storage building for from $50 to $200 a month. Renting requires less capital and the work space may be changed easily if conditions are not satisfactory.

Often a specialized weaver can easily adapt an extra bedroom or unused attic or basement space for weaving. Those who weave yard goods, as opposed to hangings and mats of limited length, must be careful to have enough space to conveniently set up the long warp without undue tangling.

Weaving is not the spectator craft that potting, iron-working, and jewelry making are: one cannot anticipate the end in weaving as in these other crafts. This quality makes it easier for the weaver to choose his place of work without having to consider its access and appeal to the public. He can work far from the beaten track so long as he has an accessible spot at which to display his work for sale.

Many, particularly the more artistic weavers, dye their own yarns to acquire exactly the harmony of color needed for fabrics or wall hangings. Dyeing requires several dye pots of stainless steel, plastic, enameled steel, or aluminum, a drying rack—often no more than a board with pegs or nails driven into it—and a space where the drippings from the freshly dyed yarn will not disrupt the other functions of the weaving room.

Plastic pails, suitable for cold dyeing, may be purchased at hardware stores for about $3.50 for an 8- to 10-gallon size, and galvanized pails cost about the same. Enamel pails of the same size may be purchased at hardware stores for around $4.50 each. Cast-iron pots, available at hardware stores for about $5 for a 3-gallon size, are sometimes used for the mordant effect they give the color.

Hot dyeing can often be done away from the weaving room, perhaps in a garage, carport, or even outdoors in good weather if a source of heat for water is available.

Modern dyes, of which the best are made in Germany, may be bought at craft supply houses in large cities or ordered from the suppliers listed for about 25¢ a packet. Dyes are also available at drug stores, department stores, and fabric and sewing centers for about the same price.

At one time the materials for weaving were limited indeed, consisting of cotton, wool, and flax. Since World War II, however, a host of new synthetic yarns, including even spun glass, have appeared on the market. In addition, modern abstract weavers consider any material fair game for the loom and have adapted all manner of things to the ancient wedding of warp and weft. Exotic grasses are a favorite among many weavers, as are small clay beads, seeds of the sort that can be included in the weaving process, materials such as wire of precious metals, strips of leather, plastics of various sorts, bits of wood, fur strips, feathers, and manufactured objects. Much of this exotic material may be gathered at no cost.

Fur and feathers may be purchased from millinery supply houses or furrier shops found in large cities, or ordered by mail from suppliers listed in the appendix to this chapter for varying prices according to the type of feathers and fur. Leather may be gotten from leather supply wholesalers, from craft shops, or from leather retail chains such as Tandy's Leather Shops, which are located in large cities all over the country. One may order by mail from Tandy's also. Write to Tandy's, P.O. Box 791, Fort Worth, Texas 76101, for a free catalog and price list.

During the 1970s weavers have sometimes produced a basic item and then had it embellished by other craftsmen, such as silversmiths and enamelers, to create a unique art object. A visit to the Museum of Contemporary Crafts and the American Crafts Council offices in New York, or to any of the university art departments and craft schools such as Penland Crafts School, Penland, North Carolina, will provide the aspiring weaver with infinite ideas about the directions being taken by modern weavers, true artists as well as the craftsmen.

Wool yarn costs from $5 to $16 a pound, and very good yarn from Sweden, for example, can be purchased at about $6 or $7 a pound. Linen yarn costs $2 to $4 a pound. Depending on the size of the yarn a pound is the equivalent of 200 to 3,000 yards. Cotton yarn is seldom used in handweaving and is not readily available. All available yarn may be ordered from the suppliers listed in the back of this chapter.

Perhaps because machine-made fabrics are so taken for granted or because hand weaving is expensive, the weaver seems to have more trouble selling his production than most other craftsmen. Unfortunately, the public often does not understand the high cost of materials in woven objects and also does not understand that a great deal of time is needed to produce a piece of work. A good grade of wool, flax, or some of the synthetic materials is extremely costly to buy and requires a great deal of skill, thought, and time to transform into a piece of art.

The general public, the largest potential market for woven art, expects to pay well for the raw materials used by the goldsmith and silversmith. It must also learn that the raw material of the weaver is far more precious than is generally realized and the weaver must help to advertise this fact.

The serious weaver can set up shop, ready to produce and perhaps to sell, for about $250 to $400 capital outlay—excluding, of course, a separate studio building. This luxury will either cost an additional $300 to $1,800 if rent for a year is to be assured or perhaps up to $6,000 if a separate studio is built. Since it is sometimes easier to work in cramped quarters than to raise several thousand dollars' capital, it is recommended that the weaver start at home and progress to more privacy as his fortunes increase.

To make the investment worthwhile marketing, the weaver might expect to charge $4 an hour for his labor if he is of average speed. If he is slow, however, he cannot expect to sell in the face of competition if he charges more than about $3 an hour. The fast weaver might charge $10 an hour.

It must be understood by the weaving artist that money represents production and design represents appeal. The most appealing design will not be sold if it is overpriced in comparison with a competitive design of equal appeal, woven by a faster weaver. Perhaps it might be well for the beginning weaver to price his art on the basis of square footage. He should examine and measure comparable finished designs and work by competitors, divide the number of square feet into the price, and attach the same price per square foot to his own work. As experience allows him to weave more quickly his income per hour will rise automatically.

Of course, the weaver must also add cost of material, plus an extra 15 to 20 percent, to pay for his time in handling, to his labor fee.

One may sell and distribute goods nationally, regionally, and locally through a sales representative. Such channels of distribution reach into consumer outlets, to architects, to businessmen, to manufacturers. Inversely, they are the main reason weavers and other craftsmen can easily order supplies without having to raise and shear sheep, mine silver and gold and iron, or cut and saw trees for material.

The traditional methods of selling woven goods consist mainly of craft shows, galleries, and a few specialized craft shops and co-operatives. In many parts of the country craft shows are held as annual affairs, drawing craftsmen as well as craft aficionados and others who will spend money acquiring craft items for households, collections, or for self-decoration. The exhibiting craftsman never knows quite what to expect from such a collective market, but ex-perience has shown that visitors at craft fairs, with a few exceptions, usually buy small, inexpensive items which sell for under $5. The weaver produces few small inexpensive items and finds himself at a disadvantage under the circumstances.

Almost every state, particularly in the Midwest, Northeast, Southeast, and the West Coast regions, has a number of craft fairs all during the year, climate permitting. A list of fairs, location, dates, fees, and commissions required may be obtained by writing the tourist development department of any state. Queries may be ad-dressed to that department, State Capitol, in the capital city of the state.

These craft fairs can be used to great advantage by weavers as an opportunity to present and display talent and techniques to the public. Often a display, if properly handled, will attract the attention of architects, gallery owners, and interior designers and thereby lead to commissions for wall hangings or other woven items. Belts and handbags might prove attractive to merchants. If a weaver has items thought attractive to architects, designers, and dress shop owners, he should make up a list of prospects and send postcards or letters especially inviting them to see his display.

A number of galleries across the country, some in small college towns and some in large cities, are quite interested in exhibiting the work of weavers, especially weaving designed as works of art rather than functional items. If quality, according to the tastes of the gallery owner, warrants it, the owner might well agree to hold a one-man show and to sell items on a continuing basis after the show. Gallery owners are businessmen, however, and will sell the weaver's production at a price 50 to 100 percent more than what he pays the weaver. Some artists bitterly resent this markup, feeling that the man who sells their art makes as much as the artist who conceives and produces it. Such resentment is based on a misconception. Most of the money made by the gallery must be used to display the weaver's work, pay for help in the gallery, finance advertising and receptions, and generally build a market. Usually the gallery owner personally receives very little of the markup. Without his merchandising efforts the weaver would sell much less of his work.

Weavers and other craft artists have on occasion organized craft cooperatives as a way to avoid the gallery markup. Craftsmen members of a cooperative will learn that sales monies in excess of what the artist receives will be needed to pay for a place in which work may be displayed, pay for help in the co-op store, finance advertising and receptions, and, with what little is left over, maintain the store and pay utilities. Unless the craftsmen members of a cooperative are willing to understand and apply business principles to the endeavor, they will be far happier turning over the task of merchandising and sales to a businessman. Also, they will have much more time in which to create and will sell more items.

A number of architects across the United States, as well as interior designers of homes, business and industrial buildings, have demonstrated much interest in woven wall hangings for their commissions but complain that the cost is generally too high for a client's budget. A suggested solution to this problem is perhaps the production of limited editions by weavers. For instance, once a good design is worked out it can be repeated for a limited number of hangings, with an affidavit or other assurance that only a specified number of clients will share this particular design. Since this method has been practiced successfully by artists in a number of crafts, there is no reason why it cannot also be applied to weaving with equal success. Indeed, smaller wall hangings for residential or office use might well be sold by one of a number of mail order houses specializing in art objects, as have items of hand blown glass, ceramics, and silver. A search of mail order advertisements in shelter, art, collectors, and social magazines, which may be found at any public library, will yield the addresses of such special mail order houses. They may then be written to, enclosing with the letter a photograph of the projected work of the weaver.

For weavers who choose to produce originally designed yard goods for clothing, draperies, and upholstery, there is yet another alternative. The Countess Von Eckmann of Sweden has built up an international market for hand-woven woolen material produced by the women of her home province. Her method is to have this really beautiful material made into women's suits and coats of original design which, along with yard goods, she takes to various cities in America, England, France, Germany and one or two other countries every year or so. These are shown and sold for very good prices, at selected spots to affluent women who come by invitation only. After expenses the profits are put back into further development of the hand weaving industry in Southern Sweden. This method and logical variations might suggest a direction to the modern weavers of America.

Although the concept has not yet been developed, there is a great potential market for weaving through large national and regional department store operations. Most of the big stores in large cities have interior decorating services and special galleries within the stores for the exhibition and sale of expensive art objects and antiques. The buyers for these operations are continually seeking new and unique items. Perhaps weavers, their agents, or the American Crafts Council should explore this route of marketing and merchandising. Of course, as with art galleries, such stores will add a rather large but justifiable markup, but this will in no way diminish the price the artist might get for his work through selling directly to a customer.

Regardless of how a weaver sells his work, as an artist he should make certain that each item he produces has some sort of hallmark on it identifying its source. This can be done by weaving a signature of some sort in the item, by stitching on a small cloth label, which can be bought at fabric and sewing centers for less than $5 per hundred, or by weaving into the fabric a small strip of silver with the artist's hallmark stamped upon it. Identification is not only important to building a reputation and identity; it will also help raise weaving from a craft to a true art in the eyes of the public.

SOURCES OF SUPPLY

Contessa Yarns
P.O. Box 37
Lebanon, Connecticut 06249

Craft Yarns of Rhode Island
603 Mineral Spring Avenue
Pawtucket, Rhode Island 02862

Dharma Trading Company
P.O. Box 1288
Berkeley, California 94701

Fibrec Dye Center
2795 16th Street
San Francisco, California 94103

Field Loom Reed Company
Box 2036
Charlotte, North Carolina 28201

Leclerc Corporation
2 Mont Calm Avenue
Plattsburgh, New York 12901

Lily Mills Company
Department HWSA
Shelby, North Carolina 28150

Jeane Malsada Studio
P.O. Box 28182
Atlanta, Georgia 30328

Morgan Inkle Loom Factory
Railroad Engine House
Guilford, Connecticut 06437

S&S Arts & Crafts
Colchester, Connecticut 06415

Train Tex Industry
6501 Barberton Avenue
Cleveland, Ohio 44102

CHAPTER II

The Tapestry Maker

TAPESTRY is not new to the arts. During the Middle Ages it was considered de rigueur that every lady of noble family learn to make the complicated pictorial tapestries, some of them quite large, which are exemplified by the magnificent pieces in the Musée de Cluny, by the Bayeux tapestries, and by many others depicting battles, maidens, unicorns, and other fabled subjects. The art appeared, however, much earlier in the form of decorated feather cloaks in Latin America, in decorated wrapped baskets in many places, and, much later, in the blankets of the Navajos. And while medieval tapestries, Navajo rugs, and all the other forms had very practical uses, all became art forms in the various cultures in which they flourished. Indeed, the French nobility during the reigns of Louis XIV and Louis XV supported factories which specialized in making huge tapestry wall hangings which added to the glory of French arms and established the richness of noble chateaux. Before World War II tapestry had been revived as a modern art form and by 1970 it had become accepted as a lively arm of the reviving craft movement.

For the most part modern tapestry is used, not to cut the chill emanating from thick stone building blocks, but to enliven a room with color, texture, and abstract design. Tapestry is also quite adaptable to other functional forms because its own form is unlimited. It can be woven to fit a round or square or oblong shape. When used for clothing it does not need to be cut to a pattern for it can be woven to a pattern, each shaped piece then being stitched together. The same applies to tapestry used for upholstering chair

seats. It applies also to tapestry handbags, women's hats, and the numerous other articles now hidden in the creative depths of some tapestry maker's mind.

Tapestry is a flexible, fluid, adaptable form of weaving, the potential of which is only beginning to be understood in the 1970s.

Like more abstract loom-woven pieces, tapestry can be given, in one piece, variations in texture as well as form and it can be endowed with a fluid dimension which will add interest to the fabric for any number of special uses.

Training for tapestry making can be found in a number of places. An essential part of training is to study ancient, medieval, and Louisian pieces, preferably the pieces themselves in the museums of the world, but, if this is impossible, in the numerous books which have been written about tapestry in its various forms. The modern artist in tapestry must not be at all provincial in his knowledge of technique. He should look into the somewhat primitive but effective methods of the Navajo as well as the most sophisticated collective technique of seventeenth-century French and Belgian tapestry factories. All of them will stimulate his imagination.

Most of all he should study design through all the ages and all the cultures to which he can be exposed. After such study the tapestry maker will have a well of knowledge from which he can draw ideas for his own work and use these ideas separately and in combination to create new pieces of rare distinction.

The technique of weaving tapestry is not difficult to learn but experience is a necessary concomitant to perfection and an essential part of training. As with any art, tapestry making requires discipline based on dedication and enthusiasm. Discipline can most easily be learned in a weaving course in a good crafts school or in a college.

And schooling offers other important advantages. It provides background and training in creating good modern design, which is learned not only from design but also from drawing and painting, which in turn improves the powers of observation so that the student can learn to see design wherever he looks.

In addition a school provides opportunity for communication between learning craftsmen and artists. Artists must work alone in the ultimate creation of art, but communication is stimulating, widens the capacity for ideas, and encourages the imagination. It screws to the sticking point the courage which produces new ideas and launches the artist and his patrons on adventures of the soul.

Blessed is the tapestry maker because his equipment is inexpensive. The simplest, most primitive loom is quite suitable for any type tapestry, from Navajo rugs to odd-shaped modern pieces. A vertical tapestry loom may easily be made in a home workshop from two-by-twos or two-by-fours, several ¾-inch dowels or sticks, and a few nails. The materials for the loom probably will not cost over $10 from a local retail lumber store, and much less if scrap lumber is employed. The sketch shown here will give adequate instruction in making such a loom.

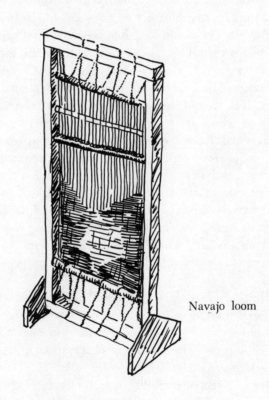

Navajo loom

Of course, a 10-treadle 8-harness loom will also serve for weaving tapestry but since only two treadles and no more than four harnesses are needed, the result is no better than that from a homemade loom. New looms can easily be made to accommodate extra-large designs.

The simplicity of the loom allows the tapestry to be produced in a minimum of shop space. There needs to be only space for the loom and for pegs or shelves for storing yarn.

Because of limited returns on the investment when selling tapestry work, it is advised that the artist either find suitable space in the home for his studio, or that he rent part of space used by other craftsmen for just $5 or $10 a month. The money needed to build a special studio would take years to replace through sales.

Pegs for hanging yarns may be easily furnished by nailing a 6- to 8-foot board, at least 2 inches wide, on a suitable wall and boring holes with a half-inch brace and bit or electric drill into which half-inch dowels 6 inches long may be driven. Dowels, in 3-foot lengths which can be cut with any type saw, are available in hardware stores or craft stores for about 35¢ each. As the sketch shows, a yarn board is quite simple to make.

Some modern tapestry, as in olden pictorial hangings, requires a multiplicity of color tones, sometimes available from yarn manufacturers but often requiring that the yarn be dyed by the artist.

Commercial dyes, available from sources listed in the appendix to this chapter, cost from 25¢ to 35¢ a packet. More adventurous weavers will also want to try their hand at vegetable dyeing. Some natural dyes, such as walnut and marigold, may be collected from one's own back yard. Others may be ordered from botanical suppliers listed in the appendix. Dye pots, or pails, exactly like those described in Chapter I of this section, may be bought at hardware stores for from $2.50 to $4.50 each, depending on type.

Depending on design concepts and the degree of sophistication desired in design, the yarns needed may be easily obtained from established sources of supply, as listed in the appendix of this chapter, or may have to be sought much like the widow's mite. Woolen and linen yarns are easily acquired, but more exotic fibers of plastic or glass or cattail leaves will be rather difficult to find at times. Most large cities, however, have distributors for all manner of strange materials, and weaving instructors generally are knowledgeable about all sorts of strange sources of supply.

Tapestry yarns, identical to weaving yarns, are rather expensive. High quality wool yarn will cost from $5 to $16 per pound, linen from $2 to $4. Other supplementary materials will vary in cost depending on the quantity desired to properly execute a concept. The tapestry maker should haunt millinery shops, furriers, and such chain stores as Tandy's, seeking scrap materials and leftovers which can be bought at various prices. Of course, natural materials such as grasses, vines, and cattails may be gathered in the yard or along the roadside at no cost whatever.

Including enough yarn and dye to make several tapestries about 2 feet by 4 feet, the tapestry maker should be able to collect his material and equipment for around $100.

Tapestry may be sold generally through the same channels as other forms of weaving. The tapestry maker who wishes to become professional should take color photographs of each piece he produces to be collected into a catalog of sorts. He can seek one-man shows in galleries; he can solicit commissions from architects, dress shops, decorators, department stores and other normal outlets; or he can combine with other artists to form a cooperative. Like other artists he may wish to make the craft-art fair circuit which provides at least one fair a week in certain areas of the country where exposure of an artist's work can possibly earn him several hundred dollars of income a week. When not showing at fairs he can be producing for future fairs. Of course, he should offer items of a type to fit the needs of the market he solicits.

Craft shows, with dates and fees, are listed by the tourist development departments of state governments or by state Chambers of Commerce. Write directly to state capitals, or acquire the mailing addresses of state Chambers of Commerce from local chambers.

Limited editions, though not so suitable for tapestry as for some other arts, should also be considered as a means of building sales volume and income from architects, decorators, or mail order businesses.

Tapestries, like other woven goods, should be signed by the artist in a distinctive manner.

SOURCES OF SUPPLY

Brodhead-Garrett Company
4560 East 71st Street
Cleveland, Ohio 44105

Crafttool Company, Inc.
1421 West 240th Street
Harbor City, California 90701

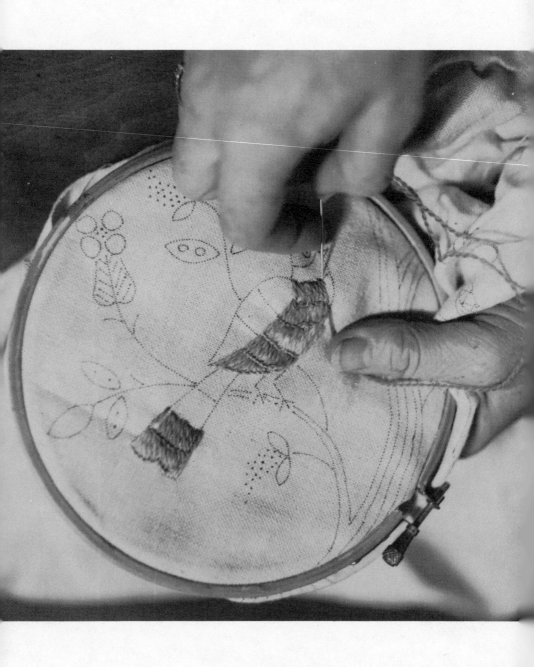

CHAPTER III

The Embroiderer and Needlepointer

EMBROIDERY claims a most respectable history in most areas of the world and among cultures of varying sophistication. In generations not so long past it was a craft often used by impoverished gentlewomen to eke out a living by decorating all manner of linen goods with finely stitched designs. Needlepointing is a form of embroidery which is somewhat akin to tapestry in its appearance but using to a large degree the technique of embroidery. The difference between the two is mainly that embroidery is more flexible in form, uses finer thread and a number of different stitches and is applied to the surface of an object already made. Needlepoint, on the other hand, completely covers the surface of a piece of fabric and forms its design by using different colored yarns applied solidly only in cross stitch.

In the last generation or so machines have been developed which can nearly duplicate hand embroidery and needlepoint much more cheaply and far more rapidly than can the handcraftsman. The quality of the machine work, however, is certainly lacking in character, thus leaving open an opportunity for the handcraftsman to produce the finest of this type of work.

Embroidery is not so much a matter of making as of decorating. The modern embroiderer can follow the example of genteel predecessors and decorate the same items which have been decorated with embroidery for centuries. These include handkerchiefs, shirts and blouses, towels, pillow covers, pin cushions, samplers, bed sheets, and other forms of personal and household linen. Gloves, knee-socks, and baby clothes may also be embroidered very elegantly for special gifts, and a small but charming medium for embroidery might be leather book marks decorated with silken thread.

While most embroidery now being done—much of it in such exotic places as the Philippines, Hong Kong, and Yugoslavia—is of traditional design for traditional items, it must be stressed that modern design and imaginative application will be needed to keep embroidery alive as an important craft. Some sort of formal training in art and design, therefore, will be most valuable to the embroiderer and needlepointer who wishes to seek or supplement a livelihood.

Needlepoint lends itself to slightly different items. Furniture upholstery has always been a favorite item for the amateur needlepointer and continues to be a good salable item for needlepointers who wish to sell their production. There are many other things suitable to needlepoint, however. One popular item is the wall plaque or sampler with a pictorial or literary subject, decorated with various designs and framed. Large handbags and knitting bags can be made most handsome by needlepoint. Small cocktail coasters, table mats, or mats for lamps and vases may be designed and executed by the needlepointer. And the craftsman who learns to work out his own designs may execute the more complicated parts of seat coverings, et al, to be sold through craft shops to less talented amateurs who wish to fill in the solid color background on such items.

Again, as with all modern craftsmen, the needlepointer should realize that new markets can be built through the use of modern design. Design is essential to success, as has been proven in the case of tapestry. Traditional needlepoint designs will certainly sell, but the taste of the American public is changing toward modern, abstract design. The needlepointer who recognizes this trend will benefit himself and the craft movement.

Training for embroidery and needlepoint should be sought mainly in the design school, for design is really more important than the comparatively simple techniques needed. Techniques, however, should be thoroughly understood in order to adapt designs to them.

Basic design may be learned in almost any formal art school, either the ones connected with art museums in larger cities, or in universities, most of which are listed annually by the American Crafts Council, which sells this list by mail.

Technique may be learned from skilled embroiderers and needlepointers, many of them amateurs, who are capable of creating their own designs, or from any one of a number of books listed in the bibliography to this chapter. An especially good book on embroidery is *Embroidery Stitches*, a paperback published by Simon & Schuster, which sells for $1.95.

In both these ancient arts, however, experience is by far the best teacher of techniques, and practice will soon let the beginner know if he has the careful patience needed to spend long hours on creating designs from tiny, often monotonous, stitching.

Equipment for both embroidery and needlepoint is simplicity itself. It consists mainly of needle and thread and, in the case of embroidery, a number of embroidery hoops of various sizes.

The embroiderer needs a number of various-sized needles to use with either coarse or very fine thread, some of it silk or synthetic, some cotton and some wool, depending upon the article to be decorated. Needle and thread are available at almost any general store, variety store, or department store, or at any of the legion of special sewing shops which now are found in large or small towns (the Singer stores are a good example). If one is not near a store he can order this elemental equipment from Sears, Roebuck or Montgomery Ward. Cost is negligible: 25¢ per dozen for assorted-sized needles, 30¢ to 60¢ for a spool of thread, or perhaps slightly more for special embroidery thread, again depending on the size of spool or skein.

Embroidery thread is produced in so many colors and tones of these colors that special dyeing is hardly necessary to even the most meticulous designer.

Also needed is that traditional equipment of the needle-plyer, the embroidery hoop. This consists of two small wooden hoops, one of which fits tightly inside the other. The area of cloth to be embroidered is stretched over the smaller hoop, and hoop and cloth are then forced inside the larger hoop to hold the cloth taut while it is being decorated. In the days when embroidery was a common household activity, these hoops were sometimes attached to beautifully constructed stands which held the work at a proper height for a sitting woman to decorate comfortably. It is believed that such stands are no longer available, except rarely in antique shops, but the hoops, in a variety of sizes, are readily available from a number of sources. Sears, Roebuck and Montgomery Ward and like organizations offer them in retail stores or in mail order catalogs. Large department stores, small variety shops, or specialized hobby shops often stock them. The special sewing shops usually have them or can order them for a customer who is not too impatient.

The embroiderer of ambition might wish to acquire several sizes of these sets of hoops to fit any type work. The hoops can be bought at a cost of from about 50¢ to $1 depending on size.

An embroiderer, then, can set himself or herself up in business with a capital outlay of perhaps 25¢ for needles, a couple of dollars for thread, another couple of dollars for hoops and, if original items are to be made, perhaps $5 for cloth. Of course, the cost of cloth is eliminated if the embroiderer is decorating handkerchiefs, shirts, mats, or other items furnished by the customer. Surely no other business requires a capital outlay of merely $5 or $10 to start production.

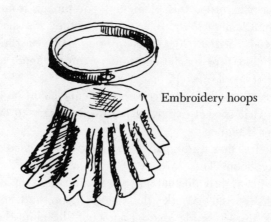

Embroidery hoops

The investment in time for learning and reading is really far more important than the money required.

Needlepointing is a slightly more complicated field in which to enter. As with embroidery, needles are the essential tools, but larger needles, generally known as tapestry needles, are required. The same sources that supply embroidery needles also offer this type of needle. Cost, also, is about the same—about 40¢ for a package of needles.

No hoops are required for needlepoint but a special type of coarse canvas is needed for the usual needlepoint designs, although regular heavy canvas can be used for special designs. Needlepoint cloth can usually be found at needlework centers, craft and hobby shops and, of course, in the needlework section of department stores. Such cloth, of about 26-inch width, is fairly expensive, costing about $6 a yard. But a yard of the stuff is sufficient for a number of samplers or chair seats or handbags, so that the average cost of canvas for an average item can be figured at $1 to $1.50.

Special wool thread, known as tapestry yarn, is also required for needlepoint, as it is tightly spun, harder than the familiar knitting yarn, and costs a bit more as a consequence. Normally it sells for about $1.50 per skein. It is available from the same sources where one finds canvas and needles.

A minor item, graph paper, is needed to work out original needlepoint designs. This, of course, can be found in any school supply section of drug stores, department stores, variety stores, book stores, or office supply outlets, all of which are established in most towns of any size. Graph paper costs no more than 50¢, depending on the size of the pack. It is an important adjunct to needlepoint, however, for it enables the serious artist in this somewhat overlooked medium to create original, unique designs.

All in all, the needlepointer can set up shop with a minimum outlay of from $10 to $15, depending mainly on the number of skeins of colored yarn needed to execute a design. Both embroidery and needlepoint are fortunate crafts in that no shop as such is needed for either. They hark back to the pre-industrial age of home crafts. Both may be done sitting down, with a table or stool nearby for keeping yarn and cloth and needle where they can be easily reached. A comfortable chair or sofa and a good light, with a desk or table to work out designs, are all that is needed to make any room into an embroidery or needlepoint shop.

Marketing these two related crafts, however, is sometimes more difficult than with the more vigorous crafts which require special shop space and expensive equipment. Needlepoint and embroidery are still considered to be in the never-never land between craft and hobby, and many potential customers feel that they should not pay high prices for an art which, if they had the initiative, they could do themselves. The definition of both these activities as crafts must depend almost wholly on original design, with embroidery and needlepoint being merely the media for the design. So, craftsmen in both fields should concentrate on bright, modern design to demonstrate to the world that both arts can be considered true crafts.

Communicating such an idea is not too easy at this time, either, but there are ways.

Publicity can open doors if the craftsman has something new to offer. Women's page editors, who are sometimes fading away in a world exposed to Women's Liberation, or their counterparts on any-sized newspaper, radio, or television station, especially educational television, can make such publicity possible. So can advertising in the want ads of smaller newspapers or hobby magazines such as *Antiques, Crafts Horizons,* or other regional magazines with women's audiences and a classified ad section. Cost of such advertising will, of course, vary with each publication. Rates may be determined by calling or writing the advertising department of the publications which is listed in each issue.

There are other means of exposure, though, which are shared by other craftsmen. Crafts and art fairs, common to many communities, especially in New England, Florida, California, and most large cities, provide an excellent opportunity for embroidery or needlepoint to be displayed to the public. In addition to displaying finished work, a small hand-lettered sign on a fair booth might ask for commissions for embroidering gloves or shirts, or making needlepoint chair seats or original designs. Sketches of new designs might also be displayed. Craft fairs are generally listed by state and city Chambers of Commerce, the addresses of which can be obtained by calling any local chamber.

Embroidery specialists might take samples of their work to lingerie, shirt, and bridal departments of large stores asking for commissions, or to furniture stores to sell them on the idea of making hand-embroidered pillows on consignment.

There is a market of sorts for embroidery in the craft cooperatives in youth areas of Los Angeles, San Francisco, Atlanta, New York, and other large cities which attract young people. Many of these cooperatives sell hand-embroidered dresses for women, Russian shirts for men, and even embroidered jeans for both sexes.

Needlepointers might follow the same plan by calling on interior decorators, furniture departments of large department stores, and quality upholstery and reproduction shops. In addition, a market for handbags and knitting bags might be found in women's wear shops; semi-finished pieces, which need only a background filled in, might be sold, outright or on consignment, to hobby and craft shops, the independent ones as well as the related sections of large department stores.

It should be remembered, however, at all times, that under such circumstances the craftsman is really selling design rather than work which can be made and sold much more cheaply by special machines.

Embroiderers and needlepointers are also in demand at a few interior design shops, sewing centers, and craft shops to teach their crafts, thus opening up a market for their work as well as bringing in welcome income—indeed, teaching at a set fee per hour per pupil can often be more lucrative than selling one's work.

In common with all crafts, embroiderers and needlepointers should devise a way of signing their work, with the name of the town in the signature if possible and practicable.

Prices charged for embroidery and needlepoint must, of course, vary according to the quality and complexity for the piece, the time needed to complete it, the cost of material, and, also, what the market will bear. An embroiderer who produces for sale might charge between $3.50 to $4 an hour for work, plus the cost of materials and other costs. Chargeable time should also include the time needed to work out original designs. If limited editions are produced the design time may be spread over the total items in the edition. Prices may vary upward as the embroiderer establishes a reputation or if demand for a particular artist's work rises.

As with anything, it is more difficult to sell embroidery for a higher price than the local market generally pays for comparable work, but the skilled artist with special talents can make more per hour if he insists on his higher price to reflect higher skill.

Needlepoint and embroidery lend themselves very well to being enjoyable, part-time sources of income, and with proper attention paid to design, a number of these specialists might well gain recognition as important artists working in important crafts.

SOURCES OF SUPPLY

Craft Yarns of Rhode Island
603 Mineral Spring Avenue
Pawtucket, Rhode Island 02862

Dharma Trading Company
P. O. Box 1288
Berkeley, California 94701

Dick Blick Company
P. O. Box 1267
Galesburg, Illinois 61401

Jeane Malsada, Inc.
P. O. Box 28182
Atlanta, Georgia 30328

S & S Arts & Crafts
Colchester, Connecticut 06415

Vanguard Crafts, Inc.
2915 Avenue J
Brooklyn, New York 11210

CHAPTER IV

The Macrame Worker

SAILORS invented macrame. It falls into the same category as scrimshaw, building ship models in bottles, and other creative activities developed to while away the months and years in lost areas of the world far away from the family and the glitter of settled and civilized lands. Shipboard television, radio, and movies have largely replaced creative arts aboard the fast, modern cargo ships of today.

Macrame survived, however, because it became a specialty of a group of nuns in Flanders who made articles of macrame for sale. This art of creative knotting was adopted by the revitalized crafts movement after World War II and has gained some status in the textile arts since that time.

There is much to be done with macrame, which consists of knotted cord and nothing but knotted cord, although the size of the cord may vary and several colors may be used by the skilled macrame worker to create quite stunning designs. Possibly the most popular products are belts, usually white or of one solid color, knotted into repetitive designs to the desired length. Many macrame belts are tied together, while others are started on a regular belt buckle. Other items created in macrame include lamp-shades, wall hangings, handbags, women's hats, women's open-work ponchos, even skirts and whole dresses if the cord is soft and the knots not too tight. Macrame is also suitable for watch bands, bracelets, cigarette pack holders, and any number of types of containers.

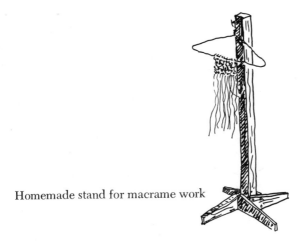

Homemade stand for macrame work

Training for macrame is available from time to time from the summer craft classes offered by most city school systems, in summer camps for young people, and as a part-time service in many hobby and craft shops around the country. For the most part, however, the macrame workers of America seem to be self-taught; the simplicity of technique and material, plus the lack of organized classes, recommend self-instruction. Several very well written and well illustrated instruction books on macrame are available and are listed in the bibliography to this chapter.

Equipment for macrame working is readily available. No looms, needles, heddles, or reels are required; only 10 dextrous fingers and a mind which can create variety out of simple cords and knots. The craft is started on a stick or a horizontal bit of cord or perhaps a belt buckle, and the work is done on a vertical plane, the initial rod, cord, or buckle being fastened to a nail in the wall or the stand of a floor lamp or any object which will allow the worker to use both hands to knot the cord from top to bottom. Some workers may design a very simple stand which may be set upon a table or the floor, as the example illustrated here, but it is necessary only in the absence of an already available place from which to hang the work. Such a rack can be constructed at a cost of about $2, or less if scrap lumber is available.

Workshops are quite unnecessary for macrame. The art may be pursued in the living room or kitchen or even on the beach so long as there is a place to hang the work while knotting. Indeed, some macrame artists working on large ponchos and the like can tie their knots evenly without the need of hanging the work.

While macrame requires only cord to work with, the types of cords can vary greatly. One might employ quarter-inch manila rope or silken embroidery thread depending on the use and artistic concept of the piece being made. The coarser the cord, however, the more rapidly the work progresses and anything made of embroidery thread, however beautiful, will take an inordinate length of time to execute and probably even more time to sell for a price which would pay for the labor and material involved. Rope, though, which goes rather quickly, can be profitable material when used for large items such as macrame door mats or indoor rugs of fairly small size.

The most popular, and perhaps profitable, material for macrame work is strong, twisted cotton mason's cord, available at any hardware store for about 75¢ for a ball containing 50 to 75 feet. This material is ideal for washable belts, handbags, and other containers and for vests or ponchos. It may be dyed easily to incorporate color into the design or it may be purchased in a few limited colors, yellow or blue for the most part, at hardware stores or hobby and craft shops.

Hemp twine, which can be bought at hardware stores, office supply stores, ten-cent stores and variety stores, also offers an interesting material usually in a hempen color. Binder twine, also made of hemp or jute, while rough on tender fingers, can be found at farm supply stores in large balls or reels of 500 feet for about $4 a unit. Hemp or cotton quarter-inch rope, twisted or braided, is found at almost any hardware store for around 3¢ a foot, and braided nylon rope is available at hardware or marine supply outlets for about 5¢ a foot.

More elegant materials for macrame include wool tapestry yarn and cotton crochet thread, the tapestry yarn costing about $2 per skein and the crochet thread costing around 65¢ for a ball of 250 feet. Both these materials turn out beautiful items, but being small they tie into small knots which require many more knots per item and much more time to finish than mason's cord or heavier material.

There are real problems to making money by marketing macrame. The medium itself is somewhat limited in expression, for one thing; it demands its own somewhat monotonous scheme of general design. And while it may offer interesting texture and some color and some adaptation to a number of different types of items, it does not offer the individuality, the distinction, the versatility of other textile arts. One person's macrame is very likely to look like another's if the skill of the two artists is equal.

Nevertheless, macrame does find some market and while it seems to be one of the crafts which flowers and dies and reflowers, there probably will be a small, steady demand in each community for certain articles made of macrame. Undoubtedly it will continue to be taught in many summer camps and craft programs because its techniques are not too difficult to learn and its capital requirements are small. How, then, can the macrame worker earn a return on his investment of time and material?

Well, first of all it must, as in all things for sale, be exposed to the market it wishes to reach, possibly men who need belts, or women who want wall hangings or vests, or mothers who wish pretty diaper bags. Probably the market will be young, for almost everything is new to youth and the disadvantages of macrame might not affect its appeal to young people just becoming enthralled by handmade objects well designed and well executed.

The small craft cooperatives often found in washaterias or small rented shops in youth districts (formerly known as hippie districts) offer a fine place to display macrame work to an interested audience. Such cooperative shops are found in almost every large city and simply must be sought out with samples and negotiated with for display space.

As with weaving, pottery, and silversmithing, the craft fairs of New England, Florida, California, and many communities across the nation offer an excellent medium for selling macrame. And, as with certain other crafts, the artisan might solicit orders from the men's and women's clothing shops in his community and sell to these retail outlets directly, perhaps on consignment, which means that the articles are consigned to display only and the artist gets paid when the article is sold and the merchant has subtracted his margin from the sale price. Gift shops located around resort areas or in entertainment areas in larger cities also offer possibilities for the macrame worker to sell his production.

One must look at macrame realistically, however, as a means of making money. It does not have a wide, steady demand among the public. It takes an inordinate amount of time to finish even small articles, not counting the time required to conceive new designs, shop for cord, and find selling outlets. If the macrame worker earns the same hourly rate, say $3 to $10 an hour, as the weaver or blacksmith, then his production, except in the case of items made of rope, must require an outrageously high selling price. Because of this it is not recommended as a full-time craft and source of livelihood. It is, nevertheless, a most interesting hobby.

Perhaps this fact is the source of real income from macrame; the skilled worker can give lessons to teach other aspiring craftsmen of all ages to make their own belts and handbags and lampshades. There is a distinct market for teaching in many areas of the country.

Many, many shopping centers in the country include craft and hobby shops. Larger cities have shops devoted to selling the material for knitting and crocheting, both allied to macrame. As a means of attracting customers and making them into regular customers these shops also offer lessons in certain of the crafts including macrame.

Even though the macrame worker finds it difficult to market his work to return $3 or $4 an hour he might find it relatively easy to give lessons at $1 an hour per student and realize from $5 to $10 an hour from his teaching. This activity will pay him adequately for his time and also serve to subsidize his work which he can then afford to sell at a price the market is willing to pay.

Jobs teaching macrame may also be sought at summer camps, at public parks in large cities which offer a recreation program during the summer, at YMCA summer courses for children, and in the recreational programs, both adult and youth, of churches of every denomination. The pay will not be as good as that realized from teaching in a commercial establishment such as a craft shop, but the work is most satisfying. These jobs must be asked for, so the hopeful teacher must make personal application to summer camps and YMCA headquarters in his area.

Or, for the sheer pleasure of it, the macrame worker can continue to do his work and sell his production whenever he can for whatever he can get in his own area.

SOURCES OF SUPPLY

CCM Arts & Crafts, Inc.
9520 Baltimore Avenue
College Park, Maryland 20740

Craft Yarns of Rhode Island
603 Mineral Spring Avenue
Pawtucket, Rhode Island 02862

Jeane Malsada, Inc.
P. O. Box 28182
Atlanta, Georgia 30328

Lily Mills Company
Department HWSA
Shelby, North Carolina 28150

Sax Arts & Crafts
207 North Milwaukee Avenue
Milwaukee, Wisconsin 53202

Triarco Arts & Crafts
P. O. Box 106
Northfield, Illinois 60093

Vanguard Crafts, Inc.
2915 Avenue J
Brooklyn, New York 11210

CHAPTER V

The Stitcher and Seamstress

IT is said that the sewing machine was the first domestic machine invented and widely accepted into the home. The sewing machine, which predated other appliances by a generation or more, has been and is being manufactured in every industrial nation in the world and for several generations has been accepted and used skillfully by many nonindustrial peoples from Seminole Indians in Florida to Polynesians in the South Pacific. Wherever sewing has been an integral part of the traditional or acquired culture of a people, the sewing machine has found its place in the home. Possibly it has been so universally accepted because, whether operated by human muscle or electric motor, it continues to duplicate the elemental rhythms of humankind. It is comforting, much like the regular rhythm of the heddle in weaving or the steady ring of the anvil in blacksmithing. Although it has not entirely replaced the needle in certain types of stitchery and sewing, it has greatly speeded the production of the seamstress and stitcher without eliminating the value and beauty of handwork.

There is a minor difference between the stitcher and the seamstress. The seamstress traditionally makes clothing for women, as the tailor does for men, and the stitcher makes all manner of things of cloth, mostly functional but frequently decorative. Also the seamstress often cuts her clothing from predesigned patterns, although sometimes doing her own designing, while the stitcher makes things of different bits of cloth according to her own design. Both crafts are almost wholly practiced by women and both are true home crafts. Both, but especially the seamstress, suffer the competition of machine manufacturing.

Seamstresses offer a great variety of work within the narrow limits of clothing, both men's and women's. Of course, they make all manner of dresses, skirts, slacks, and shirts of cotton, wool, linen, or synthetic fabrics. Most are made to fit the figures of patronesses, although some of loose fitting, costume style are made hopefully to fit the personality of the patron.

In past years seamstresses were in great demand to make special gowns for weddings, balls, and other special events. Today's seamstress, though, largely makes informal, unusual clothes not offered by the factories, with which she cannot possibly compete in terms of labor and material costs. The modern seamstress is mostly a special craftsman for a special market, often young.

A very good and easily salable item sold in both gift and clothing shops is the fancy party apron, sometimes with ruffles and sash bow, a very elegant workaday item indeed.

There are still, of course, traditional seamstresses who make and fit garments according to pattern and material furnished by the patron, selling only their skill at the sewing machine. But only a few seamstresses of modern or traditional bent are able to make enough money at the craft for more than a supplementary income. Some become both seamstress and stitcher.

Stitchery does offer more creative potential to the craftsman than making clothes and in some cases the two arts are combined. Possibly the best-known product of the stitcher, traditionally as well as contemporarily, is the patchwork quilt. These beautiful creations, made to a number of set patterns with intriguing names, were once a collective effort among the women of backwoods and mountain communities, each stitcher bringing her patches already assembled into a predetermined design. After stretching the foundation sheet on a large wooden frame, the stitchers sat with the frame resting in their laps and fastened the patches on the foundation sheet with delicate hand stitching. When they had finished this, the lower sheet was sewn on, the resulting bag filled with cotton, wool, or down, and the two sheets quilted together to keep the filling evenly spread inside the quilt. Modern stitchers usually make quilts by themselves, dispensing with the quilting frame and sewing designs and patches together with a sewing machine, then quilting by hand as in the olden days. Handmade quilts still find a good market and sell for a good price.

But modern stitchers produce far more variety than patchwork quilts. Some make patchwork sheets and then cut and sew these into aprons and skirts; some make stuffed pillows in the shapes of birds, animals, or people with details of another color cloth stitched on; and some specialize in stuffed toys for babies and college girls. Potholders, appliqued with modern design, make charming gifts for housewarmings or bridal showers and usually find a ready market. Other such traditional items as tea cozies usually sell well at gift shops because they do fulfill a function and are in short supply. West Coast stitchers and artists in universities make pillows of quite unusual design, shaped and stuffed to resemble textile sculpture. Wall hangings, pictorial or abstract, also find a limited market, especially for children's rooms.

There is little formal training available for seamstresses or stitchers beyond high school level except, of course, the essential studies of art and design and the instruction of experience. Art and design may be learned in the art departments of many universities across the nation, or at such specialized art schools as the Art Students League in New York, the Atlanta Art School, the Chicago Institute of Art, and other schools connected with the great art museums in Los Angeles, San Francisco, Philadelphia, Washington, D.C., Boston, and Cleveland. Again, as with all the modern crafts, original design will play a large part in the success of the individual artist—far more than the techniques of stitching or operating a sewing machine.

And while it does not exactly constitute a formal curriculum, beginners in stitchery or sewing can learn basic techniques at sewing centers operated by the Singer chain or as independent businesses in most towns of 20,000 population or more. Singer, for instance, gives very good basic instruction for operating a sewing machine as part of the purchase price of a new machine. The same instruction is usually available to non-purchasers of sewing machines for a nominal fee. Department stores in large cities usually offer the same services in their sewing departments. Instruction is mostly needed to teach sewers to use the many attachments with which modern sewing machines are equipped; the basic sewing of a seam is simplicity itself to learn.

Some instruction in stitchery is also available at sewing centers and at special craft supply shops which are found usually in large cities and which specialize in sewing, knitting, crocheting, needlepoint, embroidery, etc. Sometimes churches and adult education programs offer sewing instruction. Indeed, there are probably more women taking sewing instruction now than ever before as the prices of women's and children's clothing, draperies, and curtains go up, driving women to make their own. The same conditions create a very good market for the truly expert seamstresses who are called upon to make the special items that the amateur cannot always make herself.

Equipment for stitchery offers no problems of capital or availability. Needles and thread, enough to sew together dozens of pillows and wall hangings, can be bought for only $2 or $3, which covers a wide variety of thread. Although an old shoe box will suffice, a sewing box or basket is really quite necessary. A fine sturdy basket may be purchased for only a couple of dollars. All of this may be found in the sewing department of large city stores, ordered by mail from Sears, Roebuck or Montgomery Ward, or acquired in the ubiquitous sewing or craft center.

A couple of pairs of good-quality scissors are also necessary, one large pair of shears with 4-inch blades for cutting shapes and a small pair of what are known as embroidery scissors for cutting small pieces and trimming thread. Good-quality scissors, Wiss or brands of similar quality made in Sheffield, England, or Solingen, West Germany, will cost about $8 for the large pair and $3 for the embroidery scissors. This essential sewing tool is available by mail order or at sewing centers, hardware stores, variety shops, and department stores. A tape measure, which may be bought for a dime, and a yardstick, which may be bought for half a dollar or acquired free at many hardware and paint stores, will be needed by the stitcher from time to time. Then, of course, a drawing pad and pencils and perhaps graph paper will be needed to work out designs and cut out patterns. All of the ancillary items may be purchased at variety or department stores or drug and grocery stores for minimal cost.

Although quilts may be made without a frame, the old-fashioned quilting frame used by early backwoods stitchers can save much time and guarantee more accurate stitching, particularly when more than one person is working on the quilt. The frame is quite easy to make at home.

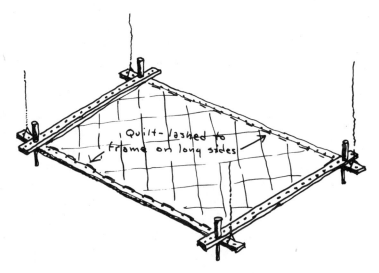

Quilting frame. Corners may be pegged or tied.
Hangs from ceiling or rests on knees of quilters.

It consists of two one-by-one-inch boards 6 feet long and
two 8 feet long, nailed or screwed together at the corners to form
a 6- by 8-foot rectangle. The frame will be a little easier to use
if the corners are shiplapped so that the sides of all boards are
on the same plane. After being assembled the boards are each
marked down the center with a pencil and 20d finishing nails are
driven through the board along this line so that the points of the
nails protrude about an inch on the other side. The cloth being
worked is stretched and fastened by forcing the nail points through
it. The frame then may rest in the laps of whoever is stitching
the patches to the foundation sheet.

A variation of this simple frame was also used by mountain
quilters. Sometimes the 8-foot boards were tied, instead of nailed,
to the corners and the cloth stretched by sewing it with an over-
hand stitch to all four boards. Such a design allows the 8-foot
boards to be untied after one or two courses of quilting squares

have been sewn down and the finished portion may be rolled up over the board to provide easier access to the next two or three courses. The thread binding the ends of the quilt to the frame is snipped by scissors to allow rolling up.

The seamstress needs more complicated equipment, some of which may also be adopted by stitchers when adequate capital is available. Basic, of course, for the seamstress is a good-quality sewing machine, either new or secondhand.

There are legions of sewing machine manufacturers in the world, mostly concentrated in the United States, the countries of Western Europe, and Japan. Each one of these areas has manufacturers which turn out good-quality merchandise and others which produce very cheap machines—poorly designed and poorly made but which sell for a low price. Machines to be used for professional sewing should not be bought on the basis of price but on the basis of reputation of the manufacturer, quality of construction, and versatility. One of the best available is the Singer, the only one now made in the United States, which is offered in a number of different models selling at different prices but all offering good value for the price. The differences in price are based on degree of versatility, not quality of construction and design. There are also some excellent sewing machines made in West Germany, England, Switzerland, and Sweden. The products of Japan seem to be improving steadily. Singer, however, seems to be the world leader in design and engineering and in pioneering with new machines which do a fantastic job in making hidden stitches for hems, in finishing buttonholes, in machine embroidery, and in other refinements which until a few years ago were found only on clothes mass-produced with industrial machines. Nowadays, perhaps as a further reflection of the rising cost of women's and children's clothing, home sewing machines made in the United States are capable of turning out, if the operator is skillful, the same complicated machine stitching formerly done only by industrial machines.

Sewing machines may be purchased new for as little as $40 or $50, but the machines of this price generally are not a good buy. One should consider a machine made only by a reputable manufacturer, and the simplest model in this category will sell for about $100. It will not have the refinements of more expensive machines but it will do a most satisfactory job in stitching and buttonholing and will last for a long time. For $150 one can acquire a machine which does zig-zag hemming and flexi-stitch, which are especially useful when working with knit materials. An additional $75 is needed for a machine equipped with an exchangeable disc control which allows almost any type stitch known to seamstresses.

Machines which can be used for embroidery and very fancy stitching akin to embroidery cost from $350 to $500 for a portable model. If a fine cabinet is desired then the cost might go as high as $250 for cabinet alone, making the complete machine cost around $700. But fancy cabinets do no better sewing than portable machines, and the portable machine is quite sufficient for even the most sophisticated seamstress.

Of course, the main difference between complicated and uncomplicated sewing machines is the number of attachments for special functions which are included with more expensive models. These attachments can usually be bought separately so that the beginning seamstress with limited capital can start her craft career with a less expensive, basic machine and acquire the attachments, one by one, at a later date. Attachments for special stitching can be bought for from $5 to $25 each, depending on the manufacturer and the model.

The beginner must realize that shopping is essential before a sewing machine is purchased. Machines can be seen and tried at the extensive national chain of Singer Sewing Centers, of course; at department stores, which display a variety of machines made in the United States and other parts of the world; and at independent sewing shops. Mail order catalogs from Sears, Roebuck, Montgomery Ward, John Plain, and other firms should also be examined after one has actually looked at various models in stores. Discount firms, most of which also offer mail order service, and which are found in virtually all larger cities, should be checked out on price before a final purchase is made.

A new sewing machine is generally furnished with perhaps half a dozen bobbins, those shiny steel spools which are hidden beneath the needle and are wound on the machine with the same thread as the spool on top of the machine. Most seamstresses, in order to save the time of unwinding and rewinding bobbins with different colored thread, are continuously adding to their supply of bobbins. New bobbins may be bought at fabric and variety stores at a cost of about 40¢ for a package of three.

Other equipment of a necessary but minor nature is needed by the seamstress. Scissors are needed, of course, the same variety used by the stitcher. A good supply of thread in different colors, in spools which sell for about 30¢ each, should be accumulated, and a basket or box in which to keep the thread is a great convenience and labor saver. A regular sewing basket, which sells for from $2 to $10; a good large wooden cigar box, which can be begged at no cost from tobacco stores, drug stores, and the cigar counters of fine clubs and restaurants; or specially made sewing boxes—all are efficient storage places for thread and the other concomitants of sewing.

Certain shop equipment, not designed for but usually adaptable to the needs of sewing, is of prime importance. Chief among this is a sturdy table on which a portable sewing machine may be used or a sturdy cabinet, furnished with ample drawer space, if a cabinet model is used. Also, the seamstress, working grandly with yards of material instead of the scraps of the stitcher, must have a large, clean space on which to lay the material out flat and cut it according to paper patterns. A dining room table is most suitable for cutting, and so is a kitchen counter. This job can be done on a clean floor, but a table of some kind will add greatly to efficiency.

A comfortable chair is also an important necessity and good light, from a window in daylight or from a strong electric light at night, is needed without equivocation. Such furniture is usually found in the home, but if not it can be acquired either new or secondhand from furniture or junk shops. Table, chair, and lamp should be available for a total of $100 new or for as little as $25 secondhand. New or secondhand furniture should be picked carefully for sturdiness and durability.

Most stitching and sewing is done at home rather than in a regular shop. A studio, however, is coveted by even the most homebound craftsman because it provides space in which work in progress may be left overnight and where the accumulation of material and small equipment may be stored safely and handily. If possible it should be further equipped with a dresser providing drawer space and with either a shelved closet or a wall cabinet where sewing machine accessories, thread, material, and other equipment may be kept convenient to the sewing machine and the table on which it sits.

The studio does not need to be large but it should be roomy enough so that there is ample traffic space between the furniture and easy access to storage facilities. A room about 15 feet square should be ideal if lighting is suitable. Often an unused servant's room, an extra bedroom, or windowed space in an attic is ideal for a sewing room. If at all possible it should be the private domain of the seamstress and stitcher, with access to others by invitation only.

When a private studio is not possible, the craftsman should have certain places in the sewing room which are private, where the machine may be stored when not in use, where work in progress may be neatly put away, and where thread and bobbins and scissors may be kept safely for use only by the seamstress.

The material for stitching and sewing poses different problems for the two crafts. Customers of the seamstress usually purchase their own material, patterns, thread, zippers, and buttons and hire the seamstress only to do the work. Sometimes the work requires cloth-covered buttons which are made with very simple equipment that lasts a lifetime. For making such buttons, the seamstress will require a supply of metal button bodies in various sizes and the covering equipment, consisting of a small metal swage and a crimper, which is a small, short rod that is struck with a hammer. Button-covering equipment may be bought at sewing centers or other sources where sewing equipment and material is available. It costs less than a dollar and may be used for years without wearing out. Grommets for laces and the clamps with which grommets are crimped onto the cloth are also found at sewing centers for between $1 and $2. This equipment, too, defies wearing out, though it does get permanently misplaced if one is not careful.

Much time can be saved in the process of sewing if one

maintains a good supply of all the miscellaneous items needed to finish clothing—such things as pearl and metal buttons in different sizes, hooks, snaps, seambinding, and thread in a garden of colors. A $5 investment will yield an abundance of such miscellany, and its readiness can save many trips to the sewing center when the time involved may be better applied to production and profit.

Stitchers, of course, produce works of art as it were, original items for which they must provide their own material. Usually no great amount of material is needed for such items as pillows, wall hangings, or even quilts, and much of the material used will be quite small in size, no more than scraps of cloth she can find or accumulate, keeping them in a scrap box much as a blacksmith develops his invaluable scrap pile of odd bits and pieces of iron. Even old neckties make fine scraps for all sorts of stitchery including quilts.

The stitcher, however, might wish to keep certain large pieces of material around to serve as the foundation of whatever she may wish to make in the future. This may be sailcloth, Indian Head, sheeting, satin, velvet, or wool, depending on the artistic taste of the stitcher. For this reason it is impossible to state the cost of purchasing such material. The stitcher must shop carefully, pick out what she thinks may have a future use, and buy it on sale when possible. Cotton cloth of good quality now sells for from $1 to $1.50 a yard. Wool, silk, and velvet cost $8 to $10 a yard and on up.

Like the seamstress, the stitcher should also include in her materials various buttons, ribbons, and bows, some that will take her fancy when no project is underway, some that she will salvage from discarded dresses or pillows or other things ready for disposal.

Seamstresses cannot display their work too easily except on their customers. Those few who make special skirts and shirts and costume-like clothes sometimes display these products in hippie-type boutiques and craft cooperatives. A few dress shops in larger cities might be persuaded to display blouses and ponchos on consignment, but there is a disadvantage in the dealings of a seamstress and a regular retail outlet. Working independently, the seamstress can furnish excellent workmanship directly to her customers at a price less than that charged by stores. If, however, she sells to the stores at the same price, the store must add its margin and often puts the final price far above that of comparable workmanship turned out by regular clothing factories.

Selling the seamstress's work, then, is generally a matter of word-of-mouth communication. Possibly one of the best means of selling sewing is to solicit the business of a team of high school cheerleaders, and do so well that the team recommends the seamstress's work to the next year's team ad infinitum. Good workmanship in this field can also lead to commissions for graduation party dresses, bridesmaid dresses, and a host of other special clothes over the years.

Many sewing centers and material shops, such as the Walter J. Penney chain, encourage local seamstresses to post their names and telephone numbers in a special bulletin area in the shop. The seamstress can find no better advertising medium than this. It costs nothing and is exposed to the potential market at the marketplace. Some seamstresses also advertise in the want ad sections of local and neighborhood newspapers. Rates for these papers may be learned by calling the classified advertising office of each.

Stitching, being as much art as craft with its original designs and execution, may be sold much as the other textile crafts, such as weaving, are sold. Gift shops make fine outlets for pillows and quilts, wall hangings, cocktail aprons, appliqued dish towels, and perky potholders. Many gift shops are constantly looking for a supply of such items, which sell at a good price, and the stitcher should seek out several in her community, take samples by, and do a selling job on the proprietor. If the work is good, display will be all the selling required. If the shop is already well stocked with similar items the stitcher should go back, again with her samples, at a later, more propitious time.

The craft fair is also a good medium for selling stitchery. Work should be displayed at a fair in the same manner as weaving, tapestry, or ironwork, perhaps hung from a cross-pole on the booth or laid out on a large table. Original design, good colors, a variety of items, and, especially for stitchers, a sense of original humor will attract customers almost every time. Also, the artist should have some feeling for his clientele; is it old or young, rich or modest in income? Items which fit the tastes and pocketbooks of specific areas will sell more quickly.

Some galleries are interested in giving special shows for stitchers and in providing continuous display for wall hangings and sculptural pieces. If the stitcher does not know any gallery owners personally she should seek some out, introduce herself, show them samples and photographs of her work, and ask for display. Art teachers will know where galleries are located, who operates them, and what the specialty of each is.

The phenomenal interest in sewing which is apparent in every section of the country offers another source of income to accomplished seamstresses and stitchers. Sewing centers and craft shops need teachers, and those artists who find satisfaction in teaching should investigate the possibilities by visiting stores and the recreational departments of county, state, and municipal governments which conduct regular classes in various crafts.

Teaching might be paid for with a salary, or income might be derived from charging each student a fee for each lesson.

Salaries for teaching must be negotiated and vary from place to place according to circumstances. If fees are the basis of income it is suggested that each student pay $1 for an hour's lesson.

In most parts of the country seamstresses may expect to be paid about $4 an hour for sewing when the customer furnishes pattern and materials. If pattern and material are furnished by the seamstress she of course charges the customer for these and adds a 15 or 20 percent fee to compensate for the time needed to obtain them.

Stitchers should aim at being paid on the basis of about $4 an hour, although this reflects only labor and not the artistic value of the stitcher's work. If a stitcher comes up with a good design, she should test the market a bit and perhaps can get paid considerably more than $4 per hour. On the other hand, $4 an hour for a particularly complicated piece of work might well make the cost of the piece too high to attract a costumer. Pricing stitchery must be done on a practical basis, but experience is needed to gain the best prices.

Both stitchers and seamstresses should sign each piece of work turned out. The easiest way to do this is to buy a roll of name tapes through a sewing center or in response to advertisements in sewing magazines and pattern books. These labels are not distinctive, but they cost only a couple of dollars for a roll of 100 labels.

A much more artistic signature can be embroidered on a small piece of ribbon which may be sewn into the work in an inconspicuous spot. The seamstress who has a machine capable of embroidering can do this on her machine. Stitchers can embroider initials at some inconspicuous spot on a pillow, apron, or quilt, or they might wish to devise a signature symbol which may be embroidered on the work. Some sort of identification for the artist is important, however, and can do much to build a reputation and gain commissions based on the desirable qualities of the work. In effect a signature is the best sort of advertising and well worth the investment of effort needed to create it in an artistic, distinctive manner.

SOURCES OF SUPPLY

Cloth of all sorts may be bought from local department stores, fabric centers, and such large chains as J. C. Penney, Walter J. Penney, Sears, and Montgomery Ward. Thread, needles, and halter-making equipment and other items are usually found at the same sources.

CHAPTER VI

The Lacemaker

BOBBIN lacemakers are somewhat rare in the United States at this time although lacemaking is a flourishing craft in most of the countries of Europe. It is a form of weaving without a loom that was developed centuries ago in Flanders and thence spread into the surrounding nations, including England. Bobbins in several distinctive national forms, fine linen thread, parchment, brass pins, and all the other tools of the craft are readily available in Europe and from one or two suppliers in the United States.

Like most forms of weaving, lace is now mass produced in the United States so much more cheaply than by hand that the only competitive advantage held by the lacemaker is original design and the beauty of handwork, which can never really be matched by the machine. Lace is used for traditional purposes even today. It is used mostly as a trim for lingerie, dresses, and blouses, for very delicate but nonfunctional handkerchiefs, for dainty mats on which to set drinks, and for table mats, and napkins for special dinner parties. It can also be used for small tablecloths but the time necessary to make a lace tablecloth by hand would make the item so expensive that it is not likely a market will be easily found.

Wall hangings may also be made, not from the fine thread usually used for lace but from heavy mason's cord which sells for about 75¢ a ball. Wall hangings are made quickly because of the heavy cord used and it is a good item on which to learn the craft. It requires special large bobbins, however, but these can be improvised from lengths of wooden dowels, available at hardware stores, retail lumber outlets, and craft shops. Tenpenny nails can also be used as bobbins for coarse lace work.

Mason's cord may also be used to make coarse table coverings, perhaps in color, or even bedspreads, which might find a rather good and lucrative market.

Indeed, the time necessary to make even a yard of lace trim an inch wide by hand puts handmade lace into the luxury classification, which perhaps explains why it is more a hobby than a means of livelihood in the United States and most countries of Western Europe. A real expert can turn out a yard of trim in an hour, after the pattern has been designed and punched in parchment and bobbins wound and pins put in place for starting. But most lacemakers, even those with considerable experience, can turn out only 12 to 14 inches an hour, which makes the product very expensive indeed merely from the standpoint of labor. The craft, however, is challenging and fascinating and makes a fine hobby which can bring in a little income from part-time work or from teaching.

The main problem of the beginning lacemaker is finding a place to learn the craft. There are a few books, mostly from England, which describe the techniques and tools in detail, and there are regular classes in England, but none known to the author in the United States.

Two books on lacemaking are listed in the bibliography to this chapter. *Bobbin Lace, Step by Step,* by Osma Gallinger Todd, is available from the Osma G. Todd Studio, 319 Mendoya Avenue, Coral Gables, Florida 33134. The other, published in England, is *Handmade Bobbin Lace Work,* by Margaret Maidmort. This book is available in the United States only from Robin and Russ Handweavers, 533 North Adams Street, McMinnville, Oregon 97128. Both the Todd Studio and Robin and Russ might be able to advise aspiring lacemakers where the lacemakers of the United States are located so that they may be asked for instruction. Someplace, 2990 Adeline Street, Berkeley, California 94703, which sells lacemaking supplies, might also be of help in finding lacemakers in various parts of the country. Most lacemakers seem quite dedicated to their art and will probably be most willing to help aspiring lacemakers get started.

Equipment for bobbin lacemaking is small but specialized. Bobbins, of course, are essential, because a piece of lace only an inch wide requires about 2 dozen bobbins, and wider pieces can require 5 or 6 dozen for one design. Most bobbins available in the United States are made in Sweden and sell for about $3 a dozen. English bobbins are of a different design and are not available in this country except through antique dealers. Those antique dealers who sell English furniture sometimes find a drawer full of old bobbins which they sell for practically nothing, most not knowing what they are.

Rosewood bobbins, also made in Sweden, may cost up to $1.25 each, but while pretty they are no more efficient than the standard birch bobbins.

English bobbins are longer and thinner than the Swedish variety, and the English type is made of many materials which reflect the avid interest of English lacemakers in their art. Some are made of common woods like beech, birch, or maple. Others, though, are turned in ebony, rosewood, mahogany, bone, or ivory. In the nineteenth century many had the name of the lacemaker engraved on them, and these are fast becoming collector's items. And about the year 1818 a candidate for Parliament, the Hon. John Osborn, distributed lace bobbins with his name on them instead of campaign buttons.

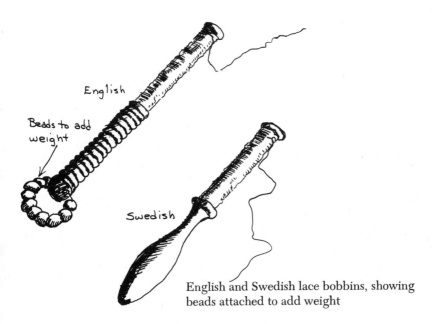

English and Swedish lace bobbins, showing beads attached to add weight

While any size thread may be used for lace, the traditional thread is of light linen. It may be purchased from the suppliers listed earlier in this chapter for a cost of $1 to $2.50 a spool. Of course, common sewing thread of cotton or silk or synthetic material will make lace also. The linen thread, however, is quite durable as well as traditional.

Lace is made by weaving the design much like a cat's cradle made of string to amuse children, but with pins substituted for one's fingers. Brass pins are preferable because they do not rust, but heavy bank pins, which are found at office supply stores for about 50¢ a thousand, may be suitable. Brass pins are available from lace supply houses.

Designs for lace must be worked out on special graph paper which has the lines crossing at either a 45° or a 50° angle. Regular graph paper will do for the 45° angle merely by visualizing lines which bisect the regular 90° angles of the squares. For designs requiring the 50° angle, though, a special paper must be drawn up, a somewhat tedious but not a difficult task if a protractor, a rule, and a sharp pencil are available. Once a master graph paper is drawn it may be easily reproduced in a Xerox-type machine.

After being worked out on graph paper, the design must be transferred to a strip of heavy parchment paper about 2 or 3 inches wide and 12 to 18 inches long. Transfer is accomplished by placing the graph paper over the parchment and pricking through both with a pricker, a small tool resembling an awl. Prickers may be bought from lace supply houses for about $1.50 each, but they are easily made by inserting a large darning needle, eye first, into the end of a quarter-inch dowel 4 or 5 inches long. Lines showing the relationship of threads to holes must then be drawn on the parchment with a pen or fine pencil, ink being preferable. Any heavy paper or light cardboard may be substituted for parchment paper, but nothing holds up quite so well as the parchment. Parchment sometimes may be found at art supply stores or office supply stores for about $1 for a 27-inch by 33-inch sheet, which yields enough paper for several dozen patterns.

Another essential bit of lacemaking equipment is the roll-shaped, straw-stuffed pillow which is the lacemaker's workbench. The pillow is available in different sizes, the smaller ones being suitable for relatively narrow lace trim, the larger ones necessary for handkerchiefs, table cloths, runners, and larger items. Small pillows are about 8 inches long and 9 to 12 inches in diameter. Pillows are stuffed tightly with straw to provide a body into which the pins will stick securely without falling out at a crucial moment. Pillows are covered with a heavy Indian Head material or heavy linen.

When in use the pillow is held in the lacemaker's lap or set on a table. The parchment pattern is secured to the pillow around its circumference with several pins and other pins are inserted in the previously pierced holes which form the pattern. Threads from the bobbins are looped on the pins, and the bobbins are allowed to hang over the circumference of the pillow toward the lacemaker. As the lace progresses the bobbins are unwound.

Pillows are the most expensive piece of the lacemaker's equipment. Small pillows, available from the three supply houses listed above, cost about $20 and large ones about $30. Pillows can be made at home for less money if good straw is available for stuffing, but unless the straw is stuffed properly the pins will not hold and the pillow will be useless.

One other piece of equipment is valuable but not absolutely necessary. This is the bobbin winder, a small machine which winds the bobbin neatly when a crank is turned. It sells for about $15. Its main advantage is that it keeps the thread clean; thread often becomes soiled when wound on the bobbin by hand.

A lacemaker can start her activity with a capital expenditure of

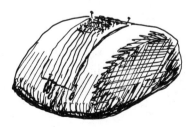

Lacemaker's pillow

from $40 to $60 depending on the sizes of pillows desired and the number of bobbins needed.

Lacemaking can be done almost anywhere, living room, bedroom, porch, or patio. No special shop is needed.

As with other textile craftsmen, the lacemaker should try to charge no less than $3 an hour for her time plus the cost of material. Lacemaking is such a slow and tedious operation, though, that a charge even of $3 an hour makes a narrow piece of handmade lace sell for almost $10 a yard; the lacemaker cannot expect too many customers to pay this sort of price. She can sell a few wall hangings, tablecloths, or other items made of large cord which are woven much faster than lace trim, and she can give lessons.

Although some women in Europe make a living making lace all day every day, not many American women have the time or the patience to follow this example, nor can they find a market which will pay them adequately for the time needed. But women, and perhaps some men, will find lacemaking a fascinating and satisfying hobby, especially when a daughter's wedding gown can be trimmed with handmade lace in the classic tradition, or when an old friend can be given a rare handmade lace handkerchief for Christmas. And if enough ladies can be persuaded of the virtues of lacemaking as a hobby, a condition certainly prevalent in Europe, then the rare but accomplished lacemaker in America will be needed to give lessons. She can explain the equipment and its use, demonstrate how to create new patterns, and show how to manipulate the bobbins to make these patterns a reality in linen thread.

Lessons can be given as part of a craft program for young and old sponsored by government bureaus, churches, YWCA, or Girl Scouts. They might become a prime attraction for a craft shop, and the lacemaker should approach craft shops in her community to sell them on the idea. About the only risk involved in teaching is in time spent seeing if enough students will be willing to pay $1 an hour to learn an ancient craft requiring great skill and taste. Teaching might also uncover a purchaser for a few yards of exquisite handmade lace for some special purpose.

SOURCES OF SUPPLY

Robin and Russ Handweavers
533 North Adams Street
McMinnville, Oregon 97128

Someplace
2990 Adeline Street
Berkeley, California 94703

The Osma G. Todd Studio
319 Mendoya Avenue
Coral Gables, Florida 33134

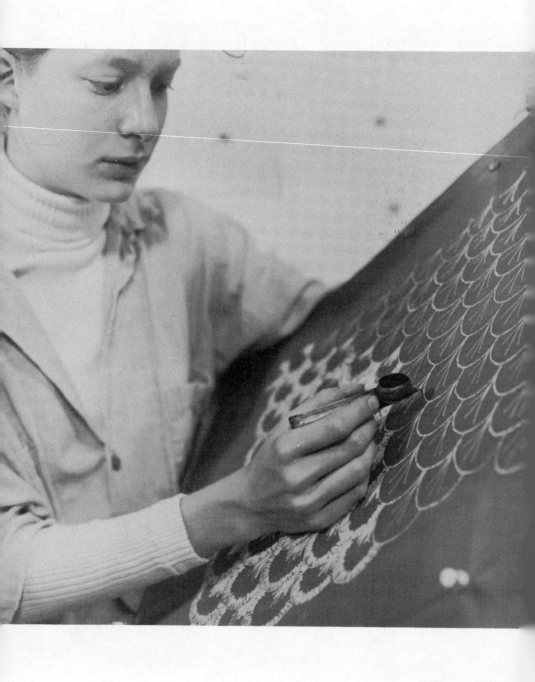

CHAPTER VII

The Batik Printer

BATIK dyeing is probably the most outstanding example of the cosmopolitan attitude of the crafts in America, the melting pot. And it is possibly the most outstanding reflection of the influence of rapid, easy communication all over the world in the age of the renaissance of crafts.

Batik is an ancient craft in the East, practiced widely in the islands of Indonesia, such as Bali and Sumatra, places which until a few years ago were considered only as settings for the stories of Maugham and Conrad, places exploited by European rubber barons, exotic fever places better read about than visited. But all this has changed. Since the intimate exposure of the Orient to Americans during World War II and the improvement in transportation in the last generation, the Orient is now closer to New York or San Francisco in terms of time than Boston was to New York at the beginning of the industrial revolution. As a consequence batik has become an American craft, executed by Americans and adapted to American design and functions.

Essentially batik is done on the principle of etching, with cloth being substituted for metal, dye replacing etching acid, and wax protecting the material from the dye. For in batik one spreads wax where he does not want the dye to penetrate, dips the cloth in dye, washes out the wax, and repeats the process, using another color of dye.

In Indonesia, currently as well as 400 years ago, many batik designs are quite traditional and executed in only two colors by several processes. The most common process, done by rural villagers, used animal fat instead of wax on a coarse cloth instead of fine silk. The finest, before the coming of democracy, was done only by licensed artists in the king's court and each printing was considered a masterpiece. Short cuts were developed in later times, however. Instead of painting and then scribing areas of wax on both sides of the material, some modern batik printers actually print the designs with wooden blocks on which the fine lines are delineated with raised wire mounted in the blocks. Still later, when industrial processes reached Indonesia, very beautiful batik has been mass produced on huge rotary printing presses. The artist, though, during his training, is concerned only with handmade batik, the training needed, and the equipment required.

As with so many of the textile crafts, batik is used mainly for wall hangings, an item not wildly popular with the public even though it is steadily receiving more acceptance as the public is exposed to the medium. And much as the saris of Hindu women have been adapted to Western modes, batik is also used for women's gowns. Batik dyers in the United States can take advantage of such fashion by designing batik sheets that can easily be adapted to clothing without great interference with the design. Some modern American batik is used for tablecloths, for luncheon mats, and for covering divider screens. It may also be used for women's head scarves or large colorful handkerchiefs. Draperies are ideal subjects for batik designs.

As with most modern crafts, training in batik consists of learning design applicable to the material and the relatively simple technique. Such training is found in the art schools of universities around the country, as shown in the American Crafts Council listings, which may be ordered directly from the ACC, or in a few craft schools such as Penland Crafts School at Penland, North Carolina, Haystack School at Deer Isle, Maine, and others in California and the Southwest. Many municipally operated craft schools, most of them open year round, also offer excellent training in batik, for from $1 to $2 a session. A telephone call to the recreational department of any city will yield the place and cost of craft lessons. Much can be learned from studying books on the subject, some of them listed in the bibliography to this chapter, and by visiting museums and exhibitions which display fine examples of batik. Background in techniques, acquired directly from experience or indirectly from books, will do much to help one appreciate the delicacy of the design.

Equipment for batik working is as simple as is the technique. The tools used by Indonesian masters are rather difficult to acquire but modern versions of these ancient tools can be bought inexpensively from batik suppliers listed in the appendix of this chapter.

Two types of tjanting

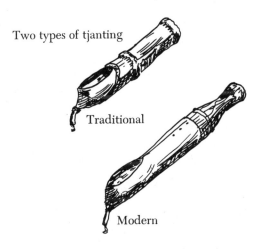

Traditional

Modern

For instance, the stylus used in Indonesia, called *tjanting*, is made of bamboo with a copper spout and a handle. The copper basin of this peculiar tool is filled with melted wax and applied to the white cloth through the spout. Several tjantings are needed for each piece of work, so that different sized spouts may be used to make relatively wide or narrow applications of wax. The American version, however, is easier to find and works just as well as the Indonesian. It sells for about $1.50.

Of course, melted wax—half paraffin and half beeswax—is an essential of batik. Paraffin may be picked up in most grocery stores at about 50¢ a pound. Beeswax sells for about $1 a pound in craft and art supply stores.

Possibly the most convenient melting equipment for wax is an electric frying pan which may be purchased at hardware and department stores for about $16 to $18 new. These pans can sometimes be picked up for a mere $2 at a flea market or secondhand store which deals in such equipment.

Fairly good-sized pots, perhaps two or three, are also needed for immersion of the fabric first in starch, to stiffen the material before wax is applied, and for dyeing. Starch costs only about 30¢ for a 1-pound box in almost any grocery store. Dye, preferably German dye, sells for about 35¢ a packet and is available at craft shops or from the mail order suppliers listed at the back of this chapter.

Regular dyes must be applied cold to preserve the protection of the wax. American dyes must be bought carefully, however, and experimented with because some, from all manufacturers, tend to run and thereby destroy the precise designs in batik. Modern Indonesians use a very fine German dye which is sometimes available in some large metropolitan areas of the country. It sells for about the same price as American dye.

The German dye is especially good because one dye will yield four or five different tones or distinct colors when vegetable mordants are soaked in it. The variety of mordants is great, consisting of such interesting substances as mimosa leaves, oak chips, beet slices, and other vegetable matter. Mordants may generally be acquired in the kitchen or yard of the artist or a friend. Mordants can seldom be bought because they are simply not offered for sale.

Five-gallon, galvanized mop pails are suitable for starching and dyeing if smaller pieces are being worked. Ten- and twenty-five-gallon galvanized wash tubs may be used for larger pieces. The five-gallon pails may be purchased at hardware stores for about $1.50 to $2 each. The tubs cost about $3 for a ten-gallon size and $4 to $4.50 for the large twenty-five-gallon size.

After starching or dyeing, the material must be stretched tightly to eliminate any wrinkles while drying. This is done on a large wooden frame which may be identical to the quilting frame illustrated in Chapter V or may be modified somewhat to facilitate the job of stretching. Indeed, instead of inserting a series of small nails through the frame, one may nail on a number of spring clips used to secure papers in office files. These cost about 5¢ apiece for a 1½-inch clip. Clips should be placed about 1½ inches apart, as shown in the illustration. Also, adjustable frames may be made, as shown in the sketch, for about $2 worth of 2-inch by 1-inch lumber, available at any retail lumber dealer. Pushpins, available at art supply

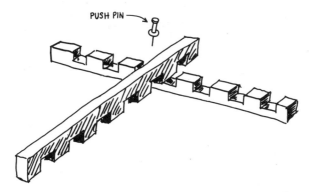

PUSH PIN

Construction of adjustable stretching frame for batik

or office supply stores at about 1¢ apiece, may be used instead of nails for small items.

Modern American batik may be done on cotton, linen, or silk. The beginner will probably wish to start his career with cotton, which is the least expensive of the three. Cotton bleached muslin sells for about 40¢ a yard on bolts that are only a yard wide and therefore suitable only for smaller items. Bleached percale sheets, however, may be bought for about $3 each. If the batik dyer is located in an area where textile mills are found he might investigate these mills as sources for bleached cotton sheeting of several widths at reduced prices, especially for odd-length remnants.

Linen is readily available in the fabric departments of large department stores for from $3 to $6 a yard for material 36 to 45 inches wide. The difference in price reflects the difference in quality, width, and heaviness of the linen.

The pure unadulterated silk needed for the best batik is considerably harder to purchase and more expensive than cotton or linen. Most stores and fabric centers no longer offer pure silk. The source for it now is either Europe, Hong Kong, Japan, or India, and the supply from these places is rather undependable. Pure silk may be bought from Hong Kong for from about $2 to $3 a yard for the 40-inch width. Silk from India should be somewhat less expensive if a source can be located, while silk from Japan and Switzerland should cost slightly more. The serious batik dyer should talk to craft teachers in universities, municipal craft centers, and craft schools to learn where silk and other materials may be gotten. The sources and prices are changing every day.

Ordinarily, very little space is needed for batik dyeing. However, large pieces require a large drying frame and a large table for applying wax prior to dyeing. If done at home the kitchen, all things considered, is a convenient shop merely because of its linoleum or tile floor which resists dyes and wax. There must be an available counter or table large enough to spread the material flat to apply the wax and to support the drying frame or stretcher while the material is being fixed to it. The stretcher can be leaned against a wall while the dye dries.

The equipment for starting work in the art of batik may be gotten for less than $25, a relatively small investment in the craft field. The question from the business standpoint is whether or not the monetary return from batik makes even a $25 investment worthwhile.

Probably not, from the standpoint of livelihood. A very few batik artists in the whole nation of 210 million might make a decent living by selling batik items, but even this is doubtful. Certainly it cannot be done except in the large metropolitan centers. As a hobby, or as a part-time professional craft, batik dyeing can offer great satisfaction and a little supplementary income. The exotic origin of the technique, the rich transparent color, the painstaking application of wax are all satisfying factors which outweigh the tedium of starching, dyeing, and stretching the wet fabric. And the results, in scarves, draperies, or wall hangings in one's home can be distinctive and gratifying.

The batik dyer can hardly expect to charge more than $3 an hour for his time because demand for batik is not enough to make the supplying of it more valuable. Yet, on larger items the process requires many, many hours and the finished item will hardly be worth enough to most people to pay the cost. Batik requires a special, sensitive market, but even the individuals in this group cannot use batik for everything; there comes a point of saturation.

Batik, however, like glass, weaving, and stitchery, can be produced in limited editions for wall hanging, scarves, and similar items. This means that all items in the edition can be prepared together. Perhaps six or eight or more scarves can be waxed on one piece of fabric at one time; the whole piece of fabric can be dyed and stretched at one time; then the separate scarves can be cut apart and hemmed. Such rudimentary mass production can make each hour far more productive than if scarves are made one at a time, and the charge per hour can be consequently higher, perhaps $5. Limited editions can be sold to women's dress shops or to special mail order houses if the quality of design and work warrants it.

As with other crafts batik can be displayed and sold at art and craft fairs in any community and it is displayed by some galleries. A list of fairs in each state is usually available through the state Chamber of Commerce or from the department of state government dealing with tourist development.

Batik patterns designed especially to be made into clothing might be displayed at fabric or sewing centers, possibly on consignment. The managers of these stores must be called upon and shown samples.

As with other nonprofitable but interesting crafts some income may be derived by the skilled batik artist through teaching the art in craft schools. Those courses administered by municipal governments sometimes need teachers who will be engaged on a salary arrangement. Craft shops, and possibly sewing centers and fabric shops, might hire a teacher of batik if the artist can show that any students coming for lessons will probably buy equipment and materials from the sponsoring shop. Stores usually pay a salary to teachers, varying from one locality to the next. Those teachers who, through personality, imagination, and skill, can draw larger classes can demand higher salaries. Teaching also provides an appreciative audience to which to display one's own work.

Training and experience in batik dyeing offers another advantage to those artists who wish to enter professionally the field of textile manufacturing. It offers superb training in designing mass-produced fabrics, for which there is a great demand. Batik patterns themselves may be sold to fabric manufacturers on a royalty basis or for a negotiated fee. Or, if the job is appealing, the artist may wish to get on the payroll of the design department of a large textile manufacturer. Designs may be sent to the design director. Alternatively, application for a regular job may be made to the personnel director of the desired company or to the personnel department of a management engineering firm, some of which are found in most large cities.

Whatever the artist does, he should be certain to sign his work in some way as a means of building a reputation and gaining valuable recognition locally or nationally.

SOURCES OF SUPPLY

Aiko's Art Materials Import
714 North Wabash Avenue
Chicago, Illinois 60611

Fibrec Dye Company
2795 16th Street
San Francisco, California 94103

Glen Black
1414 Grant Avenue
San Francisco, California 94133

Poly Products Corporation
13810 Nelson Avenue
Detroit, Michigan 48227

Triarco Arts & Crafts
P.O. Box 106
Northfield, Illinois 60093

CHAPTER VIII

The Tie Dyer

ALTHOUGH its origins go back thousands of years to the Orient, tie dyeing became popular in America during the height of the so-called youth rebellion in the late 1960s. It manifested itself at first not as an art but as a mode of personal decoration that was new, different, and seemingly unconnected with the traditions of the past. During this period thousands of students dressed themselves in tie-dyed T-shirts and tie-dyed jeans. When the manufacturers of youth clothing saw the extent of the fashion they quickly produced all manner of items which were printed to simulate tie dyeing and thus spread the exposure of the medium even more.

Once established, tie dyeing was adopted by the textile artist, its value as a design medium recognized, and its potential developed in the art schools of universities all over the country. Its adoption ties in well with the innovative spirit of the textile artist found in universities and modern craft schools in the United States. Also, its simple technique has made it popular with hobbyists all over the country. Indeed, tie dyeing probably makes a much better hobby than a professional craft as its market is not large and the techniques and inexpensive materials and equipment attract far more artists than the market can absorb.

Original tie-dyed items are still popular to a degree with young people in the 1970s; such items include striped jeans (often discolored with bleaching agents rather than colored with dyes to make a design), shirts for men and women decorated with sunbursts, and scarves. Many of these items follow the original American designs in two colors. In the last few years, however, the sophisticated

artists have endowed the original amateur's designs with a mass of color and combinations of stripes and sunbursts and all manner of marvelous effects harking back to the Oriental origins of the art. As a consequence the serious tie dyer can produce very attractive fabrics suitable for wall hangings, tablecloths, place mats, coaster mats, and materials for long dresses, shirts, slacks, umbrellas, and bedspreads. The more sophisticated designs of the neo-tie-dyer require more sophisticated techniques and a deep sense of design, but the medium may still be learned quickly and done well with little training so long as the artist has a basic talent for design.

Training for tie dyeing is neither of long duration nor difficult. Basically the process consists of tying string, or wrapping a rubber band, tightly around bunched fabric, then dipping the fabric, a bit at a time, into a pot of dye. The dye penetrates that part of the fabric which is not tightly bound and leaves the tightly bound portions undyed. If a long piece of fabric, or the legs of jeans, are tied in several places then dyed, the result is irregular stripes of color. If a square piece of cloth is tied in the middle and more ties placed around the bunched fabric to its edge, the result is a sunburst of irregular stripes of color radiating from the center tie. A combination of several colors and stripes and sunbursts can create, with successive dipping in different colored dyes, a most attractive design, each design being unique.

This technique can be learned in the art schools of universities all over the country, either in design classes or in textile classes. It may also be learned in craft schools such as Penland Crafts School at Penland, North Carolina, and in the museums and very good craft schools administered by municipal, state, and county governments such as the Chastain Crafts Center in Atlanta. Usually there is someone with experience in the basic technique of tie dyeing in almost every group of college or upper-high school students, and since equipment is as simple as the technique, these amateur artists can give lessons at home.

A number of books describing techniques are found in the bibliography for this chapter.

The equipment for tie dyeing is virtually limited to string, dye or bleach, and one or two galvanized, plastic, or enamel pails for dyeing. String may be found at any hardware store, drug store, office supplier, or ten cent store and costs about 65¢ a ball. Rubber bands can be bought at the drug store or office supply store for around 15¢ per hundred. Dye may be bought at drug stores or department stores for about 25¢ a packet; fine German dyes can be purchased at about the same price from mail order suppliers listed in the appendix to this chapter.

Galvanized or plastic pails may be bought at hardware stores and sometimes at grocery stores for about $2.50 for a 10-gallon size. Enamel pails are found at the same sources for about $4 to $5 each. Many artists prefer the enamel pails because the inside, usually white, will not become discolored from successive dyeings and will reflect the true color of the dye before the fabric is dipped in it. Small cooking pots or bowls may be used for small items.

Tie dyeing can be done almost anywhere in the home. All that is needed for shop equipment, really, is a water tap with which to fill the pails to mix the dye. Of course, some facilities for drying must be in or near the working area, but these might consist of a mere clothes line, a gas or electric home clothes dryer, or an indoor clothes drying rack, the folding type of wood or steel, which may be bought at hardware or department stores for from $5 to $10 each. Those who wish to try tie dyeing in a commune might easily resort to the old frontier method of drying by spreading the fabric over a bush.

Almost any organic material except wool is suitable for tie dyeing, and new techniques might be suitable even for wool. The only requirement for the fabric used is that it take dye, a criterion which eliminates many of the new synthetic materials. Prices for different materials run from 60¢ a yard for 45-inch-wide unbleached cotton muslin to $3 or $4 a yard for hard-to-get silk.

All of this material except silk is available at sewing centers, fabric chain stores such as Walter J. Penney, and the fabric sections of department stores. If the artist lives in an area where textile mills are found he might check the mill-end stores which sell remnants at an excellent discount.

If the tie dyer wishes to try his art on readymade clothing such as jeans and knitted T-shirts, he must pay from $5 to about $9 for the jeans and about $3 for a pure cotton knitted T-shirt. It is probably best, however, to seek commissions for tie dyeing jeans and shirts. Otherwise the artist must expend too much of his capital in stocking numerous sizes of both items, and sales will likely not be brisk enough to support such capital outlay.

Craft fairs are good places to display and sell tie-dyed items. A list of these may be acquired from state Chambers of Commerce, the addresses of which are available at any local chamber of commerce, or from the tourist development department of state governments, which may be written to at state capitals.

Also, tie-dyed items are popular with the young clientele of craft cooperatives which may be found by searching in the youth areas of most large cities or on college campuses.

Local dress shops might be interested in stocking tie-dyed scarves and shirts. The interest from dress shops will vary from locale to locale, so shop owners must be approached by making personal calls on the operators and managers with samples. Some managers will dismiss the idea rather rudely, but others will be most cooperative and helpful and will freely offer suggestions on which items will sell and which will not, which materials will sell best, and how items should be priced. Clearly, then, it will be well worth the tie dyer's time to make personal visits to shops. He can learn a great deal about the marketing of his craft if he does not take rebuff too personally.

Because of competition, both from the hosts of skillful tie dyers and from other crafts which compete for the discretionary dollar, the tie dyer cannot expect to earn more than $2 or $2.50 an hour for his work, with perhaps an extra bonus tacked on the hourly fee for a particularly attractive piece. Tie dyeing offers more satisfaction as a hobby, or as one of several crafts done by a craftsman, than as an exclusive means of livelihood.

Because the tie dyer cannot expect a very high hourly fee for his work, he must plan his production carefully so that he can produce more items per hour. This might be done by investing in additional dyeing pails, which may be left full of dyes in a number of colors to eliminate the time needed for frequent mixing; or he might dye a number of scarves or other small items at one time, cutting them apart after dyeing and drying. The more time he can devote to production while minimizing the time needed for preparing to produce, the more profit he can expect.

Tie dyers, however, even the ones who have not reached the apex of design and craftsmanship, can sometimes find teaching jobs at which they can make supplementary income from a small salary and which will develop their own skill while teaching neophytes. One can apply for teaching assignments at craft supply shops, municipal craft programs, and summer camps.

All tie-dyed items should be labeled or signed in some way by the artist as a subtle sort of advertising. Cloth labels available at sewing centers, or by mail order in response to advertisements in sewing and craft magazines, sell for about $5 for a tape which has a hundred labels. These are easily stitched on each item.

SOURCES OF SUPPLY

See Sources of Supply for Batik Printer, Chapter VII.

CHAPTER IX

The Silk Screen and Block Printer

THE artist who attempts to make a comfortable living only through printing original designs on cloth with silk screen, linoleum, or wooden blocks is indeed flying into the face of competitive adversity. Printing presses—huge rotary machines which are continually being refined to print faster—hold a virtual monopoly in the marketplace for printed fabrics.

For generations, mass-produced, printed fabrics have replaced, through reproduction, the fine, primitive designs of African tribes, the noble handmade batik of Indonesia, and even the painted buckskin of the American Indians. Of course, the original beauty of the handmade designs cannot be exactly duplicated by the machine, but the production of thousands of yards of print material in an hour's time gives the printing press an overwhelming advantage in productive cost when compared to the tedium of printing even one yard of material by hand.

All this does not mean that hand printing should disappear as an art form. It is still an important and satisfying craft. But the reality of the machine makes it difficult for the handcraftsman to make a living producing printed fabric.

Printing by silk screen or block is alike in principle, being different only in the equipment needed and in technique. Silk screen printing requires the forcing of ink, or viscous dye, through a fine silk fabric which has been overlaid with a stencil that forms the design of each color. Its equipment consists of the screen stretched tautly on a wooden frame, stencil paper and knives to cut the stencil, dye or ink, and a rubber squeegee with which the ink is forced

through the screen. The process is conducted on a table large enough to hold the fabric being printed from the floor.

Block printing, on the other hand, is accomplished by carving the surface of blocks of linoleum mounted on wood, or of solid sugar pine, into designs, one for each color, applying dye to the consequent raised surface of the block with a roller, and transferring this dye to the cloth by placing the inked block face down on the cloth and hammering it with a rubber mallet.

Both processes can produce designs of any number of colors by successive printings, carefully planned and executed, which place the color to create abstract, traditional, or pictorial patterns.

Printing is related to batik and tie dyeing in the manner of items produced by the handcraftsman, with perhaps a little more emphasis on designs which may be used for personal clothing, draperies, or other items which are made of yard goods. The textile printer also makes wall hangings, small items such as scarves and kerchiefs, table mats, tablecloths, napkins, pillow covers, and, on occasion, upholstery material for special decorative effects. Hand printing can be particularly effective for upholstery fabric because the printer can design blocks which will print to fit the peculiar shapes of chair seats, backs, and upholstered arms. With a little imagination and a good sense of design the hand printer can decorate virtually anything made of woven fabric.

Both silk screen and block printing are included in the curriculum of the textile sections of most university art schools and craft schools such as Penland at Penland, North Carolina, and Haystack at Deer Isle, Maine. Both are also taught very effectively in the crafts schools operated by many municipal governments, such as the crafts program of the Parks Department in Atlanta. A list of universities with art departments and craft schools may be ordered from the American Crafts Council for a small fee, as shown in the appendix of this book. Information about municipal and county-operated craft schools may be gotten by telephoning county and municipal governments. Most government-run crafts programs charge a small fee for lessons, usually from $6 to $15 for a six-week course, the difference in the fee being determined by the cost of materials needed. As might be expected, the materials for fabric printing are not as expensive as the materials for silverwork, gold work, and jewelry making.

Homemade silk-screen frame with silk and stencil installed, and squeegee

Equipment varies for silk screen and block printing. The silk screener requires a frame, which might be homemade, bought from an art supply store, or ordered from a supply source for from $5 to $25 depending on size. Screen cloth, which costs about $2.50 a yard, and stencil paper, which costs about $2 a roll, are required. Also needed is a sharp knife (or razor blade) which can be bought at art supply or office supply stores for $1 to $1.50. Screen cloth and stencil paper are usually available also at art supply stores or may be ordered from firms listed in the supply source appendix for this chapter.

The silk screener also needs a piece of plate glass 2 feet square on which to mix ink, a putty knife, and an ink roller. Plate glass may be purchased at any glass supply house for about $3 to $4. It can be obtained, too, in automobile junk yards by asking for the flat window of a wrecked or junked car, at variable costs depending on locality and circumstances but probably for much less than the cost of a piece of plate glass. Good-quality putty knives are available at hardware stores for about 75¢. Ink rollers may be bought at most art supply stores or ordered from the supply houses listed in the appendix to this chapter. If the silk screener or block printer lives in a fairly large city he might be able to purchase a roller at a printing supply house. The cost at either source will be from $3.50 to $5.00

depending on size and quality. Fabric printers generally use a roller from 6 to 9 inches long. Dye is forced through the silk screen stencil with a wooden squeegee which has a rubber lip across its bottom. Squeegees may be bought at art supply stores and craft shops or ordered from art supply mail order houses, as listed in the appendix to this chapter. They cost from $2.50 to $7.50 depending on size.

A stencil type dye is needed for silk screening on fabric. It may be bought in tubes or cans of various sizes and costs about $6 a pound. Art supply stores and mail order art supply dealers usually stock a good selection of colors in silk screen fabric dye.

For block printing the artist needs a supply of sugar pine (not white pine), knot free, up to 11 inches wide and at least 1 inch thick if large blocks are to be carved. This may be bought from lumber supply houses in large cities that specialize in special woods, from the supply sources listed in the appendix of this chapter, from art supply stores and craft shops. Sugar pine generally sells for about 35¢ a board foot.

When linoleum is used, it may be bought at one of the proliferation of flooring supply outlets, usually found in large cities, at hardware stores, or at retail lumber dealers. Art supply stores, mail order art supply firms, and Sears, Roebuck, Montgomery Ward, and other general mail order houses also sell linoleum. One must get a fairly thick, smooth-surfaced linoleum for printing. It generally costs about 25¢ a square foot, or may be purchased for less if scrap is available from a flooring supply store, lumber dealer, or a home builder.

Linoleum, of course, must be mounted on a block of wood before carving or printing. Regular floor tile glue, which sells for about 50¢ a pint, may be used for mounting, and the block may be any kind of wood if it is at least 1 inch thick. Suitable wood for linoleum blocks may be found at the site of a house being constructed, where scrap is free (cuttings from stair treads being preferable because of thickness), or obtained from a local retail lumber dealer. One should ask for five quarter stuff. It sells for about 40¢ a board foot, or less if scraps are available.

Plate glass is also needed by the block printer, as is a putty knife and ink roller.

Of utmost importance to the block printer, however, is a set of from 6 to 12 high-quality carving tools. The best carving tools are made in England, Germany, or Switzerland, although some are also made in Sweden and Italy. These imported tools may sometimes be found in large hardware stores but are more likely to be available in art supply stores or from mail order supply houses listed in the supply source appendix of this chapter. At least one mail order firm—the Woodcraft Supply Company in Woburn, Massachusetts—stocks both Swiss tools and the superlative Marples tools from England. Imported carving tools of professional quality cost from about $3 to $7 each depending on size and design; some special types cost as much as $16. The block printer may generally be adequately equipped with about $25 worth of carving tools.

It is essential, too, that he have a set of sharpening stones. A general bench stone about 8 inches by 2 inches by 1 inch can cost up to $40, but satisfactory stones are available at much less cost. The block printer will need a bench stone with a coarse and a fine side, which costs about $4 for an India stone, about $10 for an Arkansas soft stone, and about $18 for an Arkansas hard stone. In addition a soft round-edged slipstone of white Arkansas is needed at a cost of about $4, and a hard slip will be necessary for an additional $8.

The block printer will also require a rubber mallet which may be found in hardware stores or at Sears, Roebuck for about $5.

The same sort of dye is used for block printing fabrics as for silk screening.

Since printing is a rather messy operation, special shop space is advised for the silk screener and block printer. A detached shop is not essential, certainly, but a special room is more a necessity than a luxury. First of all one needs a table on which to work. This may be an ordinary kitchen table for silk screening, with a surface of at least about 4 feet by 6 feet so that there will be adequate space for the screen, possibly for the glass on which the ink is mixed, and for cutting stencils. Such a table can be bought at furniture stores or Sears, Roebuck, unpainted, for about $15 or from a secondhand furniture store for about $10. If possible a wide shelf might be attached to a wall of the room for cutting stencils and mixing ink. This shelf might have shelves underneath it for storing ink, screen

Design for homemade shelf-table
for silk screening and block
printing

cloth, stencil paper, and knives. The whole structure may easily be
built from ¾-inch plywood for between $15 and $20. Refer to the
sketch shown here for design. A good light, costing from $5 to $10,
is also necessary.

The room itself should be no smaller than 12 feet by 12 feet, for
there must be clean floor space on which to unroll a bolt of cloth
if the printer intends to print yard goods for clothing or draperies.

A fully equipped silk screening shop will probably cost between $50 and $100 to set up, depending on how handy the artist
is in constructing tables, screen frames, and what all, or how lucky
he is in adapting surplus furniture and scrap lumber to his needs.

Block printing requires about the same amount of shop space
and tables and shelves, the main difference being that a sturdy table
is required to withstand the constant hammering of blocks with a
rubber mallet, even though no great amount of force is required.
One may purchase such a table, either new or secondhand for about
$5 more than the silk screener's table, or he may construct his own
with 4-inch by 4-inch legs, 2-inch by 6-inch rails braced in the
middle and a piece of ¾-inch plywood for the top. Material for
constructing such a table may be bought at almost any retail lumber dealers and should cost no more than $15. The accompanying
sketch indicates design and construction.

As will be learned in training, the block printer must have a padded space on the table, made of several layers of cloth or paper, on which he prints, to guarantee that his pounded blocks print evenly. Scraps, at virtually no expense, may be used.

The block printer requires more capital than the silk screener to set up shop due to the expense of woodcutting tools, sharpening stones, et al. He should expect to spend at least $100 for his tools and equipment and an additional $75 may be needed for furniture, the total depending on the price of plywood and the number of woodcarving tools desired. As with most crafts, however, block printing can be started with a minimum number of tools and more tools may be acquired as capital and needs increase.

Cost of the cloth on which printed designs are applied varies according to the cloth. Plain unbleached cotton muslin may be purchased at fabric centers, sewing centers, department stores, and Sears, Roebuck for about 40¢ a yard. Linen costs about $3 to $6 a yard for good-quality material 45 inches wide, and silk, when it can be found, may run as high as $4 to $9 a yard. Cotton is excellent for gaining experience and silk may be bought in small quantities for small items such as scarves and kerchiefs. Also, the synthetic materials, even glass fabric if the right sort of ink or dye is used, are most suitable for fabric printing.

There is not a wide market for hand printed fabrics and the printing artist should not expect to earn more than about $3 an hour until he acquires a reputation based on original design, craftsmanship, and an eye for what his market will buy. To the hourly cost for labor he should add the cost of his material plus a 15 to 20 percent to markup on the materials to pay for his time in acquiring them.

Marketing hand printed fabrics follows much the same route as finding customers for other textile crafts. Art and craft fairs are good media of distribution and sales. Lists of these fairs with dates, fees, and commissions may be gotten by writing state Chambers of Commerce or the tourist development departments of state governments.

Some galleries in college towns or large cities show hand printed fabrics of unique design and style and will continue to exhibit the work of the artist if his work demands attention and sales from the public.

Also, small printed items such as scarves might be sold by showing them to dress shop managers, mostly of smaller independent shops, to offer a unique item which gives them a competitive edge. Dress shops which cater to a more sophisticated, affluent clientele will probably offer more potential to the artist.

And, since printing lends itself particularly to limited editions, the printer might investigate the special mail order houses which sell limited editions nationally. The names of these entrepreneurs may be acquired by looking for their advertisements in shelter, art, and antique magazines, which are found in most public libraries of any size.

Teaching, of course, is always a way to make a little money in the crafts. Fabric printing is interesting to many dilettantes as a fascinating, challenging hobby. Teachers of fabric printing are needed by summer camps, craft centers, and government craft programs. The would-be teacher should make a list of camps from magazine advertisements or by calling local YMCA's or churches which have summer camp programs. By personally visiting craft shops with samples of work in hand, and by telephoning local government programs, the hopeful teacher will uncover individuals who may talk about a job.

Pay for teaching varies from locality to locality. At best, however, it will probably offer no more than supplementary income.

SOURCES OF SUPPLY

Advance Process Supply Company
400 North Nolde Street
Chicago, Illinois 60622

ALD Screen Printing Supply Co.
716 Rex, N.E.
Canton, Ohio 44702

Ceramichrome, Inc.
7155 Fenwick Lane
Westminster, California 92683

Fibrec Dye Center
2795 16th Street
San Francisco, California 94103

Hunt Manufacturing Company
1405 Locust Street
Philadelphia, Pennsylvania 19102

Naz-Dar Company
1087 North Branch
Chicago, Illinois 60622

Rembrandt Graphic Arts Company
Stockton, New Jersey 08559

Weber Costello
1900 Narragansett Avenue
Chicago, Illinois 60639

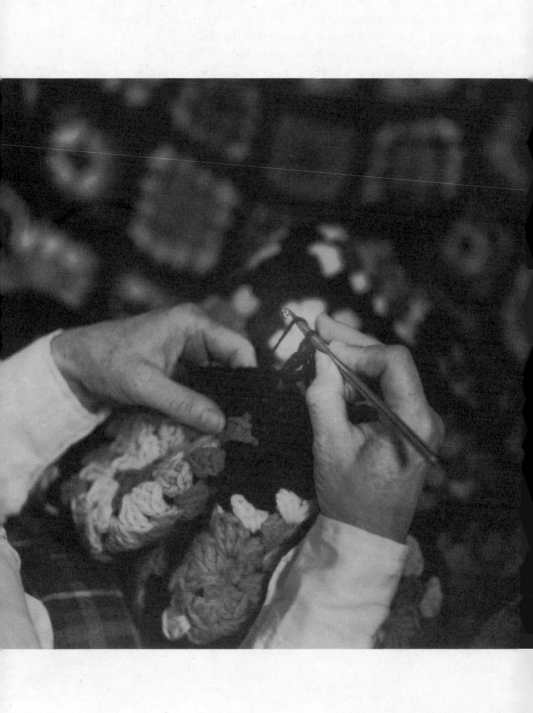

CHAPTER X

The Knitter and Crocheter

SINCE the advent of the industrial age both knitting and crocheting have become functional, widely practiced home hobbies. Knitting is the more popular of the two while crocheting is the easier. Both hobbies produce items that have been in use for ages but which are now for the most part produced by the million by knitting machines in knitting factories. Yet, despite the influx of the machine, both hand knitting and crocheting still might find a small, although undependable, market in some localities. The superior texture and design of hand knitted and crocheted items, and the flexibility which allows the handcraftsman to make each and every item unique if desired are the factors which must be used to sell hand knitting and crocheting to any potential market.

Both crafts, which use similar techniques, require yarn and needles, the knitter usually working with wool or a synthetic substitute for wool, and using two or three needles; the crocheter working with small cotton or linen thread as well as wool, and using a single needle with a shallow hook on its end.

The traditional products of the two crafts distinguish one from the other more than techniques and materials.

For instance, the knitter (the word undoubtedly shares its derivation with the word *knot*) mainly produces articles of clothing, shaped to fit various parts of the human body.

Knitted sweaters, caps, gloves, mittens, socks, and baby clothing all providing the efficient warmth of insulating air trapped in the knots, are the mainstays of the knitter's art. Patient and skillful knitters, however, are quite capable of turning out hand knitted dresses.

And many a young girl in olden times learned the craft by knitting tea cozies to insulate a pot of tea and keep it warm on a cold winter's day.

But there is a modern facet to knitting, too, fostered by the same artistic spirit and imagination that has turned the ancient weaver into an artist rather than just a craftsman. The manifestation of this is that some enterprising knitters are beginning to use the old technique to make a new type of wall hanging, sometimes small and sometimes as large as a bedspread. Some of these hangings are close knit, using small needles, which take a long time to produce. Others are netlike in quality, abstract in design with dimensions reminiscent of modern finger woven fabrics. This of course is art, purely and simply, and as it develops and gains recognition it will put knitting on a new plane in the world of art and perhaps attract gallery operators as a new source of sales.

Crocheting, on the other hand, lends itself more readily to flat articles such as place mats, afghans, bedspreads, and antimacassars (those Victorian upholstery protectors against hair oil, which now are seldom seen, and then only as ornaments). And sometimes the modern crocheter will use very coarse cotton yarn, practically soft rope, to quickly make ornamental potholders for bridal showers and unsentimental gifts for special occasions.

Knitting and crocheting are traditionally such home crafts that one seldom finds a class in either technique in the sophisticated craft and art curricula of universities, in summer camps, or even in municipal craft programs. Yet, while most women are no longer required to provide warm clothing and ornamentation for the home, hundreds of thousands of women each year seek the instruction they can no longer obtain from a mother, an older sister, or an aunt. And it should be said that although knitting and crocheting are considered women's work, many men find the gentle clicking of knitting needles or the sure progression of crocheting a restful surcease from the press of business matters or the tedium of retirement.

The instruction these people seek is most often found in craft centers in the larger cities of the nation, or, in the very largest cities, in the shops devoted exclusively to knitting and crocheting materials, which build and maintain their trade through making lessons available to potential customers. There are so many of these shops around the country that a list of them cannot practically be included in a book of this sort. They may be located by reference to the telephone book in any community, or by asking a knitting friend where she buys her material and inquiring there about lessons. Some excellent books on knitting are listed in this chapter's bibliography.

As compared with most other crafts the equipment and shop space required for knitting and crocheting is so simple as to be startling. Knitting requires two needles and a pair of dextrous hands. Shop space is not required at all, for the skillful knitter, particularly, can ply her craft in a moving automobile, a darkened movie theatre, or while submitting to the ordinarily distracting influence of a television set.

Of course, there are various sized needles for different sized yarn and for special effects in both activities. Knitting needles range in size from slim plastic or metal needles 1/16 of an inch in diameter and 6 inches long to large wooden needles up to 1 inch in diameter and 1 foot long, the wooden surface being polished smooth as glass to prevent snagging. Crochet needles come in practically the same sizes for the same reasons and range from small metal and plastic needles to large ones made of polished wood. Needles for both crafts may be found in craft centers, fabric centers, and knit shops as well as in department stores and the Sears, Roebuck catalog. Cost of needles ranges from 65¢ a pair for small sizes to $1.50 a pair for the large.

Crocheters who turn out place mats of linen or cotton thread will also need a stretcher which may be homemade from four small boards and small aluminum nails or may be bought in an adjustable form at any of the suppliers of needles for about $6 each.

Material for both knitting and crocheting is as simple as the equipment. Loosely twisted yarn, usually wool, is needed for clothing, afghans, and bedspreads. Tightly twisted cotton and linen thread, much larger than any sewing thread, is used by the crocheter for place mats and similar products. The material, too, may be found at craft shops, fabric shops, and department stores, both local and mail order. Wool, in many colors and tones, sells for around $2 a skein, with at least 6 or 7 skeins being needed to make a man's sweater. Cotton and linen thread is sold at the same type outlets for about 65¢ for a large ball of cotton and $1.50 for linen.

Wool is the traditional material for knitting and crocheting yarns. It still offers the most vibrant and exciting colors and therefore has the most artistic potential for knitters and crocheters. But acrylic and other synthetic yarns are gaining rapidly in favor. The practical adaptability of these new materials to the demands of modern life is making old, rich colors and designs less meaningful.

Acrylic simply will not dye as well as wool, but it will hold its shape after working, it may be washed in a machine and dried in a mechanical dryer, and it may be stored in any drawer or closet with no fear of damage by moths and other vermin. Also, in many cases it is less expensive than wool. Consequently, and sadly, the modern knitter and crocheter is advised to give serious consideration to the use of acrylic yarns. Sweaters and afghans made of the synthetic materials will probably sell more easily.

As a standard of cost of items made, one may consider that two 4-ounce skeins (total cost: $2 to $3) will supply enough yarn to make one vest.

Presentation to the public of knitting and crocheting is rather more difficult than for sewing, stitchery, or weaving. They simply do not lend themselves to display in craft fairs and galleries as well as a number of other crafts. Really they are too functional, as clothing and table linen, and should be seen in the shops which specialize in these artistic commodities. The only exception is to seek display in knit shops where they will be very much appreciated by the aficionados who trade there.

To sell in this limited marketplace both knitter and crocheter should take samples to show the managers of men's and women's clothing shops, gift shops which sell linen, and of course, knit shops. Some handknit sweaters are sold in very good volume at men's and dress shops and the devaluation of the dollar now offers the American knitter a real advantage in competing with the European knitter. Until 1973 European hand knitting usually sold at a lower price because of a lower labor cost. This is true no more.

Always, too, the handknit sweater, however beautifully designed and knit, must compete with very handsome and functional sweaters turned out by the woolen knitting mills. The same applies to crocheted items, which do not have direct competition from mills but which must compete with mass-produced equivalents.

Knit shops generally show more interest in buying and displaying handknit ware than do department stores, which sell a large volume of mass-produced knitted items. The knit shops offer a little less competition. Further, in a knit shop one might be offered a teaching job at a salary consistent with similar part-time jobs in any particular area. And a teaching job exposes one's skill to an appreciative captive market which might buy handmade sweaters and table items.

Both knitter and crocheter should try to demand at least $3 an hour for the labor of making all items, plus the cost of materials, plus a 15 to 20 percent fee for the time and taste spent in purchasing the yarn.

Woven label tapes with the artist's name may be ordered from sewing centers or from mail order houses which advertise in sewing magazines for about $5 per hundred labels. Such labels offer fine identification for items of clothing and large crocheted pieces but cannot always be used on table mats and antimacassars. Whenever possible, though, both knitter and crocheter should try to use some sort of signature, as a means of seeking commissions.

SOURCES OF SUPPLY

Those who produce and teach knitting and crocheting, both on a professional and an amateur basis, seem to feel that the best and least expensive sources of supply for yarns of wool, cotton, linen, and synthetic fibers are local sources. These include such ubiquitous retail establishments as:

Sears	Arlans
J.C. Penney	Woolworth
K. Mart	Kresge

Of course, Sears, J.C. Penney, and Montgomery Ward have mail order catalogs which offer, at good prices, a variety of fibers and colors, needles, and sometimes stretchers. These stores also sell instruction and design books. Local sources for the knitter and crotcheter include most variety stores, department stores, large and small, and a number of regional discount chains such as Richway, Treasure Island, and others.

CHAPTER XI

The Basketmaker

IT may seem strange to most that baskets are included in the textile crafts, that field of soft and clinging materials so different in character from the usually rather rigid baskets. But baskets, above all, are woven objects using the same basic technique of warp and weft and wrapping that is found in weaving and tapestry. Only the materials are different.

Basketry is as ancient a craft as weaving and pottery. Originally, it offered a way to supply functional containers for a myriad of uses which eventually included temporary containers for human bodies in the form of wicker furniture. Until the middle of the nineteenth century baskets were important equipment for farms, city households, and shops of all sorts. They were used to hold trash or charcoal, to gather corn and cotton, to measure grain, to catch fish, to sieve flour and meal, and to take fowl to market. In fact, baskets still retain a great deal of importance for modern society. There are machines which can mass-produce bushel and peck baskets used, until the last generation, to ship fruit and vegetables to city grocery stores.

Alas, baskets in industry are seen less and less these days, and even machine-made baskets are sometimes sold in antique shops; fruit and fowl are shipped to market largely in that most unglamorous manifestation of late twentieth century culture, the cardboard box.

But basketry has not died out. It seems to be reviving in another manifestation of twentieth century culture, the crafts renaissance. And while it is no longer used as a common container it still is functional in ways unthought of in the eighteenth century, and with embellishments of artistic worth which emphasize the basic artistry of its craftsmanship.

Modern baskets, which represent basketry of the future no doubt, appear in strange places: in a lady's boudoir where they hold jewelry; in an executive office where they contain waste paper, or on a barbecue table where they lend strength and security to paper plates. Baskets are popular for women's handbags, provide color in living rooms, and are used as lamp bases and other interesting decorations. Some modern basket makers have even produced that rather common form of transition between the ancient craft and the new art, wall hangings, made of various materials, colorful and interesting and durable as a purely decorative art.

Small flat baskets can be used as key trays, or to hold glass ash trays; larger flat baskets serve admirably as serving trays. And the rectangular lidded wicker baskets imported in some quantity from India make attractive weekend bags.

But regardless of the necessary art which must be applied to all modern crafts, baskets are still essentially containers. The artist who wishes to make his living making baskets, therefore, should address himself to the areas where containers are needed. Heaven knows, in the affluent age of the late twentieth century, people have an excess of possessions which they must store, carry, and all too often throw away; baskets offer handsome, artistic, practical containers for all these uses, just as they have since man first began to accumulate possessions. So the modern basket maker, in order to find a market for his art, must apply to the functions of his work the same depth of imagination he applies to its form, color, and decoration.

Again reflecting the astounding versatility of university textile arts instructors, the best training for making baskets is in art schools of universities (more and more of which are adding crafts courses to their curricula) and in craft schools such as Penland at Penland, North Carolina, and Haystack at Deer Isle, Maine. Basketry on the elementary level is also taught in many summer camps, in some church day camps, and in some YMCA day camps. As with a number of other crafts, instruction in basketry is sometimes difficult to find because basketmakers who can teach the craft are in short supply.

A list of universities teaching basketry as part of the textiles course may be obtained from the American Crafts Council for a minimal fee by writing to the address in the training appendix in the back of this book. Information on basketry courses in camps may be obtained by writing directly to the camps in the American Summer Camp Association List which is also available in most city or university libraries. Camps are also listed in *Vogue, Seventeen, National Geographic, Boys' Life*, and other parent- and youth-oriented periodicals which may be found in libraries or on newsstands. One other source of instruction in basketry is the crafts programs of municipal and county governments which may be inquired about by calling the recreational departments of these governments as listed in the telephone book.

A great deal can be learned about making baskets through reading the books listed in the bibliography for this chapter and by examining all manner of baskets, ancient and modern, in the museums of cities and universities. Even more can be learned by watching basketmakers work in such historical restorations as Williamsburg, Virginia; Old Sturbridge Village, Massachusetts; Dearborn Village, Michigan; Westville, Georgia; and others. Also, since American Indians made wide use of baskets, one can visit various Indian reservations and watch skilled basketmakers at work. The Cherokee Reservation in North Carolina has especially skillful basket-makers living in all areas of the reservation; some demonstrate their skill in the restored historical Cherokee Village in Cherokee, North Carolina.

The equipment needed to make baskets is most limited and depends on whether or not the basketmaker buys or makes his own splints, and what type of baskets he wishes to make.

All that is needed for making woven splint baskets from the beginning is an axe or saw for cutting small trees, a wedge and sledge to split the trees and a small, sharp knife of good quality with which to split and scrape the splints to a satisfactory finish. If bought splints are used, only the knife is necessary. Axes, available at hardware and sporting goods stores, cost from $5 to $10 depending on size and quality. Wedges, found at the same sources, sell for about $3.50 to $4; 6-pound sledges usually sell for around $10. Knives, either paring knives or pocket knives, cost from $1.50 to $8.

For making coiled baskets one needs only a large sailmaker's needle in which to thread raffia or yarn or whatever material is being used to fasten the coils together.

One added bit of equipment for almost any type basket is a soaking tub to keep splints and other rigid material flexible enough to work. This may be a 5-gallon galvanized pail which sells at hardware, department, and some grocery stores for about $2.50, or a larger 10- or 20-gallon washtub which sells for about $3.50 to $4.50. The Cherokees often use a pool in a crystal clear, cold mountain stream.

And while pre-colored basketry material is available, some basket weavers, certainly the Cherokees, do their own dyeing either with modern artificial dyes or natural vegetable dyes made from native plants and everyday materials such as black walnut hulls, goldenrod, sumac, and berries. Merely soaking oak splints in a container with a piece of iron, for instance, turns the splints black. If dyeing is done by the basketmaker, several pails or tubs, bought at the hardware or grocery store for from $2.50 to $4.50, will be needed as well as a source of heat, which might be the kitchen stove, a charcoal grill, or an electric plate.

Modern dyes cost about 25¢ to 40¢ a packet and may be bought at craft shops, drug stores, or grocery stores, or ordered by mail from the weaving suppliers listed in back of the chapter on weaving.

Traditionally the shops for basketmaking have been the front yard or front porch in the summer time and a comfortable spot in front of the fire in the winter. Space is needed, for basket making material can be quite bulky in some cases. While the actual weaving is usually done in the artist's lap, or on the ground in front of a chair, small baskets might be woven with more comfort on a roomy table, with the soaking tub handily set beside one's chair.

Of course, a separate room is always valuable but by no means necessary for making baskets. It is wise, however, to have separate storage space. This might consist of a closet or a large chest.

Materials for baskets come from all over the world. They are oak splints, willow splints, honeysuckle vine, native cane, corn husks, native grasses, palmetto leaves, palm leaves, pine needles,

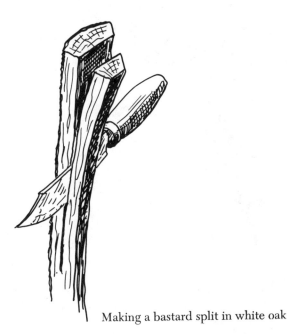

Making a bastard split in white oak

almost anything long enough or flexible enough to be woven into rigid or semi-rigid containers. Imported materials such as raffia and rattan reeds are quite popular in modern basketmaking.

Almost all these materials may be ordered from supply houses and bought from local craft shops at fairly reasonable prices, although prices are difficult to specify on a quantitative basis. Usually raffia, rattan, oak splints, and other materials are sold in pound bundles. A bundle of oak splints, for instance, enough to make a gallon-sized basket, should cost about $2. Enough raffia and rattan to make a coiled basket of the same size might cost from $2 to $3.

Of course, if the basket maker has equipped himself with axe, sledge, and wedge, he may learn to make his own oak or maple splints after instruction and experience, using what the old-timers called a "bastard" split, a term which is most appropriate until the neophyte learns what he is doing. Also, pine needles and honey-

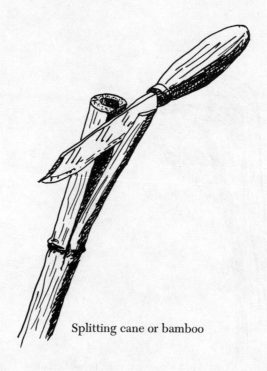

Splitting cane or bamboo

suckle vines can be gathered at any rural or even suburban roadside; cane splints, although they are available for cash, may also be made at home with a sharp knife and acquired skill. The cane used is the miniature bamboo-type grass which grows in swampy spots along the edges of creeks in many parts of the country. And, for that matter, bamboo itself, which is grown in most parts of the United States for garden purposes, may be split into the same type splints that have been used for basketmaking in the Far East for millennia.

Basketmaking is so versatile in its use of materials, so basic in its general technique, so widely applicable to modern and primitive needs that it is difficult to state exactly how much its material will cost in terms of dollars. Each basketmaker must search for the wealth of raw material in his own area, request catalogs from suppliers listed in the back of this chapter for more exotic materials, and decide for himself how much of his capital must be spent to supply himself with what he needs to make the sorts of baskets he desires.

Handsome handmade baskets are something of a rarity in the late twentieth century, but, if they are well designed, well made, and functional in the context of our times, baskets are marketable in many places. They should be shown to managers of gift shops, to managers and buyers of variety shops and dress shops (for baskets may function as handbags), or to the buyers of furniture or women's handbags in large department stores.

Craft fairs, a list of which can be obtained from state Chambers of Commerce or the tourist development department of state governments, provide excellent presentation and sales potential for small baskets. The actual weaving of baskets at the display serves as a fascinating drawing card.

For large baskets, hardware stores serve as excellent outlets. Some large leaf baskets are more or less mass-produced, but many managers of hardware stores will be interested in the beautiful, old-fashioned handmade oak baskets which sell for about $10 to $12. The basketmaker should take samples of his work to show the manager and contract, usually on a verbal basis, for at least a dozen baskets at a time.

Again, $3 an hour is a good labor fee for the basket maker to hope for, but as in weaving, his speed of production will affect the hourly fee he can expect. A fast craftsman might well make $5 or $6 an hour for his work. And for such fancy items as decorated basketry handbags or sophisticated waste baskets he can expect a higher labor fee which includes the value of his designs.

Craftsmen must realize that making a living in a way they like also puts them squarely into business, with compulsory obligation to consider such factors as competition, supply and demand, pricing, distribution, and other ghastly but most realistic considerations. As a businessman the craftsman must investigate the income and tastes of his markets, and the imagination and merchandising ability of the store managers who agree to stock his work, and then he must respond to these realities with types of baskets and other items which fulfill the desires of the market. If he satisfies the requirements of the market he might expect to make up to $10 an hour for his labor.

Reputation is a business factor also. The basket weaver might conceivably contact the news media, so his craft can be transformed into interesting copy for the public. His reputation may be built slowly by signing each basket he turns out. A signature can easily be placed on the bottom of each piece of work by writing name and town with an indelible laundry marker in some inconspicuous place. If the texture of the basket refuses such a signature, then a flat splint with the signature can be incorporated securely into almost any type or size basket one produces.

SOURCES OF SUPPLY

Bersteds Hobby Craft, Inc.
Box 40
Monmouth, Illinois 61462

Crafts of Cleveland Leather
2824 Lorain Avenue
Cleveland, Ohio 44113

Economy Handicrafts
47-11 Francis Lewis Boulevard
Flushing, New York 11361

Nasco House of Crafts
901 Janesville Avenue
Fort Atkinson, Wisconsin 53538

Vanguard Crafts, Inc.
2915 Avenue J
Brooklyn, New York 11210

2
Ceramics

CHAPTER XII

The Potter

ONE seldom sees a starving potter.

Of all the ancient crafts now being revived, pottery seems to satisfy the largest public demand. And the craft is still marketed much as it was in the eighteenth century, with established potters turning out a handsome volume of production to a fairly limited area. (Of course, a twentieth-century factor in the American potter's life is the volume of imported handmade pottery, usually very well designed, that is produced in Italy, Mexico, Spain, Japan, Hong Kong, and other countries around the world.)

It is true that before the days of mass production there was probably a larger proportion of potters in the population (usually at least one to any village of 1,000 people or more), but there is still, in the space age, a larger proportion of potters than that of any of the other crafts we have inherited from prehistory. This fact alone indicates the continuing demand for handmade articles of fired clay. And demand is illustrated in a more forceful manner when one considers that there are several potters in the United States in the 1970s who are reported to earn as much as $40,000 to $50,000 income a year from making and selling handmade pottery. Of course, such income, comparable to that of highly paid business executives, is an exception. If it were not, half the world would fervently embrace pottery as a full-time occupation whether they liked it or not.

There are many potters, however, who make a very comfortable living producing limited editions of certain artistic items and others who never went to art school but who turn out, as tradesmen (in the old-fashioned sense), most attractive articles. This group carries on the tradition of the preindustrial village potter and generally produces a limited variety of functional handmade pots which sell readily enough to provide a good livelihood. Then there are others who barely make it because of a variety of reasons: they do not know how to pot properly, or they do not know how to present their wares, how to price them, or how to design them to the tastes of their markets. This last group may enjoy being potters, but surely penury is not enjoyable even to the artist of simplest needs.

Things made of clay have always had exceptional variety in design and function. The modern potter's work is mostly functional, although more imaginative potter-artists have confiscated many forms and functions which previously were the exclusive domain of the glassblower, the enameler, the woodworker, and even the blacksmith.

For instance, in generations past no chatelaine would have considered the use of a wine decanter made of common clay. Yet at least one potter in the United States designs and throws such an item, large and interesting, embellished with all manner of decorations which reflect art and humor. This decanter serves a useful function for many people. And he sells it at a good price.

Other unusual articles of clay which are finding a good market in the late twentieth century are cases for mantel clocks (in modern, somewhat abstract design), orange juice squeezers, lamp bases in modern color and design, nut trays, large wine reservoirs, cooking utensils, and countless other items.

All of the new forms of pottery serve only to expand the variety of traditional, functional items also being produced such as bowls, tableware, cups, ash trays, sconces, flower pots, candle holders, bookends, bottles, storage and tobacco jars, tea and coffee pots, small trays, pitchers, syrup ladles, and numerous other things which are so integrated in our culture that we seldom notice them. And though the traditional articles of fired clay might sometimes seem mundane, the modern potter of artistic bent has given them new life through design and color sometimes far beyond the imagination and artistic capacity of the old village potter.

By far the most widely produced pots are the traditional pots, plates, and pitchers which are thrown on a wheel, then decorated and fired. Some potters, however, produce what is known as slab pots. These are made of flat slabs of clay joined together at the edges (sometimes, in the case, of bottles, with a thrown neck added to the cubic shape), then decorated and fired like other pots. Raku pottery is thrown or shaped like traditional pots but is fired in an open kiln in the manner of rural potters in Japan. The classic traditional pots of Taos and San Ildefonso pueblos in the Southwest are shaped by patiently joining coils of clay together with the hands, then firing in an open fire rather than a kiln.

As with other crafts, art in pottery often is substituted for function and a number of artist-potters turn out pots which are delicately shaped but which have such narrow necks that they are quite useless for anything but decoration. Others use the clay not for pots but for decorative sculpture, shaping the material with hands, paddles, and similar instruments, and decorating and firing in a kiln. The Museum of Contemporary Crafts in New York, which is operated by the American Crafts Council, has many exhibits of this type of sculptural pottery.

Pottery, however, lends itself to new designs and ideas. There is no more flexible medium of the arts than basic clay. Moreover, the very feel of it seems to stimulate ideas in the modern potter-artist's mind, and new shapes and decorations grow like magic under the craftsman's hands. Throwing a pot can be more like play than work. But the practical challenge of using different clays for thick or thin articles, the care needed to fire without warping or cracking, the mixing and application of glaze and color keep the potter's feet firmly on the ground, providing a satisfying balance between fantasy and reality.

But while pottery may seem like play and throwing a pot may appear to be so easy as to be natural to anyone, the aspiring artist who considers pottery as his possible medium should not be deceived. Making pottery is a most delicate art requiring skill, knowledge, and instinct of a rare sort. It also requires a great deal of training, formal or otherwise, and the successful potters of today have acquired, by one means or another, an extensive background in design as it may be applied to the material.

Virtually every formal crafts school, university art department which teaches crafts, and the more informal crafts courses in municipally operated centers teach the ancient art of making things out of clay. A list of formal schools and universities where such instruction is available may be ordered for a small fee from the American Crafts Council, the address of which is listed in the appendix of this book. Instruction at municipal craft centers, often excellent, may be inquired about by telephoning the recreation departments of cities and counties.

There are a number of potters in all sections of the country, some of whom sell directly to their customers, and many of whom work at or sell through restoration areas such as Old San Diego, in California; Colonial Williamsburg, in Virginia; Restored St. Augustine, in Florida; Westville, in Lumpkin, Georgia; and Sturbridge Village, in Massachusetts. One might approach these artists for private instruction. Some will willingly take on an apprentice.

Also, if an aspiring potter lives in an area which has no craft schools nearby, or he is unable to attend university classes, he can learn the rudiments of technique and terminology of working with clay by reading some of the very good books that are listed in the bibliography for this chapter. Indeed, such reading is valuable preparation for attending class or beginning an apprenticeship. For one thing, it can teach the neophyte about the various types of pottery being made in the United States, the terms of the art, and the tools.

The equipment for making pottery depends on the type being made. Of course a kiln, which fires the clay and makes it suitable for holding liquids, is basic equipment. There are a number of commercial kilns of all sizes which are sold by pottery supply sources listed in the back of this chapter. A typical electric kiln suitable for a small operation sells for about $400. Some potters, however, prefer to make either an outdoor or an indoor bisque kiln from number 2 grade common house brick, fired with natural or LP gas, or sometimes fuel oil. This type can be built for about $150 including a burner. Gas needs no burner other than a 1-inch pipe connected with the fuel source and equipped with a valve located outside the kiln. Oil burners can be bought from furnace dealers in almost any town or from building supply dealers. A little patient seeking can sometimes result in finding a suitable secondhand oil burner for a small price. A heating dealer might supply one at no charge.

Raku open kilns require no more than about 100 number 2 grade house bricks at about 5¢ each, a galvanized garbage can or similar metal container which can be bought at a hardware store for around $4, and a source for natural gas or a tank of LP gas with a 1-inch pipe connected to the source. Such a kiln, which must be outside, can be put together for under $20.

Another piece of equipment common to all types of pottery is a clay mixer in which the potter can blend his powdered clays to suit thin or thick work, and to give strength and evenness of quality to the clay. A clay mixer may be bought from pottery suppliers for around $600, a rather expensive piece of equipment. But potters, as with other craftsmen, are unusually ingenious in making all manner

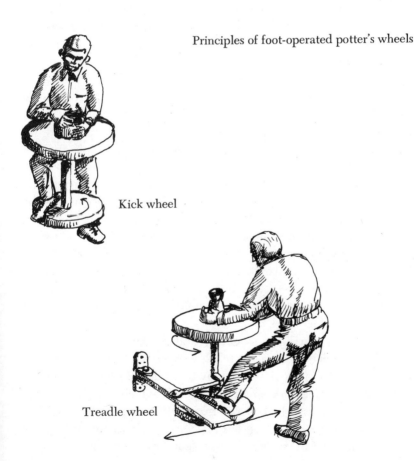

Principles of foot-operated potter's wheels

Kick wheel

Treadle wheel

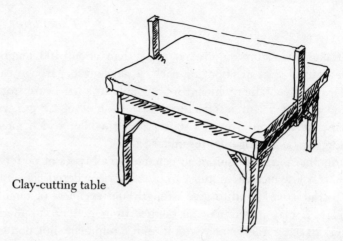

Clay-cutting table

of things. A clay mixer can be homemade out of a 50-gallon steel drum, a ½-horsepower electric motor, and a few pieces of angle iron for from $25 to $40, depending on whether the potter assembles the mixer entirely by himself or supervises its fabrication at a welding shop.

The potter's wheel, normally known as a kick wheel even though some potters prefer an electrified wheel, may be bought at potters' supply houses for $150 to $175, depending on whether or not it is motorized. The enterprising potter, however, can make his own out of various pieces of wood, steel plate, and angle iron for about $35 to $40.

Additional equipment consists of a cutting bench over which a wire is stretched tautly where a lump of damp native clay can be sliced time and time again to examine its interior for pebbles and trash. (This operation is unnecessary if powdered clay bought from potters' supply houses is used rather than native clay.) The bench can be homemade, similar to the illustration, for about $5 worth of lumber and 25¢ worth of 16-gauge wire. The bench top should be covered with a piece of canvas, which will cost perhaps 50¢, so that the clay will not stick to it.

Small tools used for modeling and working consist of wire loop tools, which cost from 75¢ to $2; wooden modeling tools, which cost about 35¢; a pin tool, which may be made by sticking a needle, eyefirst, into a wine cork; and a flat sponge, which costs about 35¢. All of these tools may be ordered from potters' supply houses.

Also, a piece of strong flexible wire, such as an old guitar string, is handy for cutting the wet pot from the wheel or slab merely by passing the taut wire across the surface of the wheel. A small board or dowel should be tied to each end to provide a hand-hold.

Bats, made of plaster of paris (to which clay will not stick), are no more than disks about 1 inch thick and 6 inches to a foot in diameter. The work rests on these bats while being thrown or worked on, and the bat can be easily picked up for moving the piece around after it is made. Bats cost from about 70¢ to $2. They can be made in a cardboard mold with about $3 worth of plaster of paris needed to make up to five or six bats. Plaster of paris can be bought at art supply stores and in most drug stores. Plaster slabs, which are 2 inches thick and usually about 18 inches square, may be easily made at home.

Additional equipment consists mainly of containers to hold the wet clay. Plastic or metal garbage cans are ideal. They cost from $2.50 to $5.00 at hardware stores, grocery stores, and mail order houses. Lids are necessary to prevent the clay from drying too quickly.

While a number of potters work at home, some sort of exclusive shop space is essential in pottery; a garage, an unused basement room if it is not damp, or a small building in the backyard would be suitable. The potter's shop must be fairly good sized, at least 12 feet by 20 feet, in order to accommodate the kiln, wheel, drying racks, and storage for clay, colors, glazes, and finished pots ready for market. For the potter comes closer, and always has, to mass production methods than any of the craftsmen in that he must make up numbers of pieces and allow them to become bone dry so that he can fire a number of them at the same time. The expense of operating a kiln for one piece would be nothing short of idiotic.

Of course raku firing must be done outside and it is also advisable to place a large gas- or oil-fired bisque kiln outside. Electric kilns are easily and safely used inside.

Setting up a well-equipped pottery operation at home can be done at a cost of about $300 if the potter makes his own wheel, kiln, clay mixer, and other equipment. If he buys all of this then his capital expenditure will exceed $1,000. To cost of equipment must be added another $1,000 for rent of suitable space for a year (although in some areas space can be rented for less money) or up to another $4,000 if a separate shop must be built. Drying shelves and tables may require another $50 for material. Materials such as clay, color, and glaze might require another $50.

Some very suitable clays can sometimes be found around a yard or in nearby woods. Sometimes a clay bed might be accidentally discovered while digging a garden. At other times one can wander down a woodland creek, checking its banks for outcroppings of clay which show where topsoil has eroded away. Such clay comes in many colors: white, gray, red, or yellow. The bad clay, which may contain sand, can be mixed with the good, which is clean and pure, to create the proper consistency for good, strong, beautiful pots. If native clay is used it is important to work it on the cutting table before making its into pots. Grog, made of ground-up fired clay, such as ancient potsherds sought by pueblo potters, may be added to common clay to give it very superior qualities.

Even the city dweller, however, can be a potter, for clays may be bought, damp or in powdered form, from a number of ceramic suppliers who do business either retail or by mail order. Wet clay can be bought in 5-pound tins for about $1.50, but it is better to buy at least 25-pound tins for about $4 or even a 60-pound tin for $7. The price differs per tin depending on the type of clay; red, or terra cotta, is the cheapest, and pure white, or kaolin, is the most expensive.

Since clay is sold by the pound and gets much of its bulk and weight from water, the least expensive form of clay is powder. It is also easier to store and is readily made into a workable form by adding water, the weight of the water being one-third the weight of the dry clay.

A 5-pound bag or tin of dry clay will cost about $1, a 25-pound container about $3. The 5-pound bag when mixed with the proper weight of water will weigh about 6½ pounds. Dry clay is certainly less expensive to buy if it must be shipped since shipping charges are based on weight.

Colors can be bought from the same sources which supply clay and equipment for from 35¢ to 85¢ per quarter-pound box. Slips, which are used to glaze, cost around 35¢ a pound.

The potter has many advantages over most other craftsmen in earning a return on his investment. If his design and technique are good and if he throws his heart into his work, he can expect to earn up to $20 or $25 an hour for every hour he produces. This is due largely to the organization the craft imposes on the craftsman.

For instance, the potter does not have to start and finish one item before going to another. He makes up a number of items on the wheel and sets them aside to dry. While these pots are drying he fires and glazes a batch that were thrown several days before. At the end of a week he has produced an astounding number of different pieces, most of which have a demand in the marketplace and most of which sell for a reasonable price.

Contrast this situation with that of the weaver. The weaver in a week's time may finish one fine blanket or wall hanging, but even at $3 an hour on the average, plus cost of materials, the blanket demands a much higher price than one pot or even a set of dishes. The price alone, regardless of excellence of design and technique, diminishes the market for the weaver's work.

Potters have many places in which to sell their work. Locally they can approach department stores, hardware stores, flower shops, and gift shops with samples and prices and expect some interest from the managers and owners of these shops. Many set up their own shops, usually around tourist attractions such as Old San Diego, which has many independent craft shops within the old city. A number of successful, though less artistic, potters make a good living selling flower pots, bird feeders, and other such items in roadside stands.

And, of course, the craft fairs found all over the country offer great sales outlets for the potter. Many potters spend half the weeks of the year traveling around to these fairs where they can sometimes take in $500 a day or more. The other weeks of the year are spent in producing.

At least one potter in North Carolina spends about 50 weeks a year producing, then sells the lot for a handsome annual income in two weeks at the crafts show in Chicago's Merchandise Mart. It must be remembered, however, that this sort of sales program requires additional capital the first year just to buy food and lodging.

A list of craft fairs can be obtained by writing any state Chamber of Commerce, or by writing the tourist development department of any state government. Lists give dates, locations, and cost of fees and commissions.

A few potters make a very good living by developing regular customers among specialized retail craft shops in some cities. There are not too many of these shops operating in the country at this time, but a few have been outstanding successes, The Signature Shops in Atlanta being a notable example.

The successful potter, like other craftsmen, must build a reputation. Part of this depends on signing each piece of work before it goes to the kiln, by scratching a signature or initials when the piece is leather dry, or painting the signature on the bottom of a pot before glaze is applied.

One successful potter foregoes the need for a written signature because of the distinction of his designs, which usually reflect in shape or decoration the shape and movement of the human eye. Another, who specializes in handled pots, pitchers, cups, and mugs, gains instant recognition by the design of the handle he applies to every handled item he turns out. This serves to emphasize the importance of good design as well as technique in selling pottery; one can make a very good living without compromising artistic principles.

SOURCES OF SUPPLY

Edmonds Scientific Company
150 Edscorp Building
Barrington, New Jersey 08007
(Pyrometers and thermocouples)

Chas. Taylor Sons Company
Box 14058
Cincinnati, Ohio 45214
(Crucibles)

Products for the Potter and Tilemaker

A. D. Alpine Inc., A.B.
353 Coral Circle
El Segundo, California 90245

Art Consultants
97 St. Marks Place
New York, New York 10009

American Art Clay
4717 West 16th Street
Indianapolis, Indiana 46222

B & I Manufacturing Company
P.O. Box 1267
Galesburg, Illinois 61401

Carborundum Company
Niagara Falls, New York 14302
(Tile)

CCM Arts & Crafts, Inc.
9520 Baltimore Avenue
College Park, Maryland 20740

Ceramichrome
7155 Fenwick Lane
Westminister, California 92683

Cole Ceramic Laboratories
Box 248
Sharon, Connecticut 06069

Nasco House of Crafts
901 Janesville Avenue
Fort Atkinson, Wisconsin 53538

Sax Arts & Crafts
207 North Milwaukee Avenue
Milwaukee, Wisconsin 53202

Seely's Ceramic Service Inc.
9 River Street
Oneonta, New York 13820

Skutt Ceramic Products, Inc.
2618 S.E. Steele Street
Portland, Oregon 97202

Vanguard Crafts, Inc.
2915 Avenue J
Brooklyn, New York 11210

Wheelcraft, Inc.
2233–140 Avenue N.E.
Bellevue, Washington 98005

CHAPTER XIII

The Enameler

WITH roots as deep in history as those of the glassworker and the potter, the enameler still holds a strong position in the crafts. His equipment is much the same, on a smaller scale, as those who work entirely with glass or clay; and his frit, the dry enamel he binds to metal with blinding heat, is similar in character to the other materials. None of his pieces, however, are of ceramic material alone for he must work with copper, brass, and even iron, which gives him cousinship to the blacksmith and coppersmith as well as the potter and glassblower.

Enameling consists of applying rather dull color in the form of finely powdered enamel, sometimes mixed with a slip for painting on. This dull material is either shaken or packed on pieces of metal in appropriate designs with as many colors as desired, then subjected to intense heat in a small kiln or sometimes, in case of iron, with a blowtorch. And then behold the color change, for the frit melts, joins the metal, and assumes a deep, transparent brilliance that almost gives it the shining beauty of precious stones.

The work of the enameler has manifold uses, some for personal adornment, some for decorating functional items, and some to add a spot of beauty to any room in the house. The ancient people of all continents treasured enameled jewelry such as earrings, finger rings, bracelets, and buckles. The modern enameler makes the same items, and such is the cyclical nature of human history that modern design, abstract though it may be at times, often resembles the designs of the past and reflects the long pedigree of enameling.

But the modern enameler also decorates objects that had no

place in ancient homes. Ash trays, for instance, made of copper and brass, and decorated with the muted or bright colors of fused glass, find a receptive market. Small shaped or cast bowls may be partially or completely decorated with enamel as may small pitchers, bowls, and flatware. Since enameled ware is as resistant to heat as glass or fired clay, the enameler sometimes turns his art to table mats, small trivets, and small stands for bowls of hot food.

Decorative enameled tiles, for hanging singly or to set en masse in a predetermined pattern, are popular items with modern-minded people who wish a spot of easily cleaned color in bathrooms or kitchens.

And buttons, decorated with floral designs, animals, or coats-of-arms, can be made to order in size and color to give an air of distinction to men's blazers or women's coats. Cuff links, too, with personal or general designs, usually attract a considerable demand.

Frit fuses as readily with iron as with the more malleable copper and brass and can easily be applied to iron objects made by the blacksmith, such as belt buckles, spoons, forks, and handles of knives.

Indeed, the use of enamel for decorating metal objects may be so universal that the enameler can greatly extend his field of decoration by learning what the silversmith, coppersmith, goldsmith, and blacksmith make and by using enamel to provide a new dimension of brilliant color to the objects made by these craftsmen. Normally the enameler has decorated small objects because his traditional equipment is small, but there is no reason that a massive wrought-iron gate cannot be decorated with enamel if the proper equipment is devised.

The techniques of enameling are not difficult to master. What separates the good from the mediocre artist in the field is not fusing frit and metal, for this is a consequence of natural forces brought together, but in planning and executing designs well before the actual enameling is done. The enameler must be a master of color and design first of all, and he must be familiar enough with his medium to visualize the finished colors after heat has changed the dull, ugly-duckling frit into brilliant colors.

Training, therefore, should consist of acquiring a thorough background in art and design with additional attention given to dress design, jewelry design, and interior design. After such basic training the would-be enameler should learn the simple techniques of how to clean his copper and iron, how to mix and apply frit in order to get as full a range of color as desired, and how to fire the piece to make it finished in all the beauty of which enamel is capable. When design and technique are learned, tried, and made satisfactory, the enameler should turn his attention to application, old and new. He should learn to observe all manner of clothes, jewelry, and house appointment. He should try, in his mind's eye, to put enameled objects in unexpected places, and honestly develop the taste that can realize unsuitability. Then he should get to work and produce, with confidence that his work will appeal to and satisfy himself first and then his market.

Training in the technique of enameling, how to mix the colors with their binders, how to clean metal so that colors will stick, how hot to turn the kiln, how to cool the enamel slowly so that it will not crack, are simple matters which can be taught to pre-teenage children in summer camp programs. They are important, basic even, but do not require long periods of training as is necessary in blacksmithing, silversmithing, or pottery. Fine enameling stems more from design than technique, and training in art is more important than training in technique.

Experience, too, even the experience of making mistakes, is important. One of the finest enamelers in the United States has built her reputation on the basis of a unique cracked pattern which appears on the surface of the enameled pieces she produces. She learned how to create this effect through an error in technique, but had the artistic capacity to realize that the error gave a unique quality to her work.

Mistakes can be made in the home kiln, but basic training is necessary first to help the craftsman recognize what caused them. Such training is available at virtually all universities which offer courses in the crafts and at all formal crafts schools. A list of these may be obtained from the American Crafts Council in New York, the address of which is listed in the appendix to this book. It is also taught at municipally operated crafts schools which may be located in each city by calling the recreation department (usually connected with the parks department) in a city.

Some summer camps, both private camps and those operated by churches, YMCA, and other organizations, offer training in enameling. The availability of this training must be sought out by mail and telephone in each locality since training in enameling is often dependent on whether or not the camp has found a teacher in the subject.

Much about enameling can be learned from books on the subject. The bibliography at the end of this chapter should be consulted.

Before he can get to work, however, the enameler must collect the tools of his trade, which are relatively simple and relatively inexpensive. Some sort of work table is needed where the artist can sit and apply frit carefully and accurately on his metal. Such a table might be found hidden in attic storage, at a secondhand furniture store, or bought new. It should not cost more than about $15 and a chair, if one must be bought, may be of the unpainted kitchen variety which sells new for about $7.50.

Frit, or enamel, may be applied in several different ways. Many enamelers carefully pour the material on the cleaned copper into desired designs, perhaps using a small fairly stiff brush or a popsicle stick to push it into precise shapes. Most professional enamelers make wide use of dental tools, probes and the like, to pack the enamel into desired patterns, especially on small items such as cuff links and buttons which might have raised edges. Dental tools are usually available without charge from any dentist's office. They may be bought new from local dental supply houses but the cost is high, and new tools are no more valuable to the enameler than old, discarded tools.

Brushes are needed from time to time with which to paint certain areas and backgrounds. Only high quality sable brushes can be depended upon.

Brushes ranging from size 00 to size 8 cost from about 85¢ to $2.50 each. A selection of about five brushes will generally suffice. Total cost for brushes will be between $8 and $10. They may be found at art supply stores.

A kiln is also basic equipment. Small electric enameling kilns which may be set up on the work table cost from $50 to $150 depending on size. Order kilns from suppliers listed in the appendix of this chapter.

A good pair of metal shears is also necessary to cut copper and brass sheet to proper size and desired shape. Shears of the finest quality will do a much better job than cheap shears. They may be bought at almost any hardware store for about $8.50 a pair. They last forever.

Additional equipment consists mainly of an assortment of inexpensive or discarded china saucers, preferably white, or some small white enameled pans in which to mix frit and binder, to blend colors, and to hold the blended colors while actual painting is going on. All that are needed may be bought new from variety stores for only a couple of dollars.

A few enamelers like to form small bowls and trays themselves, or to cast brass objects which will be decorated with enamel. This aspect of enameling is more akin to silversmithing than enameling and requires an assortment of hammers, anvils, and stakes, which can get rather expensive. Casting, of course, requires a furnace much more complex than the enameler's kiln. This equipment is described and priced in the chapter in this book under silverwork and will not be repeated in this chapter.

Any room, even the corner of a bedroom furnished with desk or table large enough to hold a small kiln and a few saucers of color, will serve as a shop for enameling. Enough drawer space should be available to store frit, binder, brushes, and cleaning solvent.

Also, there should be enough space to store pieces which have been colored but not yet fired, so that a number of pieces can be fired at one time. Unless several people are working in the same shop, more extensive facilities are not necessary.

Frit, binder, and copper or brass are the only materials of the enameler. Sometimes all of these materials may be easily found in art supply stores and craft supply shops in large cities. Otherwise they may be ordered from the list of suppliers shown at the end of this chapter. None of the material is expensive unless large pieces of copper are desired.

Copper, for instance, of 24-gauge thickness, costs about 3¢ a square inch, more if thicker and less if thinner. At times scrap copper can be bought at sheet metal shops in any community for less than it costs when ordering it from a supplier.

Frit costs about $1 per 2 ounces, and 2 ounces will cover a great deal of copper. Binder costs about $1 a pint. Various cleaning substances can be bought for about $1 a pint, either from mail order suppliers, from the corner drug store, or from the neighborhood hardware store.

A few enamelers might do well enough at the craft to make a comfortable living, but the practical craftsman will consider it a part-time occupation which can yield supplementary income only. There is simply not the market for enameled items to support a full-time effort. It is, however, a most pleasurable and challenging activity.

Some market for enameled buttons and buckles should be found in sewing centers and women's dress shops. Men's cuff links, with designs in current fashion, might be sold in limited editions in men's shops, either the independents or those which are part of large department stores. The department stores would want them in rather large quantity, so that the enamelers who wish to sell to merchant giants should be prepared to produce cuff links in gross lots at least. The same applies to buttons and buckles. The department buyer is the person to contact.

Ash trays, coasters, small serving trays, cigarette boxes, and other pieces of table furniture can sometimes be sold through furniture stores and gift shops or the appropriate department in large stores. Again, some quantity of production will be necessary if the buyers of such retail outlets are to be interested.

Probably the most profitable sale of enameling can be found at art and craft fairs. Here the enameler can display all manner of items and sell them one by one to suit individual customer's tastes. Between sales, he can demonstrate his art to draw more customers to his display. Small items which sell for less than $5 will offer more sales potential at craft fairs; sometimes one can acquire a nice commission which results from the display of his work.

It should be realized, however, that craft fairs, while they offer opportunity, also force the enameler to compete with the more popular crafts. It might be feasible, therefore, to apply early for space near the entrance of the fair, to catch the customer's dollar before it is spent for something else, or to make arrangements to sell enameled work in conjunction with other craftsmen. For instance, belt buckles or sandal decorations might be more easily sold at the leather worker's booth, and some of his work with enameled decoration might in turn be displayed and sold at the enameler's booth.

Lists of craft fairs may be obtained by writing state Chambers of Commerce or the tourist development departments of state governments.

Enamelers who are well based in design and color might be expected to earn $5 to $10 an hour so long as demand for what they are making is sustained by capricious fashion and good times. Since the craft lends itself admirably to limited editions, much as with pottery, the enameler who creates a distinctive design for any of the objects he produces might well consider concentrating on these successful designs until a drop in sales indicates a change in the tastes of the market. And if such a change occurs, it is the perspicacious enameler who has another item to fall back upon to earn income.

The artist's signature should be placed on every piece of enameling he produces—name or initials, and, if possible, the town in which he works.

SOURCES OF SUPPLY

Borax Company
Borax House
Carlisle Place
London, S.W.I.
    (Free Information Booklets)

American Art Clay Company
4717 West 16th Street
Indianapolis, Indiana 46222

Art Consultants
97 St. Marks Place
New York, New York 10009

CCM Arts & Crafts, Inc.
9520 Baltimore Avenue
College Park, Maryland 20740

Cole Ceramic Laboratories
Box 248
Sharon, Connecticut 06069

Gregory Kilns Company
8041 Hart R. D., No. 1
Mentor, Ohio 44060

Honovia Liquid Gold
1 West Central Avenue
East Newark, New Jersey 07029

Quimby & Company
Oakdale Road
Chester, New Jersey 07930

L. Reusche & Company
2 Lister Avenue
Newark, New York 07105

Technical Specialties,
    International, Inc.
487 Elliot, West
Seattle, Washington 98119

Thomas B. Thompson Company
1539 Old Deerfield Road
Highland Park, Illinois 60035

Vanguard Crafts, Inc.
2915 Avenue J
Brooklyn, New York 11210

CHAPTER XIV

The Ceramic Muralist

THE ceramic muralist is essenially a potter who doesn't make pots. He does, however, use exactly the same materials as the potter. But instead of throwing and firing a finished masterpiece, he deals with components, each a small part of the whole, and puts them together to cover a wall with color and sculptured shapes. So perhaps he might be designated part sculptor as well as part potter. As a consequence his training must be in both arts as well as in architectural design and engineering.

For the ceramic muralists of the world (and there are not too many of them) supply the needs of architects for unique external embellishment of buildings and of interior designers for interior decoration. The muralist's works consist of many ceramic tiles, some large and some small, put together somewhat like mosaic to give a massive effect which might be large enough to cover the whole exterior entrance wall of a large building. The ceramic muralist may make individual tiles to be used to decorate a kitchen, but on the whole he works on commissions for large and impressive murals.

Since tiles are flat the muralist often does not use a kick wheel at all; but some of his designs may call for round as well as rectangular tiles, so he is usually equipped with a wheel for this eventuality. He works mainly on a large bench, canvas-covered or equipped with plaster slabs as described in the chapter on the potters. He rolls out his clay like biscuit dough, cuts it to shape with his knife, and then molds the surface with wire tool and wooden paddle or forces the clay into a plaster mold he has made himself in order to create a surface design. Many ceramic murals incorporate several surface designs to create a special effect of the whole. When surface designs are repeated it is more efficient and sometimes more esthetic to use exact duplicates, hence the need for molds.

In finishing his tiles the muralist follows the same procedure and uses the same materials and equipment as the potter. He must let his green tiles become bone dry and then fire them in the kiln after applying color and glaze. All the equipment needed for this is described in Chapter XII of this section.

Generally the muralist needs a separate shop building larger than that needed by the potter. Space is required for two reasons: First, he must have adequate drying racks for a number of tiles; secondly, he needs floor space, or perhaps a very large table, on which to lay his tiles out, fit them together to check his design, and number them for final assembly in the building to make his com-

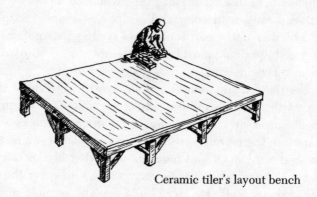

Ceramic tiler's layout bench

plete mural. Such shop space might cost from $3,000 to $5,000 to build depending on labor costs in the area where the muralist operates and, of course, on the type of building material used—concrete block, lumber, or sheet steel. The shop should be of at least 600 square feet unless the artist's location offers climate of dependable enough clemency to allow him to lay out his tile outside his shop.

Often the muralist will need an assistant or paid apprentice, at a cost which must be figured eventually in the selling price of his work.

Ceramic murals are not the sort of art to sell in retail outlets or craft fairs. They are done entirely on commission from architects and interior designers. Commissions, however, may be obtained by personal calls on architects and designers with color photographs of past works and perhaps a sample tile. Regular perusal of building news usually can guide the muralist to the architect who is planning a new building. It is of advantage to the muralist, however, to make general calls on architects and interior designers to get acquainted with the style and attitudes of each so that future calls can be limited to those architects who use modern design and decoration and who appreciate modern crafts as a medium of architectural expression.

The ceramic muralist cannot always count on working steadily. He must, therefore, ask for compensation on the same basis as the sculptor, selling his work on the basis of cost of time, talent, plant, and material. He should expect to charge about $200 a day at least for the time he spends designing and making his mural, and this time includes the hours spent in consultation with the architect and his staff.

Murals should be signed with pride—one or several tiles devoted to a distinctive signature which gives name, date, and location.

SOURCES OF SUPPLY

See Sources of Supply for The Potter, Chapter XII.

3
Metals

CHAPTER XV

The Silversmith and Coppersmith

ONE works in precious metals; the other works in a base metal of beauty and durability. Yet the silversmith and coppersmith use tools that are identical for the most part and they share the same techniques. The difference between the two is in the products they make more than any other factor. Both could work in gold sheet as well as copper or silver although the amount of goldsmithing done in the twentieth century is confined almost entirely to jewelry, which will be covered in the next chapter.

Smithing automatically suggests hammer work since the term actually means *smiting*. So the silver and coppersmith use hammer and anvil to shape great or small sheets of metal into various forms, mostly what is known as hollow ware (bowls, plates, pitchers, cups) and, to some extent in this century, into large pieces of personal jewelry of silver, copper, and brass. Not too many generations ago, the silversmith enjoyed a higher status than the coppersmith, for he dealt with lords and ladies and rich merchants. The coppersmith, often a nomadic gypsy, made, by the same process of smithing, a variety of cooking utensils, from brass-bowled soup ladles with wrought-iron handles to great copper wash tubs. But the coppersmith came to the back door and dealt with coolies, butlers, and housekeepers. Strangely, however, the products of the coppersmith are now appreciated, on the basis of form and workmanship, as much as silverware, and the status of the once lowly coppersmith is interchangeable with that of his fellow worker in precious metal. And now the silversmith often becomes a coppersmith by substituting copper for silver and working on the lesser metal with the identical tools he uses for the silver. Also, much fine hollow ware is made of copper, then plated with silver, to give as much grace to a dining room as pure silver.

Products made by silversmith and coppersmith are legion, and the history of some items stretches back into prehistoric times. There are bowls for sugar, jam, honey, vegetables, and salads along with the spoons, forks, and runcible spoons needed to move these foods from the bowls. There is tableware from which to eat and flat silver to go with it. Pitchers there are in great variety for coffee and tea, milk and cream, wine and water and all manner of beverages. Great and small trays are made with the special forming hammers of the silver and coppersmith, some to hold a silver service, some to serve finger sandwiches, and heavy tree trays on which to carve a roast of beef.

Then there are candle holders, single or multi-armed, and sconces and the accouterments that go with these gleaming sources of soft light, such as candle snuffers and wick trimmers.

More common items which once were necessary but which now are admired as well for decorative effects are copper tea kettles to use on the stove, frying pans with wrought-iron handles, boilers and double boilers, bowls for soup ladles, colanders, and cooking spoons, most with the traditional handle of strong wrought iron. Of course there are all sorts of small copper plates and containers, too, too various to itemize, for food storage and cooking. All copper cooking utensils are tinned on the inside to prevent poisoning, the tin being applied while molten with a pad of cotton waste.

Both silversmith and coppersmith often delve into jewelry. They turn out finger rings and earrings, bracelets, pendants, and necklaces, buttons and buckles and women's hair clips, all of them items which have been popular since prehistoric times. And since silver and copper are much less expensive than gold, well-designed pieces of jewelry made by silver- and coppersmiths usually find a ready market.

Metal, even soft metal, by its very nature requires more complicated equipment for shaping than the more plastic materials such as clay, fibers, or wood. For all metal must be worked be-

tween two surfaces harder than it is, even if intense heat is necessary to soften the metal before it is worked. Smithing, then, even
of soft metals such as silver and copper, requires hammers and
anvils as basic equipment, and a source of heat—at least a blowtorch and at most a furnace. And there are a number of other
special tools or materials for cutting, drilling, and joining together
one piece to another to accomplish a desired shape. As a consequence training must not only be given in learning the nature of
the material but in the proper, efficient use of a multiplicity of
tools. Further, the craftsman must master a glossary pertaining to
these tools.

Most university art schools now offer excellent training in silver and coppersmithing along with very good courses in design.
A list, quite long, of these schools may be ordered in return for
a nominal fee from the American Crafts Council in New York,
which each year makes an exhaustive survey of the sources of
training in all the crafts: who teaches them, how much the tuition
is, and what degrees are offered. Included in this list are the independent crafts schools such as Penland at Penland, North Carolina, and Haystack at Deer Isle, Maine, and others in various parts
of the country.

Also, many municipally operated craft schools offer excellent
training in silver and coppersmithing. These may be located by
talking with recreational departments of various city and county
governments, usually in metropolitan areas. Most municipal craft
schools conduct short courses of from 2 to 6 weeks, but the cost
is negligible and most do have the tools to teach the basics of the
craft. Complementary study in art, and particularly design, may
also be found in most metropolitan areas either in municipal or
private schools.

Would-be professional craftsmen sometimes tend to denigrate
the quality of training in municipal schools, but this is a mistake.
In at least one instance an outstanding silversmith in the Midwest
gained her training in working silver at a municipal craft school
after having majored in design in her college years and having
worked professionally in automobile design after college. She took
silversmithing quite by chance to alleviate the tedium of house-

work and motherhood and is now recognized as one of the best silversmiths and university teachers of the craft in the country. It all started in a municipal crafts program.

Equipment for silverworking, practically all of it hand tools, is various and for the most part rather expensive. Elemental among these are the tools with which the smith smites, the tools which justify his title.

An anvil, somewhat smaller than that of the blacksmith and weighing between 50 and 100 pounds, is essential. It must be of high quality, preferably forged instead of cast, with a hard, smooth face and good corners on the face. The anvil must be mounted on an anvil block, usually a section of an oak log of a length to put the anvil face at the proper height for the smith to work comfortably while seated, if he works seated, or at the height of his knuckles when his arms are hanging down by his sides if he prefers to work standing. If a log is not easily available, the silver-

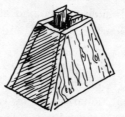

Anvil stand constructed of heavy boards

smith may be able to find the section of a bridge timber at a local highway construction company or sawmill. If this is not possible, he may make his own stand of 2-inch angle iron or of 2-by-12-inch lumber, sawn and nailed to make a truncated pyramid of the proper height as indicated by the accompanying sketch.

Large anvils, of a size appropriate for raising a silver bowl, may be ordered from a number of suppliers listed at the end of this chapter. They cost roughly $1 a pound, with a premium per pound placed on all anvils under 60 pounds in weight. German anvils, all forged, are available in the United States at about the same price.

Prefabricated anvil stands of welded angle iron are also available for about $15, but these can be made, if welding equipment is available, for about $5 worth of angle iron. Wooden anvil stands can be made for about $3 worth of 2-inch lumber, and the wooden type is preferred by many smiths.

The silver- and coppersmith also need a number of stake anvils, which are peculiarly formed small anvils with polished faces that are used for shaping the metal. These include mushroom faces, T faces, concave faces, and numerous others, all with tangs which fit into the square hardy hole of the big anvil or into a special stake anvil mount which may be fastened to a block.

A well-equipped silver- or coppersmith may have 20 stake anvils or various sizes and physiognomy, although a beginner might start with only 5 well-chosen stakes. He may expect to pay from $10 to $15 for each stake anvil.

No anvil is of any use without a hammer, and the silver- or coppersmith must have more hammers than stakes. He needs, for instance, several flat-faced hammers, cross peen and ball peen, of different weights ranging from about ½ to 4 pounds. These are used for initial shaping and hollowing, the ball peens being used to start a bowl or cup. In addition he needs shaping hammers, most of them double faced, with highly polished faces, some flat and some rounded, some pointed and some wedge shaped. These are used for embossing and crimping, for making supplementary shapes in a piece being worked, and for finishing different sized bowls. Planishing hammers are necessary to remove the marks of a ball peen and to bring the surface of the silver to gleaming smoothness. In addition, several very small hammers, for chasing (or engraving) and crimping, will be necessary.

Ball peen and cross peen hammers may usually be found in any hardware store in several weights or may be ordered from such mail order houses as Sears, Roebuck or Montgomery Ward. They cost from about $4 for small chasing hammers to around $10 for larger, highly polished shaping hammers.

The beginning smith might start his shop with perhaps eight basic hammers and limit his work while starting to the items which he can make with these. As his work grows he can purchase more hammers from the supply sources listed at the back of this chapter.

Additional hand tools needed by the silver- and coppersmith include a host of small chisels, punches, gravers, and chasing tools too various to specify. Most smiths, however, make most of these small tools from either carbon steel drill rods, which sell for about 50¢ a pound at steel supply houses, or from manufactured punches in various sizes which can be purchased at $1 to $2.50 each at most hardware stores, depending on size. Of course, some standard punches, gravers, and chisels are available at regular silversmithing supply sources at from $1.50 to $5 each, but these must often be altered to execute a particular design concept. The majority of smiths prefer to make their own in the tradition of Cellini and Michelangelo.

Though many smiths yearn for the old days of craftsmanship done wholly by hand, the practical modern silversmith who wishes to make a comfortable living knows that he must compromise his personal desires with a number of modern machine tools in his shop. One of the most important of these is a modern electric grinder and buffer, without which he must expend his capital on several apprentices, who are more difficult to find and more expensive than electric grinders. After all, grinders do not have to eat when they are not working. Grinders with two wheel mounts can be purchased from hardware stores, mail order houses, and industrial supply houses, as well as from the suppliers listed at the end of this chapter. Small grinders and buffers can be purchased for from $25 to $50. A real professional grinder, however, one suitable for dressing hammer faces, grinding special gravers and chisels —in effect one that will save time and the money needed to replace tools—will cost over $250. Many consider the larger grinder an excellent investment.

As with all metalworking, a source of heat is also needed in the shop of the silversmith and coppersmith. Either electric or gas is suitable but most prefer the quicker heating of gas in annealing the metal after it has been beaten, and made brittle between hammer and anvil. Some silversmiths, especially if they produce small items, will use a regular blowtorch fueled with gasoline, which may be used as a blowtorch in soldering large areas or set up as a lamp with a stand on which to rest the metal while it anneals. Others prefer a regular gas bunsen burner supplemented

Small homemade forge

by a small propane torch for soldering. Gasoline blowtorches sell for around $20 to $25. Propane torches with several accessories sell for less than $10 at any hardware store, with replacement tanks costing about $2. Gas burners with racks may be ordered from the suppliers listed at the end of this chapter for around $15.

And although not generally used or even thought about by most modern silver- and coppersmiths, a small forge can be a worthwhile piece of equipment in any silversmith's shop. Sometimes old portable farm forges, equipped with a hand blower, can be bought at antique shops or farm auctions for from $10 to $25. Modern gas forges can be bought at industrial supply houses or craft suppliers for from about $300 to $900, depending on the accessories. Or an enterprising smith can make his own small forge of a section of oil drum lined with clay, a few pieces of pipe, and an old vacuum cleaner or hair dryer blower. Materials for a homemade forge should not cost more than $10. Charcoal, not modern briquets but the old-fashioned kind, or metallurgical coal may be used as fuel. Forges require either an exhaust fan over a window or a chimney of some sort.

Electric soldering irons are preferred for joining small pieces. Again, quality is essential and such accouterments as temperature regulating stands, a selection of different-sized tips, and tip cleaners all enable the craftsman in silver and copper to do more good work in a given time. The beginning silversmith, then, is advised to obtain the very best soldering irons, which cost from $8.50 to $15, depending on size. Temperature regulating stands, which keep an iron hot, and thereby save the time of reheating, sell for about $25. Sets comprised of iron, temperature regulator, various tips, and other accessories can be ordered from several suppliers for a total of $35 to $40.

For cutting out shapes in sheet copper or silver, the craftsman requires both metal shears and a jeweler's saw, the latter a form of coping saw with an extremely thin, almost hair-like, hacksaw blade. Good-quality shears cost around $8 to $10. And since the silversmith must work and cut his components precisely, the better-equipped shop will have three pairs of shears: one for straight cutting, one for circular cutting to the right, and one for circular cutting to the left. Shears may be purchased at some sheet metal supply shops, at hardware stores, and from the suppliers listed at the end of this chapter.

Jewelers saws, which sell for around $4, may be bought directly from jeweler supply houses in large cities or ordered from regular craft mail order suppliers. The tiny blades, which break often, can be replaced at a cost of about 5¢ each.

Tongs or spring tweezers are necessary for handling silver or copper when it is hot from soldering or annealing. Tweezers, generally available only from jewelers or craft supply houses, cost around $2 a pair. Small tongs, available from the same sources, usually sell for about $4 to $5.

A set of files ranging from finely cut patternmaker's files in several shapes to coarse rasps are used frequently in silver and copper smithing. Patternmaker's files may be obtained from jewelers and craft supply houses, sometimes from hardware stores, and sometimes from mail order department stores. Sears, Roebuck, for instance, sells an excellent set of eight patternmaker's files for around $5. Other files, of various sizes and cuts may be bought at hardware stores and mail order suppliers for from 75¢ to $3.50. File handles, which can prevent inadvertent injury and which provide better control, may be purchased for around 10¢ apiece or made from sections of discarded broom or mop handles.

A few sets of C-clamps are usually found around a well-equipped silversmith's shop. They are easily obtained from hardware stores, mail order houses, and craft supply houses for about $1 each. They are used to clamp pieces together, for fitting, or to clamp a wooden fork, for sawing, to the edge of the workbench.

A small machinist's vise, with jaws of about 3 or 4 inches width, is also necessary. Vises are easily found in hardware stores or mail order suppliers. One of good quality sells for from $7.50 to $25, depending on size and versatility.

And while not essential, a small hand vise equipped with a thumb screw can be more than worth its price for certain filing and soldering operations. Hand vises may be ordered from craft supply houses, and may sometimes be found at large hardware stores, for about $5.

Other equipment consists of small but generally necessary items such as enamel pans for pickling solution (used in annealing), bowls for fluid soldering flux, saucers or pie plates to hold bits of solder and silver, rolls of small wire, pliers and wire cutters, etc. Most of these items may be found at a number of sources in any town. They range in price from about $4 to $5 for pliers and wire cutters to 50¢ for pie plates.

Some silversmiths will wish to cast certain items or to cast ornaments for larger items. This requires a gas forge or electric furnace which costs from $250 to $900. Crucibles sell for about $5 to $10 depending on size. Molds are made by the craftsman from plaster of paris, available at a nominal price from craft suppliers listed at the end of this chapter or even at drug stores or hardware stores.

Minimum shop space for silver- or coppersmithing should be about 400 to 500 square feet if the smith works alone. An additional 100 square feet should be added ideally for each additional craftsman. The space should be well ventilated and well lighted. Aside from the equipment already described, it must have a sturdy workbench for each person in the shop and adequate racks or shelves to store hand tools, stakes, and supplies.

Since silversmithing is something of a spectator's craft, the location of the shop in an area frequented by tourists might turn into very good advertising well worth the higher rent in such an area. If such a location is available and affordable, the smith should have his bench in the front of the shop behind a large window in full view of passersby. Shop space of this nature will rent for from $3 to $5 a square foot annually. Space in different type areas may rent for as low as $2 a square foot. All rents will vary according to different areas of the country, but rent will be based on the age and condition of the space and its exposure to people—both factors which are worth deep consideration. Rent money is nothing more than an investment. If the rent is cheap but doesn't give an adequate return for the investment then it is far better to risk higher rent and better return per dollar. Extra sales volume will more than pay for extra rent.

Workbenches equipped with drawers, shelves, and racks may be ordered ready-made from a number of craft suppliers for from $150 to $300. Most silversmiths, however, prefer to make their own benches with lumber from any retail lumber store at a cost of $25 or less. Many craft suppliers sell modular units for workbenches. Drawer cabinets sell for from $50 to $100, shelved cabinets from $35 to $75. Maple bench tops sell generally for about $5 a square foot.

The silversmith's workbench must be equipped with a canvas apron which attaches to the bench front and ties tightly around the waist of the craftsman. This is to catch silver filings so that they can be collected at the end of the filing and poured carefully into a jar or can for sale as scrap or for melting down and casting.

A well-equipped silversmith or coppersmith operation will require at least $5,000 as an initial investment.

The smith who wishes to work in copper and plate his work with silver will need an electric plating unit. These cost from $150 to $300. They may be ordered from some of the craft supply houses listed at the end of this chapter.

Material for silversmithing is mainly sheet silver of various thicknesses which is measured by gauges. Ten-gauge silver means that it is 1/10th of an inch thick; 8-gauge is 1/8th of an inch thick; 14-gauge is 1/14th of an inch thick. The same standard of measurement applies also to copper.

Sterling, or pure silver, is sold in sheets or strips of different weight at generally about $25 to $50 a square foot, depending on thickness. German silver, an alloy of copper, zinc, and nickel, sells for about $5 to $15 a square foot depending on thickness. German silver is suitable for a number of items made by the silversmith and coppersmith.

Copper, as may be expected, is considerably cheaper than silver. Depending on thickness it costs about $10 to $20 a square foot.

Silver and copper may be ordered from craft suppliers listed at the end of this chapter. Sheet copper, however, can be bought in large pieces of scrap from sheet metal shops in large cities at about the same price if bought in enough quantity.

About the only other materials needed are silver solder, which costs about $2.50 a pound, soldering liquid at about 90¢ a pint, and pickling compound at $2 a quart.

Hand silversmithing, like many other crafts, suffers the competition of several large companies which make all manner of hollow ware partly by the work of skilled hired handcraftsmen, for sale in department and jewelry stores. To meet this competition, the individual silversmith must concentrate on unique design and superb craftsmanship. He must expect to sell his work through a retail operation connected with his workshop, through interior decorators, or through small but generally exclusive gift and decorator's shops. The smith must take one or two samples of his work and photographs of other pieces to show the managers of these shops in order to make an outright sale or to place his work on consignment, which means that the merchant will add 30 to 100 percent to the price as his margin and pay the craftsman when the piece is sold.

The coppersmith might do very well taking purely functional items such as frying pans, tea kettles, and similar objects to exclusive gift shops and the cookware departments of local department stores. He should take samples and photographs to show managers and buyers. If the sale is made he should expect an order of several dozen items and must be prepared to specify a delivery date. Work in making such items, particularly if there are duplicates involved, should be planned so that all cutting can be done at one time, all shaping at one time and all soldering at one time. This will save time and increase profit.

Craft fairs are not good retail outlets for the silversmith unless he makes small silver jewelry which can sell for between $5 and $10 per item. Hollow ware is generally too expensive for the craft fair trade.

Coppersmiths, however, might do very well at craft fairs, especially if they demonstrate the craft at the display booth. A list of craft fairs can be obtained from state Chambers of Commerce, the addresses of which are available at local Chambers of Commerce, or from the department of tourism in any state government.

The best sales outlet for silversmiths is undoubtedly a retail space in the shop itself, much like in the shops of eighteenth century America and Europe. This is especially true if the shop is located in a spot frequented by local shoppers and tourists.

Both silversmiths and coppersmiths should plan to charge at least $5 an hour for labor plus the cost of material with 15 percent added, plus the hourly cost of rent. Faster workers, who produce more quickly, might expect to charge from $10 to $15 an hour plus the costs of material and rent. All, however, will be selling in a competitive atmosphere. The craftsman should modify his prices, up or down, to generally match competitive items, even if mass produced or imported, so long as quality of workmanship and design are consistent with his own. Good design and workmanship do bring higher prices.

Every coppersmith and silversmith should take pains to acquire a small signature stamp or engrave a signature on each piece of work he does. The signature should include the name of the town in which the shop is located.

Because the university art schools and craft schools are beginning to turn out some fine silversmiths, the public is becoming more aware each year of the beauty of handcrafted silver. This growing awareness bodes very well for a comfortable living for modern silversmiths who have a good sense of design, the common sense and experience needed to master the medium, and the methods of selling the products.

SOURCES OF SUPPLY

Abbey Materials Corporation
116 West 29th Street
New York, New York 10001

American Art Clay Company
4717 West 16th Street
Indianapolis, Indiana 46222

Art Consultants
97 St. Marks Place
New York, New York 10009

B & L Manufacturing Company
P.O. Box 1267
Galesburg, Illinois 61401

Bead Game
505 North Fairfax Avenue
Los Angeles, California 90036

Broadhead-Garrett Company
4560 East 71st Street
Cleveland, Ohio 44105

CCM Arts & Crafts, Inc.
9520 Baltimore Avenue
College Park, Maryland 20740

California Titan Products
2501 Birch Street
Santa Ana, California 92707

Crafttool Company, Inc.
1421 West 240th Street
Harbor City, California 90710

Dremel Manufacturing Company
4915 21st Street
Racine, Wisconsin 53406

Economy Handicrafts, Inc.
47-11 Francis Lewis Boulevard
Flushing, New York 11361

Gloria's Glass Garden
Box 1990
Beverly Hills, California 90213

T. B. Hagstoz & Sons, Inc.
709 Samson Street
Philadelphia, Pennsylvania 19106

Hillquist Lapidary Equipment
    Company
1545 N.W. 49th Street
Seattle, Washington 98107

Jewelry Craftsman, Inc.
141 North Wabash Avenue
Chicago, Illinois 60602

Quimby & Company
Oakdale Road
Chester, New Jersey 07930

Southeast Smelting & Refining
    Company, Inc.
1712 Jackson
Dallas, Texas 75221

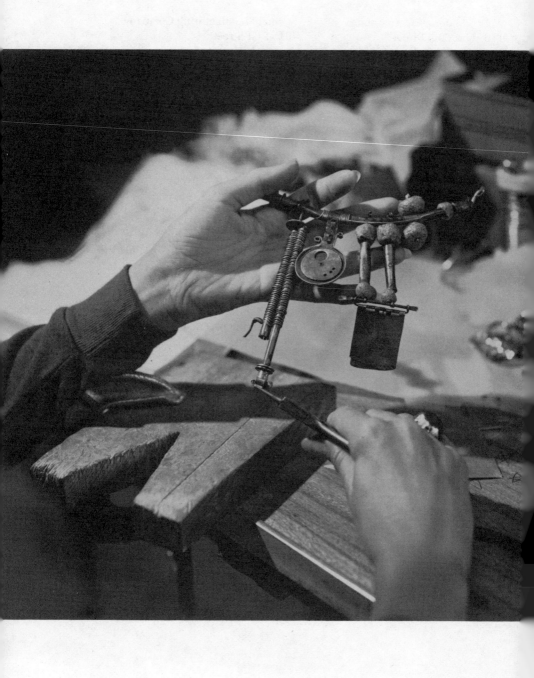

CHAPTER XVI

The Jewelry Maker

THERE has always been a good market for jewelry, even in times of economic depression. In the 1970s in America, where affluence and discretionary income are higher than ever before, the jewelry maker of skill and taste should do quite well. Indeed, the proof lies in the proliferation of small jewelry-making shops in shopping centers near affluent neighborhoods in cities all over the country. Jewelry still is, as it has always been, largely a gift of love. The young lovers of today more and more demand rings and bracelets and earrings of a unique design which is theirs alone. And they can afford such luxury.

Of course, Tiffany's, Cartier's, Bailey, Banks and Biddle, and other national jewelers with large city headquarters have for generations furnished special designs and settings for extremely wealthy families. Most of what these great houses have furnished has been of traditional, rather grand design costing up to six figures. Now, however, simpler, more modern jewelry in gold, silver, and even copper is being designed in smaller shops and selling well.

Taste in jewelry items has not changed much over the centuries even though design has changed greatly. Rings of gold and silver and sometimes copper, set with precious or semiprecious stones, are still greatly sought by women young and old, and by some men. Bracelets find an excellent market for either everyday wear or formal wear. Necklaces and pendants, clasp pins, brooches, and hair clips are popular items. And while the diamond stomacher of Victorian times is seldom worn today, modern fashion has, for a while at least, created a demand for jeweled breastplates and body armor which may last for a few more years. Also, headbands of precious metal set with precious stones or plain are popular to a degree, replacing the grand coronet and tiara of former days.

In a day of miracle medicines there is some demand for small pill boxes, made of silver or gold and sometimes set with semi-precious stones. Occasionally a jewelry maker with imagination may design a fancy cigarette holder, a jeweled safety pin, a portable ash tray, or other products of sheer fancy. But for the most part the good craftsmen are kept busy designing and making the staples of the craft, chiefly rings and earrings.

Because jewelry making is a popular craft, both as a hobby and as a profession, training is widely available in most universities with crafts curricula. A list of these schools may be obtained from the American Crafts Council in return for a small fee. The subject is also taught in formal craft schools such as Penland Crafts School at Penland, North Carolina.

Most municipally operated craft schools also teach the fundamentals of jewelry making. These schools may be investigated by calling the recreational department of any medium- to large-sized city government.

A few established jewelry makers will sometimes take on talented apprentices. Those who wish to learn the art can find no better training than to study under a master who will not only teach technique but who can also provide direction in the practical aspects of operating a full-time shop. These include how to figure the cost of labor, how to sell, how to keep track of money, how to make out tax returns, what quantities of material to order, where good bargains in supply stores may be found—the commercial minutiae that will turn a craft into a good livelihood.

Working in small items, the jewelry maker needs little of the elaborate, expensive equipment of the silversmith. Most jewelry makers' shops may be fully equipped for no more than $500. Yet, once the craftsman is established, jewelry probably brings a greater return on the initial investment than almost any other craft.

Basic equipment is a miniature anvil, either set in a hardwood block or clamped to the bench top with a C-clamp. This tiny tool has a face no longer than 4 inches, with sometimes a horn on one or both ends, or with no horn. Like the silversmith's anvil, it must have a hardened face polished to absolute smoothness which the craftsman is careful to maintain in its pristine condition. Such anvils may be purchased at jeweler's supply houses in large cities or ordered from craft supply houses listed at the end of this chapter. They cost generally from $8 to $15, with the higher priced anvils generally of better quality. Most jewelry makers also use a surface plate which is a 4-inch-by-4-inch block of hardened steel ½ inch thick, which is polished to a mirror finish. These cost about $18.

As any anvil requires a hammer, the jewelry maker works with light ball peen hammers of from 8 ounces to 16 ounces in weight. These are sold at most hardware stores or may be obtained at craft supply houses for from $4 to $6. Other hammers include a chasing hammer which sells for around $4, and plastic and hardwood mallets which sell for from $3 to $5.

Pliers of various sorts, all polished as highly as the anvil face, are quite necessary. These should be ordered from jeweler's supply houses or from craft supply houses, although sometimes they can be acquired in a well-stocked hardware store. Jewelry maker's pliers sell for from $6 to $9 a pair.

Numerous files, all small and specialized, are required to shape the dainty products of the jewelry maker's art. These range from a set of patternmaker's needle files, round, flat, or triangular, to a variety of oddly shaped files called *rifflers*. Small files are sold in sets of from 8 to 16 and cost from about $9 to $50 per set. They may be ordered from the supply sources listed at the end of this chapter.

Several types of vises, all small, are necessary. There should be a bench vise which clamps to the edge of the bench and which may be removed easily when not in use. Bench vises are available from craft supply sources and sell for around $30. For a few dollars extra, one can buy an adjustable swivel vise, also designed to clamp on the bench, which may be set at any angle to make it easier to work and shape small pieces of jewelry.

At least one hand vise, which costs less than $10, is needed, and the well-equipped shop will also have several other specialized hand vises and locking pliers, with jaws designed to hold pins or small flat pieces of metal or rings. These sell for from $6 to $10.

An engraving block which can be turned in any direction for accurate engraving, is probably the most expensive piece of equipment the jewelry maker must have. It may be bought at jewelry supply houses in large cities or ordered from craft supply houses for about $115. Various accessories for the block sell for around $1 each or may be bought in a kit of 20 to 25 pieces.

At least one small mandrel 12 inches tall is needed to shape bracelets, and some jewelry makers desire an additional oval mandrel of the same size. These may be ordered from jeweler's or craft supply houses for around $25 to $30 each.

Instead of using soldering irons, the jewelry maker usually solders with a propane blowtorch equipped with a special blow pipe which mixes gas and air. Propane tanks can be bought at most hardware stores for about $2, with enough fuel to last for two continuous hours. Blow pipes must be bought from craft or jeweler's supply houses for around $15. Other equipment for soldering, including a borax slate, copper pickle pan, asbestos stick for soldering rings, and various tweezers and tongs may be ordered from the same places that sell other jeweler's equipment for a total of about $20 to $25.

For making and shaping some bracelets, pins, and buckles, a set of dapping tools is required. These consist of various-sized dapping punches, which look like a rod with a ball bearing on its end, and dapping blocks which have concavities to fit the punches. Blocks cost from $20 to $30. Punches sell for $1 to $3 apiece, or a set of 36 punches for around $25.

Cutting of gold or silver is done with the jeweler's saw, which costs about $8, a jeweler's hacksaw at around $4, or jeweler's shears, which sell for $5 or $6. All of these special items must be purchased from craft or jeweler's suppliers, some of which are listed at the end of this chapter.

Chasing tools are usually bought in sets of 12 or 24 from $17 to $35 a set. Many jewelers, however, make their own chasing tools from drill rods, available at steel supply houses at about $1 a foot for ¼-inch rod.

To measure ring sizes the jewelry maker must have a set of

standard ring sizes and a ring stick, both of which may be bought for $15 to $20.

Burnishers, of glass and hardened steel, are available from craft supply houses for from $2 to $4 each.

Homemade jeweler's workbench

Some shops do casting of silver and gold, which requires a small electric or gas furnace and crucibles. Such furnaces can be bought from some craft supply houses for about $80. Often, however, gold and silver in small amounts can be melted in the crucible with a propane blowtorch.

Of course a small workbench of proper height with several drawers for keeping tools is also essential equipment. This may be made by the craftsman for about $15 worth of lumber and half a day's work, or it may be bought from craft supply houses for about $150.

As with everything else the jewelry maker works with, he can also get by with very little shop space, 200 square feet at a maximum, although if he wants display space for his finished art he should consider about 500 square feet for a minimum.

Size, however, is not as important to the jewelry maker as is location. Ideally, he should have his shop in a shopping center patronized by affluent women or young people who will spend money for jewelry instead of food or high rent. If the shop is located in an office district it will only be able to sell small items which are low priced, and much of the art of the craft must be inhibited in order to maintain sales volume.

Numbers of jewelry makers in large cities work in office buildings and design and make items for jewelry stores and a select clientele. Most of these members of the craft, however, are older men or young men and women who have taken over a well-established trade that automatically renews itself so long as the work is well done. The situation of these craftsmen is entirely different from that of the art craftsmen entering the trade in the 1970s. If one is to get quickly established he will find that the proper location of his shop will do much to expose his work and art to his particular market.

When available, store space can be rented in a shopping center for about $5 a square foot on an annual basis. Alterations, if needed, and the building of display cabinets, will probably cost another $2,000 unless the craftsman is ingenious enough to make his cabinets from discarded or secondhand furniture. Display cabinets must be enclosed since the valuable items displayed are quite small and easily pilfered. One stolen diamond ring could cost a year's rent.

Light and ventilation, especially if casting is done in the shop, must be good. Placing the workbench close to the front window will act as a drawing card for potential customers.

An important piece of equipment for the shop is a small safe in which to keep stones and gold. This can be bought through any locksmith for from $100 to $300 depending on size. Some office supply houses also sell small safes.

Jewelry makers usually work only with gold and silver and precious or semiprecious stones. All these materials may be ordered from jeweler's supply houses or specified craft supply houses listed at the back of this chapter. Silver sells for about $6 an ounce.

Gold, once selling for only $35 an ounce, now fluctuates in price almost every day so that quotations will have to be requested before buying.

Precious and semiprecious stones vary greatly in price according to type of stone, size, and quality. If possible it is better to examine stones before ordering unless the supplier has proven to be dependable. A number of small stone dealers in the country travel around and show stones to the jewelry maker in his shop. Names of these firms can be gotten from university instructors, other jewelry makers, and, sometimes, retail jewelry stores.

Jewelry makers will do far better maintaining a display space for selling their wares than by any other method. Some commissions from retail jewelry stores are quite worthwhile, but they will not be gained by sales calls. Craft fairs are suitable only for selling small, inexpensive items, and besides, the risk of transporting and displaying gold and precious stones in the haphazard atmosphere of a crafts fair is much too big to consider. With a shop and display room the beginning jewelry maker might start off by specializing in gold wedding bands, each unique, and by so doing capture lifelong customers who will spend more for jewelry as their fortunes prosper.

The beginning jewelry maker might expect to earn at least $10 an hour for his labor and design. Of course he must charge the customer for material, plus a 10 or 15 percent markup on top of his labor charges. As his reputation and clientele grows, however, depending on design and workmanship he might eventually earn as much as $100 an hour. After all, if he has the opportunity to design a piece of jewelry which requires perhaps thousands of dollars of gold and gems, his fee, even at $100 an hour, will be only a small part of the total, and easily accepted by a happy customer.

Every piece of jewelry made by a craftsman should be signed either by stamp or graver no matter how small the piece may be.

SOURCES OF SUPPLY

General

Brodhead-Garrett Company
4560 East 71st Street
Cleveland, Ohio 44105

Crafttool Company, Inc.
1421 West 240th Street
Harbor City, California 90710

Hielquist Lapidary Equipment
  Company
1545 Northwest 49th Street
Seattle, Washington 98107

Jewelry Craftsmen, Inc.
141 North Wabash Avenue
Chicago, Illinois 60602

Tools

William Dixon Inc.
Carlstadt, New Jersey 07072

Metals

Myron Toback, Inc.
23 West 47th Street
New York, New York 10036

Stones

Citra Trading Corporation
1200 Avenue of the Americas
New York, New York 10036

Georgia Imports
1870 Dresden Drive, G-3
Atlanta, Georgia 30319

Narinda V. Malkorta
22 West 48th Street
New York, New York 10036

Natraja Jewelers
382 Central Park West, 11U
New York, New York 10025

CHAPTER XVII

The Blacksmith

BLACKSMITHS, in the proportion found two generations ago, have virtually disappeared from the American scene in the last 50 years, but the craft has grown steadily as a hobby in the last 10 years and has gained recognition as an art based on the work of a handful of artists in different parts of the country.

A link between the blacksmith of old and the new blacksmiths has been kept alive through the trade of many ornamental iron shops found in every part of the country, but most of these establishments forego the forge. Most modern decorative iron shops use a gas forge to flatten the ends of the bars before forging. But virtually all depend on electric or acetylene welding instead of classic forge welding in joining bars together, and their products are, for the most part, merely an assembly of iron bars as they come from the mill with a minimum of shaping.

A number of blacksmiths are kept busy in the industrial regions of the Northeast to design and make prototypes for many products which will eventually be produced en masse for the American market. A few still make a good living as tool dressers, sharpening and retempering all manner of industrial and construction tools. And a few do real blacksmithing. Some of these are old, some are middle-aged, and some are young people just out of college who have taught themselves to smith or have worked briefly with experienced smiths before setting up their own forges. The blacksmith shops of Williamsburg, Sturbridge Village, Westville and other restoration sites employ a goodly number of apprentices who presumably will leave to become independent

producers of wrought iron. Older smiths for the most part furnish traditional items, but a few understand contemporary design and are producing most interesting pieces for modern homes, churches, and other buildings.

There is fascination and challenge to blacksmithing, real blacksmithing, which is possibly not matched by any other craft. It has a mystic quality and is made up of many diverse elements: the fire itself, the sound of hammering on an anvil, sparks flying, the angry hiss of hot iron being quenched, the smell of coal or charcoal burning, the thrill of shaping obdurate iron after heating it to a glowing red. The quality of each new fire changes constantly; each piece of iron is a little different from all others; each hammer blow has a little different effect on the material, creating an intellectual as well as a technical challenge. The products made of iron can be light and airy in feeling or solid and menacing, depending on the concept toward which the smith works. Forging iron is a most satisfying occupation.

In olden times the blacksmith was actually thought to be in league with the magician, using the powers of darkness and light to create useful objects from a lump of iron. The atmosphere of the blacksmith shop encourages this viewpoint, and the smith himself enjoys his work because he continues to wonder at his own alchemy in changing a base metal into jewel-like creations.

Aside from dressing tools and making industrial prototypes, which may range from surgeons' scalpels to tractor crankshafts to decorative hinges, most full-time blacksmiths in America in the 1970s seem to concentrate on making traditional items for restorations or reproductions of traditional buildings. But this is a severely limited field. Although demand for reproductions will continue, it will not nearly reach the design or income potential of handwrought iron. Certainly if blacksmithing is to be included in a viable rebirth of crafts, it must produce items of contemporary design for contemporary uses. That this can be done has already been demonstrated by a handful of blacksmiths in California, New England, Illinois, and Georgia and by a few vestigial professional shops in Germany, Italy, and Scandinavia. Strangely enough, reports state that Europe, once the heartland of craft work, is now more interested as a whole in reaching the status of social progress which America now wishes to leave behind, so that the schools for blacksmithing in Europe are suffering from less and less enrollment each year. As a consequence, there are plenty of openings. Possibly the reason for this is that blacksmithing in Europe has retained the status of a trade and has not attracted artists. In America interest in blacksmithing as an art seems to be growing more rapidly each year.

But regardless of this decline in interest, Germany, Scandinavia, Italy, and, to some extent, England have found markets for many handwrought iron items for buildings of commercial, religious, and residential nature. The potential variety of these items, mostly of modern design, is manifold.

Architects may well form the largest eventual market for the new smith, once they are made aware of the possibilities of modern design in iron and the sources for such work. For instance, modern office buildings, stores, churches, hotels, and hospitals can use wrought-iron chandeliers which use the qualities of iron and the techniques of forging to complement the building. The same can be said for stair railings, window grills, balcony railing, brackets of various sorts, outside fencing and gates, fountains, and abstract sculpture.

More and more church buildings are being designed in contemporary style, creating a very good potential market for wrought-iron crosses, altar screens, and chandeliers. Wrought iron in many forms is most suitable also for traditional churches, for decorative hinges, light brackets, and various types of decorative reinforcements and holders.

Really good, artistic wrought iron can be used in many places in residences of every degree. Garden gates and garden gate latches as well as outdoor screens and fences generally find a ready market. City houses need window grills, and iron-bound doors make a handsome addition to any residence, as do handwrought doorknobs and knockers which have a distinction not found in cast brass or cast iron. The interiors of houses need fire screens, fireplace tools, sconces, candlesticks, pot racks in the kitchen, trivets for growing plants, and barbecue utensils such as forks, spoons, and knives.

Iron may also be used for small items of personal adornment.

It is suitable especially for unique belt buckles but has also been used for necklaces and bracelets, sometimes in combination with copper, silver, or gold. Curiously enough an amateur blacksmith in England in the early 1970s inadvertently developed a flourishing trade in chastity belts after he made one as a joke for a friend. His example was followed by an American blacksmith who turned out chastity belts embellished with jewels for wearing over body stockings for party dress. It is doubtful that the chastity belt is headed for a revival, but other fads might create temporary special markets for the blacksmith in years to come.

Possibly the last nationally recognized blacksmith in America was the great and talented Samuel Yellin of Philadelphia. His shop, which employed up to 40 blacksmiths during its heyday, still stands in Philadelphia as a museum. In it are displayed samples of the gorgeous ironwork designed by this master of the craft. His shop turned out items as small as switch plates for electric lights and as large as the gates for the National Cathedral in Washington, D.C. Yellin created his own designs for the most part, working with iron rather than pencil and paper, and his designs fit the styles of his era, which lay between 1900 and his death in the 1940s. He and the equally great artist Fritz Kuhn of Germany founded a link between the master blacksmiths of the past and the renaissance of the crafts in the late twentieth century. Both should be studied by any aspiring smith of the future.

Whence came such artists in iron? Where do they learn the complicated, fascinating techniques which allow them to burn base iron into art?

One of the basic requirements for learning to work iron is an all-consuming interest in the art, a dedication, almost an obsession, that is common to all the good and all the great smiths of all time. Such interest seems to be part of a man, a seed of creativity waiting to be germinated by the heat of the forge and the water of the slack tub. It seems akin to the genius of Mozart and Cellini and Leonardo, waiting for exposure to the challenge of art to start the seed growing toward eventual flowering. More artists have this seed within them, it seems, than may be realized. But the realization of potential is easily lost in modern times because of the lack of exposure to the practice of the art. There are simply not many blacksmiths around to stimulate latent, inherent interest. And, even two or three generations ago, blacksmithing, under pressure from industry, had become more a trade than an art, not attracting to any great degree the artist who might have kept the forge alight.

But there are growing opportunities to see forges in action and learn the techniques of blacksmithing. Since 1970 more and more universities have either established or announced plans to establish courses in blacksmithing as part of the crafts curriculum in art schools. These universities may be found north and south, east and west, and though still few in number are known to the metal-working professors in most university art schools. The aspiring blacksmith should inquire about ironworking courses in graduate or continuing education programs. Also the American Crafts Council in New York publishes up-to-date lists each year of available craft courses of all sorts. These lists may be purchased for a nominal fee. The American Crafts Council's address appears in the appendix to this book.

Learning blacksmithing at a university may seem a far cry from the invaluable seven years' apprenticeship served by the great smiths of former years, but university training in America can be especially valuable to the new smith. For the most part our American universities are the source of inspiration in the continuing development of new concepts of design which may be adapted and accepted by modern folk.

Universities also offer the advantage of exposure to other crafts such as pottery, weaving, and precious metal working, all of which can give ideas to the blacksmith.

A few craft schools, notably the Penland Crafts School at Penland, North Carolina, and Haystack School at Deer Isle, Maine, are setting up facilities and short courses for teaching blacksmithing. Such schools, as well as universities, will contribute much to the future of blacksmithing as soon as instructors well trained in the art are available. The universities with courses in iron working in 1973 are lacking in instructors who know all aspects of the art, particularly forge welding, tempering steel, and the importance of good shop coal. The instructors teaching blacksmithing, however, are well grounded in using metal-working tools, and they are particularly well trained in modern design and the attitude which allows a material to create its own forms. This is of extreme value to the new blacksmith; perhaps it is the one factor which will give the ancient craft immortality in the ages to come. Fuel and welding and tempering are part of this, of course, but they can be learned with experience and exposure.

There is at least one school in 1974 devoted exclusively to blacksmithing. This is the Turley Forge in Santa Fe, New Mexico, with facilities for rather limited enrollment for successive six-week courses. It is also possible to make arrangements with some of the few, full-time professional smiths to work as an apprentice for varying periods of time, not for instruction so much as for exposure, observation, and an opportunity to ask questions. Some professional smiths are rather difficult to find as most have enough commissions from private individuals and architects to keep them busy without advertising their whereabouts. They are too busy making a living to teach. But most of them are proud of their craft and their skill and will welcome visitors and answer questions with courtesy and interest. Visits to these shops can yield much basic direction to supplement the teaching found in universities. Such establishments can be found relatively easily in New England, but are also present in North Carolina, California, New York, Georgia, New Jersey, and the Southwest; they may be hidden in other areas, particularly the Appalachian regions of the East and in the Ozarks.

More information about sources of learning blacksmithing may be obtained by writing the newly formed (in 1973) Artist-Blacksmiths Association of North America, 873 Spring Street, N.W., Atlanta, Georgia 30308.

Retired blacksmiths, though usually not artists, are a marvelous source of basic information on fuel, tools, and techniques, and most love to indulge themselves by talking about the art. Most, too, are pleasant about it, and most, even though retired, still are very much interested in learning themselves, whether from a student, an amateur, or another professional. This universal interest in the craft probably demonstrates more than anything the tenacious fascination of ironworking. Those who are exposed to it soon find that it offers a never-ending challenge which is both physical and intellectual.

Another source for exposure to tools, techniques, and blacksmiths is the restoration sites which are being set up in all parts of the country. Some of the blacksmiths at these sites are true professionals of the old school and others are skillful amateurs. Most can contribute a bit of lore that will be helpful to the starting blacksmith. Blacksmith shops of the traditional type are found in practically all regions, especially in Virginia, New England, North Carolina, the Southwest, Florida, Georgia, and Canada.

Undoubtedly the finest training available in all aspects of ironworking, both traditional and modern, will be found in England and Germany, where professional training is still available in the 1970s, even though interest in the art in Europe among young people is diminishing. Yet, a few technical schools in these countries teach a full term in the art, and this teaching is available to Americans. The German government offers around 70 full scholarships each year for Americans to attend German universities and art schools, including the very fine Northrhine/Westfalen Technical School in Aachen. Applications for these may be made through any college or university dean, and information may be obtained through the German Embassy or any German consulate in the country. England is not quite so generous in its scholarships but information on technical schools which teach blacksmithing may be gotten from the British Embassy or British consulates. There has been a renewal of interest in Britain in blacksmithing through the good offices of the Bureau for Small Industries of the British government and good instruction is available.

Where scholarships are lacking from foreign governments students might look into the possibility of Fulbright scholarships which may be applied to technical as well as academic schools abroad. The same is true of several other nationally administered foundations.

Virtually no texts on blacksmithing have been published in the last generation in America, and texts published before the 1930s, all now out of print, are extremely difficult to find. They may be found in libraries in larger cities and the libraries of technical colleges such as the Georgia Institute of Technology, Massachusetts Institute of Technology, and others. These old books are well worth studying, and some are very well written.

There is one recent book published in America (Bealer, *The Art of Blacksmithing*) which examines tools and techniques from the historical viewpoint, and three small but extremely well done books published by the Bureau for Small Industries in England (*The Blacksmith, The Decorative Wrought-Iron Worker*, and *Decorative Wrought Iron*)* should be included in any modern blacksmith's library.

Knowledge, however, will not produce ironwork by itself. A well-equipped shop is needed for that. The blacksmith shop possibly requires more capital investment than any of the other crafts, and the equipment is more difficult to acquire.

A good blacksmith shop will never be fully equipped. The special work of the smith, some of it perhaps never conceived before, requires special equipment to create a certain effect on whatever is being made—an effect more often than not locked in the smith's creative mind, impossible to express except in iron, and requiring a tool never before seen.

On the other hand, a good smith will never lack equipment no matter how specialized it must be. The blacksmith is unique among the craftsmen in that he is capable of making his own tools, as well as the tools of the other crafts. But while a few smiths of modern times continue to make their own hammers and tongs, most find that they can purchase such tools in a number of satisfactory forms and sizes more economically than they can be made. The same attitude may be applied to many other items of smith equipment.

Possibly the most basic piece of equipment is the forge with its accompanying source of air, either a blower or a bellows.

The forge itself may be built of brick, stone, or wood lined with brick and stone and clay. The forge is no more than an open hearth, usually about 3 to 4 feet square, with a firepot, molded from clay and brick or stone, some 8 to 10 inches deep and 9 to 12 inches across, depending on the type work, heavy or light, which will be wrought. It will be well for the beginning smith to carefully examine any forges he can find and use them as mod-

* These are available by mail order from the address given in the Bibliography.

els for his own. Forge design has not changed essentially since Roman times, and all of them built of brick and stone and clay may be altered from day to day if necessary to fit the type of jobs for the day.

A brick forge, permanently situated in the shop, is undoubtedly the most satisfactory type for a professional. If the smith is not a good enough mason to build it himself, he must consider the hire of a mason as part of his initial capital investment. It will cost between $600 and $1,200 to have a forge properly built.

Any forge must also have some form of *tuyere,* or blow pipe, through which the air is directed to the fire. Tuyeres, or tue irons, with duck's nests or grates and ash chutes are in very short supply in the Age of Aquarius and must be hunted diligently in antique shops, junk yards, and abandoned industrial blacksmith shops. Or they may be improvised or made from scratch or cast in iron from a pattern furnished to an iron foundry. The smith who starts a shop should know from his training what is needed to equip an efficient forge. It will require time and money, however, to find or have made what he needs.

Many modern smiths use gas forges which are easily available, easy to use and maintain, have no problem with obtaining fuel, and are clean and easily set up. For the smith who will make small items a gas forge is ideal. But the gas forge is not capable of forge welding, and if forge welding is required, the old-fashioned coal forge is a necessity. A modern blacksmith might consider having both a coal and a gas forge. Gas forges may be purchased in various sizes from the supply sources listed at the end of this chapter. They cost about $250.

Another essential piece of equipment for any blacksmith shop is a good anvil. Quality may be determined by a number of factors: weight; whether it is cast or forged; condition of the face and horn; tempering of the face, etc., all of which may be judged from experience gained during training. Anvils in good condition sometimes may be found in antique shops, in abandoned farm blacksmith shops, and occasionally in industrial supply houses which deal in blacksmith tools. New cast anvils, generally considered inferior to forged anvils, are manufactured by only one company in the United States known to the author and may be ordered through suppliers listed at the end of this chapter. Good-quality forged and cast steel anvils are still available from a number of companies in England, Sweden, and Germany. These may sometimes be ordered from steel supply houses or directly from the manufacturers. No anvil of less than 100 pounds is suitable for a professional shop. Larger anvils of up to 400 pounds are needed for large work such as gates, fences, grills, and large chandeliers. Generally, good-quality anvils sell for about $1 a pound.

A variety of anvil tools are also needed by the blacksmith. These include hot and cold hardies or bottom cutters; bottom fullers in several sizes; bottom swages, in some instances, depending on the type work done; anvil bicks; bending forks; small stake anvils; and possibly others for special jobs. Anvil tools are more difficult to find, either new or used, than anvils. Most, however, may be made in the shop. When available at the sources listed at the end of this chapter anvil tools cost from $5 to $15.

A good variety of set tools are also necessary. Set tools are such items as punches, top fullers, top swages, hot and cold sets (which are cutting tools), set hammers, flatters, and perhaps other special tools. These tools are all equipped with handles so that they resemble hammers. The handles are for holding, however, so that the tools may be set on the work in progress and hit with a hammer. Prices are about the same as those for anvil tools.

Hot and cold chisels, small fullers, punches, and small sets, to substitute for the set hammer, are easily made from drill or chisel rods by the smith himself. Or they may be bought from hardware stores at $1 to $4 each. If the smith intends to make hammers, axes, or tomahawks, he may make himself a number of drifts of various sizes by which the eyes of these tools are finally shaped.

Hammers and tongs, or course, are needed in several varieties and shapes. Hammers should range in type from ball peen in weights of 1 to 3 pounds to cross peen or straight peen in weights of 3 to 6 pounds. Long-handled sledges of from 6 to 10 pounds are also quite handy at times. A well-equipped shop should have at least five hammers for each smith and possibly up to ten, some of which may be used for shaping. Heavier silversmithing hammers are quite suitable for shaping iron. Regular forging hammers may usually be found in local hardware stores at a cost of from $4 to $10.

Tongs of different sizes and variety still may be found in America or Europe and purchased through steel supply houses or from industrial supply houses which deal in secondhand equipment at a cost of around $5 a pair. An accomplished smith traditionally makes his own tongs, and the beginning blacksmith might choose to follow this custom and make for himself the untold variety of tongs as they are needed.

Since a modern blacksmith shop is designed to yield a comfortable livelihood, the modern smith should also, as soon as possible, acquire a small trip-hammer or air hammer. Such mechanization

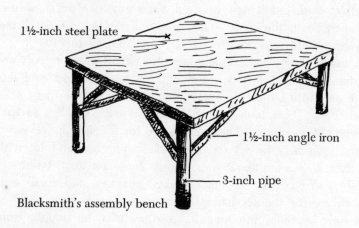

1½-inch steel plate

1½-inch angle iron

3-inch pipe

Blacksmith's assembly bench

does no harm to the quality of work turned out. It is merely a modern substitute for several apprentices, and allows the modern smith to turn out good work in many fewer heats, thereby saving a great deal of time and money in successively heating the iron being worked. Mechanical hammers such as Little Giant, of Mankato, Minnesota, are still being manufactured in the United States and may be purchased through industrial supply houses. Trip-hammers are a major investment which sell new at around $2,000, or less for used models.

As with almost any craft shop, the blacksmith shop must have at least one workbench, or adequate workspace on a large bench, for each worker in the shop. Drawers to contain small tools used at the bench are a convenient concomitant to the bench. The workbench may be of wood, made by the smith himself, or it may be covered with iron plate for assembling decorative pieces while hot. Smiths who specialize in large decorative work such as fences, gates, etc., will require quite a large assembly bench made entirely of iron with perhaps pipe or angle iron legs, or of wood with the bench top covered with quarter-inch iron plate.

Large work will require at least two smiths for safety and efficiency.

Tools must be stored properly in an efficient blacksmith shop. A very convenient device for this purpose is a tool rack made of

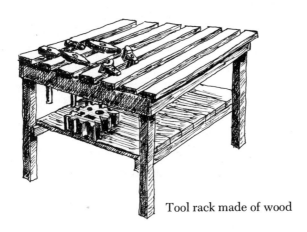

Tool rack made of wood

wood or metal with a top consisting of slots or rods with spaces between each sufficient to receive the handles of hammers, set tools, tongs, and boxes to store hand chisels and punches. Such a tool rack might be the height of the forge, perhaps 3 feet square and located close to the anvil and forge for convenient accessibility.

A vise is quite essential to the smith. Traditionally the blacksmith has always used a heavy leg, or post, vise attached to the bench or to a post set in the ground convenient to the forge. Like many of the tools of the forge, however, leg vises are in short supply in the 1970s. The heavy vises which stand up under the pounding of large hammers are quite rare, and the small vises usually found in antique shops, remnants of farm blacksmithing operations, are usually not suitable for a full-time shop. New leg vises may be found in England and Germany and may be ordered sometimes from industrial supply houses or hardware dealers at a cost of about $25 to $40 new, depending on size. If found to be unavailable, the leg vise may be replaced by a heavy machinist's vise mounted solidly on the bench above a leg or on a heavy post inserted in the floor.

The professional smith will save much time and labor if he has in the shop some form of shear cutter, for cutting iron to proper length either hot or cold. The old-time blacksmith usually made his own but commercial shear cutters, some operated mechanically and some with hydraulic or air power, are available from the United States and European manufacturers through industrial or steel supply houses. They cost about $100.

The manufacturers of shear cutters usually can furnish mechanical punches also. Mechanical punches enable the smith to punch up to a ⅜-inch hole through a half-inch bar of cold iron much more easily and quickly than punching the same hole by hand in hot iron. They save the time of heating, always unproductive however necessary, and are well worth the investment for a modern smith. Mechanical punches sell for about $50 to $150.

Also essential for a modern shop is a heavy drill press of the type used in most modern metal manufacturing plants and machine shops. Drill presses are easily found, either secondhand or new for a cost of around $250 to $350.

A grindstone or electric emery wheel, perhaps with two wheels and steel brushes and buffing pads as well as the grinding wheels, is most necessary for resharpening chisels, dressing punches, and grinding forged items to final shape and smoothness. These cost $400 to $500. A body grinder, also very useful, costs about $250.

And while the smith traditionally has cut his iron bars atwain with hot and cold sets and occasionally a hacksaw, the modern smith will find that a power hacksaw of some sort will save untold hours over the years and be well worth the investment. Power hacksaws may be purchased from the industrial supply houses found in most cities or from some of the suppliers listed at the end of this chapter. They cost from $250 to $350 depending on size and type.

Another ancient tool, the swage block, is not essential but is extremely valuable for certain types of work. Swage blocks are made of cast iron with variously shaped indentations in the four sides and on both flat faces. They are extremely difficult to find except in Europe but the modern smith can supply himself, as did the old smiths, by making or ordering a pattern of wood and having his own design cast of ductile iron at a nearby foundry. European swage blocks cost about $200 to $300.

Of course, every shop needs one or two slack tubs for quenching and tempering, one to contain clear water, the other to contain brine. This simple piece of equipment may be the half of a whiskey barrel or a metal washtub or it may be made of plate iron welded together. It should be large enough to baptize a new smith, as is the custom in Germany. Cost will range from $12 for a half barrel to $35 for a large tub made of plate.

There are a number of small tools needed by the smith which may all be acquired at one time or collected one by one over a period of time as needed. These include pliers of different types and sizes; a goodly selection of wrenches, screwdrivers, files, and rasps of different types and coarseness; taps and dies of different sizes; scales; and calipers. Most may be found at hardware stores at a cost of from $2 to $10 per item.

And, while frowned upon by traditionalists, the modern smithy founded to produce a comfortable living, might well be equipped with either acetylene or electric welding equipment or both. Neither acetylene nor electric welding is as esthetically pleasing, as satisfying to perform, or as strong as forge welding. Nevertheless, it does save much time and may often be used for small jobs where strength is not a factor in design. Also, it may be completely hidden with judicious forging. Welding machines can be purchased for from $250 to $500.

To summarize the equipment needed to start a modern blacksmith shop, let it be said that the type of work to be performed should be the basis for making up a list of required equipment and tools. The smith who plans to produce small items such as hinges, toasting forks, fireplace tools, belt buckles, etc., can start out with the minimum of forge and blower, an anvil, a few hammers, a few sets of tongs, a few set tools and anvil tools, and the ubiquitous slack tub. On the other hand, the smith who will design and produce large decorative pieces will need all the hand tools plus a number of modern mechanical tools if he is to produce enough at a satisfactory price to make himself a comfortable living. Until the aspiring professional smith decides his specialty, he cannot plan the amount of capital needed to start his operation. With luck the producer of small items may be able to found his business with an investment in tools of from $500 to $1,000. The maker of big items of wrought iron, though, might think in terms of an initial investment of from $10,000 to $20,000, again depending on luck in finding the equipment.

An important factor in running an efficient, profitable blacksmith shop is the shop building. Even the smallest shop will require a minimum of from 200 to 300 square feet which will provide room for forge, anvil, tool rack, workbench, and drill press without crowding, and in addition provide storage space for the iron stock with which he will work. If a shop employs one or two additional workers the space should be doubled. The building must be adaptable to a flue for the forge and should have adequate windows for light as well as necessary electrical connections for blower, drill press, and other basic equipment.

Adequate space can often be found quite cheaply in outlying areas in any sized town. If, however, the shop can be located where traffic of potential trade is rather heavy, the advertising value of the location will more than offset higher rent in terms of income and profit. Modern people have neither time nor inclination to seek out the better mousetrap builder. Shop space will rent for from $2.50 to $4.00 a square foot per year. Improvements, however, might require as much as $5,000.

All the equipment in the world will be worthless unless there is stock available for it to work. The modern smith can acquire old-fashioned wrought iron of generally the type used in ancient times from one supplier in the United States and from several suppliers overseas. Wrought iron, though, is expensive, particularly when ordered in relatively small quantities, and is hardly worth the extra cost in producing wrought-iron items. A type of mild steel designated as 10-20 hot rolled has qualities almost identical to those of wrought iron and offers the advantages of low price and easy availability. It may be ordered in almost any quantity and dimension from steel supply houses in every area of the country. A shop should store an adequate supply of 10-20 hot rolled steel in various sizes for the intended work. In addition every smithy should keep on hand a small supply of various sized drill and chisel rods of carbon steel to use in making necessary punches, chisels, and other tools, and to use in making axes, tomahawks, knives, and springs if these items are to be part of the shop's production. A scrap pile, consisting of the residue of the smith's work plus fortuitous finds in junk yards and around building sites, should be carefully nurtured as a source of day-by-day material.

Modern metallurgy has also produced some very interesting types of iron and steel which can be used by the artsmith for new attractive wrought items. Stainless steel may be forged into beautiful creations and polished to its original pristine brightness after the forging. It must, however, be heated with a gas forge to retain its stainless properties. Corten steel, and other alloys containing copper, which produces a rust-colored patina when exposed to the atmosphere, should be splendid stock for forging modern designs in small or large items. Neither stainless steel nor corten steel responds to forge welding, but both new steels may be electric- or acetylene-welded and the residue of the weld ground or forged so that it is unnoticeable. The modern smith who is not bound to traditional design and material should investigate the new steels now being produced and experiment with them at his own forge.

Also he might look backward to the ironwork of the Vikings and investigate the sometimes beautiful contrast created by the use of precious metal on base metal as exemplified by the gold and silver inlaid battle axes of the Norsemen. Pieces of modern design may be decorated with wrapped or inlaid copper and silver wire. In addition, wrought iron may be enameled, providing a nice touch of color to the somber gray color of iron fresh from the forge, or the design may contain spots of colored glass which may be easily fused into small split or punched openings. Such experimentation will require knowledge of other crafts that in turn will reinforce the blacksmith's reputation for versatility.

There is always a market for certain items of wrought iron, even semi-mass-produced hearth sets, sconces, and balcony rails. Art objects of wrought iron have not been a big factor in overall sales mostly because there have been few artists in the medium for a generation and those few have been kept busy executing commissions for a few customers. If the number of blacksmiths grows, as may be expected, the whole medium will gain more exposure and create a constantly growing market for wrought iron. But people must know that smiths are available to make objects of beauty from obdurate iron. The public must be taught that blacksmiths are not just shoers of horses.

Indeed, the modern smith is starting to take pains to let his chosen market know where to find him and learn what he makes. This may be done through a good location, free publicity, paid advertising, demonstrations, and perhaps even sales calls, particularly for architectural work.

All such activities may seem crass and unartistic, but they are really no more so than advertised one-man shows to sell the work of a great painter, or concerts for a master pianist. Surely the smith who wishes to find customers should utilize the natural attractions of the smithy: the excitement of fire and dangerous red hot iron, the smell of smoke, the harmonious sound of hammer on anvil, the hissing surrender of heat to the slack tub. All of these factors will serve to draw attention to the beauty of the smith's work and wondrous appreciation of his skill.

Of course, finished work should be displayed around the shop and commissions should be encouraged. The customer who buys one beautiful piece of wrought iron, however small, will probably come back for more and bring his friends.

There are other ways, however, to sell the products of a smithy. Almost every large community has a number of gift shops, some of which specialize in very high quality merchandise indeed, which would like to stock well-designed objects of wrought iron, from door hooks and bolts to massive chandeliers. Most shops will either buy such items outright or display them on consignment, which means that the artist will be paid when the item is sold.

Craft fairs are becoming, in the 1970s, more common than ever before and offer a very good entry into the market of a region or community. Usually it pays the smith to set up a portable forge at such exhibitions to demonstrate his skill while displaying objects he has made over a period of time. Also, it gives him an opportunity to gain commissions which can be executed after the fair. Lists of craft fairs in each state can be obtained from the state Chambers of Commerce or the state departments of tourism.

The smith who intends to specialize mainly in large architectural work might take an entirely different approach to sales. For one thing his large shop might be uneconomical to maintain in a high rent district where traffic is heavy and should probably be located in an outlying area. His customers, then, must be attracted by different methods. A catalog of photographs of finished work should be made ready, merely by enclosing the photographs in a loose leaf binder, to show to customers drawn to the shop. One might first appeal to these customers, architects, builders, and engineers through letters inviting them to visit the shop and by sending inquiries regarding needs. In addition the architectural smith might organize, from time to time, special seminars for architects, builders, and interior designers. Such seminars could be held in the shop where a demonstration could be given if feasible and where work can be displayed and questions answered.

A number of advertising media are available to the architectural smith. One is *Sweet's Catalog*, which is used by practically every architect and engineer practicing in the United States. It offers a medium for providing background and specifications, address and phone number, and reproductions of photographs of the smith's work.

Architectural and interior design magazines, as well as periodicals directed to businessmen, might be approached for articles which describe the smith's work.

One of the best advertising media is the smith's own work. Each piece should be stamped with an identifying mark and in some cases the town where the forge is located.

Certainly competition should be encouraged. No force will expose the fine work of the blacksmith to the public, and thus create a market for wrought iron, so well as good blacksmiths working across the land. Competition, too, will be invaluable in forcing each competitive smith to maintain high standards of design and workmanship and to reach new heights of individual design appropriate to the coming years.

Modern blacksmiths are still rare enough so that, if they are good artists and craftsmen, they can demand $15 to $50 per hour for their work. Such a high fee is, indeed, quite necessary to compensate for the large capital investment required in a shop, and to maintain an adequate stock of iron and coal.

The blacksmith of modern times is indeed an artist, and like any artist may have deeply ingrained compunctions about adopting the methods of business to help him make his mark. Such compromise will be necessary, however, if the blacksmith is to find his deserved status in the artistic community of modern times. And the use of business methods will not in any way compromise the art of the smith.

SOURCES OF SUPPLY
Wrought Iron and Steel

Brodhead-Garrett Company
4560 East 71st Street
Cleveland, Ohio 44105

Lockhart Iron and Steel Company
McKees Rocks
Pittsburgh, Pennsylvania

Local steel supply houses

Tools and Equipment

Brodhead-Garrett Company
4560 East 71st Street
Cleveland, Ohio 44105

The Forge and Anvil
3271 Roswell Road, NE
Atlanta, Georgia 30305

Buffalo Forge Company
Buffalo, New York 14203

Little Giant, Inc. (trip-hammers)
Mankato, Minnesota 56001

The Centaur Company
117 North Spring Street
Burlington, Wisconsin 53105

Mac's Blacksmith Supply
P.O. Box 64
Bridgeton, Indiana 47836

Champion Blower Company
Pottsville, Pennsylvania 17901

T & H Pettinghaus
(German imported equipment)
261 First Street
Palisades Park, New Jersey 07650

4
Glass

CHAPTER XVIII

The Glassblower and Lampworker

GLASS has been around a long time. Although it is one of the most brittle and fragile substances used functionally by man it is also one of the most widely used materials in the modern world, and has been the foundation of great industries in Europe and America.

Glassblowing as a craft is essentially the same as it was in ancient times; the same tools are used for the same purposes with only a few superficial changes in techniques, such as the substitution of gas for charcoal as the fuel in the melting furnace. And the glassblower pretty much makes the same items his ancient predecessors did. However, the men of olden times did a much larger trade in functional glass items and in window glass, which until about 1800 was blown as was every other form of glass except plate glass. Like his predecessors, the modern craftsman makes pitchers, vases, and tumblers, sometimes with color and sometimes with bubbles and sometimes with a beautiful dewdrop of air in the midst of solid glass. He makes plates, ash trays, and large bowls of heavy lead glass which can then be decorated by his fellow craftsman, the glass cutter. And he makes wine glasses and cigarette cases and almost anything that he wants once he has his furnace set up and has mastered the few, simple tools of his craft. No two pieces are ever exactly alike.

Often confused with the glassblower is the lampworker. He demonstrates all the artistic taste and imagination of the glassblower but works with pieces of already formed glass tubes which he makes plastic over a gas lamp and shapes to his fancy. Many of the products of the lampworker duplicate those of the glassblower, but generally the lampworker turns his tubes, large and small, into bits of crystalline sculpture of flowers, insects, birds, animals, and people. He can visualize an amazing variety of objects in a simple tube of clear glass, including the complicated scientific apparatus that apparently were the first items ever made by lampworking. And it is fully as amazing how he molds the semi-molten tube by blowing into its end and shaping it with one or two simple tools to create abstraction or realism.

Both glassblowing and lampworking are taught at most universities which offer crafts curricula and at the crafts schools such as Penland Crafts School at Penland, North Carolina, and Haystack School at Deer Isle, Maine. Glassblowing is not generally taught at municipally operated craft schools because of the expense of the furnace and the amount of space needed. Lampworking is sometimes taught at municipal craft schools if an instructor is available.

The American Crafts Council compiles an annual, up-to-date list of those colleges and craft schools which teach glassblowing and lampworking. It may be obtained by writing the council in New York at the address given in the appendix to this book entitled *Training*.

If an aspiring glassblower is fortunate he may find an established local artist in the field who needs assistance and he can learn the art in this best of all ways. He will, however, be competing with trained graduates from the universities for such apprenticeships. Some prior training in art and design and a tested dexterity in handcraftsmanship will help him compete.

The equipment needed by the glassblower is considerably more complicated in some ways and slightly more numerous than the one or two tools used by the lampworker. First of all, the glassblower needs a great furnace in which to melt his silica and other ingredients needed to compose the type of glass he has in mind. Such furnaces, heated by natural or LP gas, may be purchased from the supply sources listed at the end of this chapter. They cost from $15,000 to $20,000, however. As a consequence of this great expense, most glassblowers make their own furnaces out of fire brick and fire clay and concrete block at a cost of only $2,000 to $5,000 depending on size and what materials are available secondhand.

In regard to the expense of the furnace, fuel is a big factor. For the glass must be kept molten 24 hours a day and this requires from $200 to $300 a month for fuel cost alone for an average operation turning out about 15 to 20 bud vases a day.

Glassblowers also need the small uncomplicated equipment that has been used to form the material since the year 2500 B.C. Several iron tubes some 4 feet long are needed through which to blow the molten glass into great bubbles which are then shaped to the artist's fancy. Tubes of several different uses are available at the craft supply houses listed at the end of this chapter. Tubes sell for about $5 each.

A glassblower's chair, with two solid arms over which the tube may be rolled back and forth when shaping an article is essential. The chair should be a sturdy affair either made by the glassblower himself to fit his size or by adapting a good, strong office chair by

Glassblower's chair

extending its arms. About $10 worth of lumber is needed to make a a chair from scratch. Secondhand office chairs can usually be obtained from office supply stores for from $5 to $10 and converted to glassblowing chairs for a couple of dollars' worth of lumber.

Strangely, for working a red hot substance the glassblower employs a wooden paddle, resembling a ping pong paddle, with which he strokes his molten material into its desired shape. Paddles are easily made from a piece of lumber, preferably hardwood, ½ to ¾ of an inch thick and 12 inches long. This short board may be sawn with a coping or saber saw to create a handle 6 inches long and of a width to comfortably fit the individual craftsman's hand. A pocketknife and sandpaper are used to round and smooth the handle. Certain glassblowers prefer a carbon paddle which may be bought at glassblowers' supply houses for about $10. They last a lifetime.

Sometimes part of the shaping operation for glass consists of cutting with glassblowers' shears, a tool resembling old-fashioned wool shears. Shears are available from craft supply stores listed in the appendix to this chapter. They sell for about $8 a pair.

Also, for shaping necks and narrow waists on bottles and vases the glassblower requires the tweezers of his trade, a steel tool which is a giant version of common eyebrow tweezers. These cost about $5 a pair from regular supply sources.

And, for delicate shaping and crimping, the artisan in glass uses a carbon rod which he may buy for about $3.

If the glassblower works on large, heavy bowls and vases he may require an assistant to help him cut or shape and to lend a

Homemade wooden shaping paddle

hand in taking the material on its tube back to the furnace for re-heating. Reheating is done frequently when the craftsman feels his material losing its plasticity. For glass is somewhat similar to iron in that it must be worked within certain ranges of heat. The fine craftsman in glass develops the instincts that let him know through his hands as well as his eyes when his material is cooling to a consistency which cannot be worked.

Glass is quite unlike iron, however, in that it cannot be cooled quickly. It must be annealed slowly, requiring five or six hours to cool from its plastic state to useful solidity. If it cools too quickly it will suddenly crack to pieces. A special annealing oven, therefore, is an absolute necessity for the glassblower. He can make his own from fire brick, a gas burner, and refrigerator shelves on which to set his work for about $300, which includes a thermostat that slowly turns the heat down to nothing.

Professional annealing ovens cost around $3,500. These offer considerable capacity and are suitable for large operations where a number of glassblowers are working in a shop. The large ovens also are divided into several sections to accommodate a constant stream of new-made items which, during a day's time, must be annealing at different temperatures.

Equipment for the lampworker is altogether much simpler than that of the glassblower, although the two share some pieces of equipment. The main difference is in the material with which each initiates his work. The glassblower starts with raw material, silica, from which he makes his own glass in various formulae for various uses. The lampworker, on the other hand, purchases his glass ready-made in the form of tubes and solid rods of different types of glass, most of it clear but some with color.

Buying his glass ready-made saves the lampworker the rather considerable expense of a glass furnace. He has no need of iron tubes but blows through the glass tubes, since glass, fortunately, is a very poor conductor of heat. But he must have an annealing oven, paddles, tweezers, carbon rods, and shears, using them in exactly the same way and for the same purposes as his colleague, the glass-blower. His lamp is little more than a glorified bunsen burner, which, indeed, is sometimes used for working small pieces of tube. Such a lamp may be purchased from the suppliers listed at the end of this chapter. It sells for about $100 as compared with the thousands of dollars needed to purchase a furnace.

Lacking the glassblower's chair which allows the blower to rotate his work and shape round objects, the lampworker who makes large objects often uses a glass lathe on which his molten creations such as vases and bowls are kept hot. These lathes may be ordered from the sources listed at the end of this chapter at a cost of from $6,000 to $10,000.

The lampworker who turns out any volume of work makes good use of a glass saw, which costs about $1,200, for cutting his tubes and rods to convenient length. A belt grinder, while not essential, is used in large lampworkers' shops. Grinders may be bought from industrial suppliers, Sears, Roebuck, wood tool suppliers, some hardware stores, and craft suppliers for from $250 to $600.

Some considerable amount of space is needed for glassblowing, at least 500 to 600 square feet. Not only must the large furnace and annealing oven be situated immediately adjacent to the working space, but there must be plenty of vacant space for handling the 4-foot tube with the heavy weight of glowing glass on its tip, for the glassblower must sometimes execute rather active gymnastics with his tube to coax his material into the form he wishes. Then there must be space for the chair and often for a helper to stand by the chair to assist when needed. And because of the fragile nature of glass, the producing glassblower needs ample space to store his finished products. Glass cannot be piled in a corner like wood and iron, stored in a sack like jewelry, or even stacked like most pottery. Besides, each piece has a jewel-like quality which serves to inspire the next piece, and it cries for space and light to give it life and beauty.

A display room connected with the shop will do much to stimulate sales. It must be considered, however, that the cost of renting effective display space might be exorbitant for shop space, especially if several glassblowers are working in the shop. The only answer to this problem, of course, is to move the shop away from the high-rent district and expand the display room. Almost any type building will serve well for shop space if the above specifications of work space and storage space are met.

Lampworkers have the same basic needs in regard to display as glassblowers. The lampworker, however, can work on rather small items. This allows him to display many of them in a given space and also offers the advantage of working with a small bunsen burner in a rather small shop. He must have the annealing oven, but he does not need the elbow room or the large furnace of the glassblower. Many lampworkers use the back of the display room as a shop, with an annealing oven close by. Some shops which employ 10 or 12 men and which are fully equipped with glass saws, glass lathes, belt grinders, and several annealing ovens cover 10,000 square feet of space with ample storage room for many sizes of tubes, but have separate display space.

As with so many of the crafts, shop space as well as equipment is greatly dependent on what is being produced. A professional lampworker might start his career in a small booth in a resort area where he can produce small items which sell for less than $5 each. As his reputation grows, he might move into larger quarters, hire helpers, buy more equipment, and operate from a sizable shop while maintaining a display room in a shopping center or downtown store.

The glassblower acquires his material in the form of powdered silica and other materials, such as lead to give it bulk and strength, and copper oxide, iron oxide, and colored minerals to give it color. Also, some glassblowers collect old bottles, pieces of broken window glass, and other scraps of glass which are pounded into small fragments and used in the same way as silica. Silica may be ordered in drums containing different weights from the suppliers listed at the end of this chapter. It sells for about $55 a ton, which, after being mixed with the requisite minerals and coloring material, will yield from 20 to 25 bud vases, or 35 to 50 wine glasses, or 15 glass bowls of 9-inch diameter, depending of course on the thickness of the items.

Lead is often mixed with molten silica to give weight and strength to the finished product. It may be bought from metal supply dealers in almost every medium-sized to large-sized city at a cost of about 35¢ to 45¢ a pound, with the price getting higher every year. The amount of lead needed for 100 pounds of silica will vary according to the qualities the craftsman wants for his glass.

Coloring materials may most easily be acquired from the suppliers listed at the end of this chapter. They cost from 75¢ to $30 a pound depending on the material. The amount needed for 100 pounds of silica will vary according to the tone and intensity of color desired by the glassblower.

Lampworkers acquire their raw material from established manufacturers of glass tubing and glass rods, such as Corning and Kimball. The size varies from ¼-inch tube and rod to 1-inch rod and 5-inch tube, the larger tube being suitable for making good-sized bowls. Tubing and rods sell for about $4 a pound, which provides enough material for 4 or 5 small figures. Lampworkers also use rods of beautiful cobalt glass, the only type which can be joined to clear glass, to add a spot of color to otherwise clear figures. Cobalt glass is used sparingly, however, for it costs about $30 a pound.

A glassblower setting up a complete operation with ovens, furnaces, and shop and display space, and raw material will require from $10,000 to $30,000 of capital depending on the size of his initial operation, rent in the locality in which he will work, and how much of his equipment he can make himself.

Lampworkers require much less capital. Only the lamp, the annealing oven, raw material, and shop and display space are absolutely required and these may be obtained for around $5,000. As clientele grows the lampworker may invest another $12,000 in such expensive equipment as a belt grinder, a glass lathe, and other labor saving devices which also allow more latitude in design and finishing.

Both glassblowers and lampworkers require from 1 year to 3 years to become established, though, and some serious thought must be given to a source of money for food and shelter during this period. Either additional capital must be accumulated for these basic needs, or an additional source of income must be sought, perhaps teaching in a school where glassblowing facilities are available or doing any job that will allow part of the artist's time to be devoted to establishing himself as a craftsman. It can be done in glasswork as in other crafts. There are notable examples of engineers, accountants, and other professionals becoming established glassworkers a decade or more after they started in their original professions.

Becoming established in glasswork, however, requires selling based on recognition, design, and craftsmanship. Handmade glass objects are selling all over the United States, sometimes in unsuspected locations, when the modern business tools of attractive display, advertising, and organization of the work are utilized. One glassblower, who is fast building a fine reputation and a dependable livelihood, lives in an isolated mountain area in North Carolina. There are few tourists in his area so he displays his wares several times a year in big merchandise shows, such as those in Chicago, Dallas, New York, and Atlanta, and generally sells all he can produce at a good price. In addition he is commissioned by a mail order house about once a year to create an original, unique design for a bud vase, a bowl, or a tumbler. These are then sold as limited editions by the mail order firm whose customers respond to small advertisements in antique and social magazines. Of course, this method of getting established required working for several months before any income could be expected from the work, and with a family to support this artist was required to teach at a craft school for a minimum income until his first production was sold.

There is an outstanding lampworker in Atlanta who over the last 10 years has built an international reputation with all manner of items of original design, many of which sell for a good price. Demand for his work is such that he employs 10 artists to help him execute his designs and 3 people to run his retail outlets. Much of his volume is repeat business orders received from satisfied customers. To encourage this response, the lampworker once a year prepares a folder, beautifully illustrated with photographs of new creations, and mails this to previous customers all over the world. Much of his work is bought to serve as special presentation gifts to government officials and outstanding citizens.

One of the secrets of this artist's success is that from the very first he recognized the need for good display in an area where affluent people would be exposed to his work. At first he started in a small store with display space on a main street with his workshop in the rear. As the demand for his art grew he purchased a large shop in an Atlanta suburb and rented display space in one of the largest and most popular shopping centers in the city. His success should encourage any aspiring craftsman, and his understanding of business principles should serve as an example to any craftsman who wishes the same success for himself.

The two glassworkers described have received very good prices for their work, with most of the price being paid for design and the remainder going for labor, equipment, and material. The beginning glassblower or lampworker might expect to pay himself from $3 to $5 an hour and to multiply this by 2½ to arrive at a fair retail price. This price will pay for his labor and other expenses and yield a profit which should go into capital for replacing equipment, for hiring additional workers, and for other expenses such as taxes and legal counsel. As demand for his work grows he can raise his salary and, using the same formula of multiplying by 2½, increase his operation to meet demand. An adjustment in price might be needed in a highly competitive situation, but good design and craftsmanship are usually above competition.

For the beginner, in whose case an ideal and expensive retail operation may be out of the question at first, display opportunities can be obtained through getting department store buyers, gift shop operators, art gallery operators, jewelry store buyers, and other appropriate retail operators interested in his work. The people involved in these operations must be approached individually and personally with samples and photographs. They may be expected to include their own required margin in the final retail price, and these experts can be extremely helpful in helping the artist determine what he should charge for his work. If the artist has the capital to open his own retail shop he will have to add a similar margin to his basic costs to pay for rent, salary, advertising, and utilities.

Items of glass should be signed by the artists just as paintings are signed. This can be done with some small, inconspicuous signature worked into the hot glass or with a stamp which can be pressed into the base of a bowl or vase. A signature might be scratched into the hot glass with a pointed carbon rod or engraved with an electric hand grinder. It should show the town of origin and the date, also, as a means of building recognition over the years.

Most of the successful glassblowers and lampworkers in the United States make a living exceeding $25,000. They also have done much to widen the market for art and functional items of hand-crafted glass, and while doing this have created opportunity for more glassworkers. The field is not crowded at this time and likely will never be.

SOURCES OF SUPPLY

Brodhead-Garrett Company
4560 East 71st Street
Cleveland, Ohio 44105

The Glass Works
Box 202
Warner, New Hampshire 03278

Crafttool Company, Inc.
1421 West 240th Street
Harbor City, California 90710

The Hinckley School of Crafts
Box S
Hinckley, Maine 04944

Eisler Engineering Company, Inc.
750 South 13th Street
Newark, New Jersey 07103

Paoli Clay Company
Route I
Belleville, Wisconsin 53508

5
Leather

The Leatherworker

LEATHER, like fibers and clay, wood and iron, is one of the basic craft materials in the history of man. Despite the introduction of substitutes for leather which have been created by science and industry, real leather made from the skins of cows, pigs, goats, sheep, crocodiles, and snakes still plays an important part in human activities. Most shoes, particularly those for men, are still made of leather. So are a large part of women's handbags, most billfolds, the finest luggage, men's belts, watch bands, fine upholstery, and countless small items made of genuine leather. There are so many items in fact, that most could not be furnished to the world without the leather imitations which are so widespread in modern Western society.

The leatherworker, who in the old days was known by the rather poetic name of *cordwainer*, works essentially with one material. There are so many different types of leather, though, as with wood, that much of the leatherworker's initial education should be devoted to learning the various types of tanned skins, the qualities and uses of each type, and, of course, the ways of working each. The variety of leather ranges from rawhide with the hair left on, which is completely unworked, to the most supple of lamb, baby pig, and kid, suitable for gloves and clothing.

Leather lends itself well to handcraftsmanship, but is peculiarly unsuited to mass production methods. Each hide is different in size, texture, and durability from any other. Each type of hide yields different material for different uses. Cutting it into components for all its uses requires ultimate human judgment and control.

This challenge in itself is only part of the very deep pleasure of working with leather. There is the marvelous smell of the material, particularly in oak tanned leather, in the rare piece of Indian tanned smoked buckskin, or in Moroccan leather which, for the most part, is tanned by the age-old methods which have made Moroccan leather as popular with Roman and Arabic conquerors as with modern man. The smell of leather is elemental, evoking folk memories of ancient security when leather sandals protected feet from desert thorns and bullhide shields protected life against enemy swords and arrows.

Then there is the feel of leather, the softness of buckskin and lambskin, the stiffness of cowhide, the silky smoothness of a hide tanned with the hair on, and the fibrous quality of split hide and suede.

And the appearance of various types of tanned hides is inspiring. Some, such as pigskin, have a most distinctive texture, a natural pattern resulting from bristle growth. Others, like cowhide and calfskin, show untold nuances of color in various parts of a single natural colored hide, a harmony of tones that brings delight to the eyes. Over this natural color the tanner can apply dyes, some ancient and some modern, to provide brightness or dignity or to simulate the shining surface of gold and silver and bronze.

Leather can be carved and painted, stamped and molded, stitched and laced, punched and cut. Altogether it is a fine material for handcrafting, and a good craftsman with imagination and a sense of design can make a good living by creating all manner of functional and decorative objects from this ancient material.

Belts are basic in the production of the leatherworker. They lend themselves to endless designs for use by men and women and are probably the biggest sellers among the items produced by the hand leatherworkers of the world. Each must have a buckle of some sort which the leatherworkers acquire from industrial buckle companies or from artist-blacksmiths, silversmiths, enamelers, or jewelry makers.

Handbags for women, and of late for some men too, also constitute a large proportion of the production of hand leather shops, large and small. Styles may change in the design of such items from year to year, but the need for leather handbags, purses, and wallets has remained constant since ancient times.

Footwear, of course, is traditionally made of leather and the demand has continued from primitive times until the present. Factories produce most of the shoes used by men and women but the leather craftsmen of the 1960s and 1970s have produced sandals of unique design which have found a good market, especially among young people.

Leather clothing for both sexes has been most popular, following European tastes. Skirts, slacks, coats, and jackets are all popular and profitable items. They are made of various types of soft, comfortable skins: suede, calfskin, goatskin, and sheepskin in a variety of colors. A passing fashion, which has been popular in the early 1970s, is leather hats, sewn or laced together to simulate the bolero hats of Spain. Even the tradition-bound leather craftsmen of Tangiers produce quite a large volume of leather hats which sell readily to young American tourists who wander into this time-bound enclave of Arabic culture.

The modern craftsman in leather also satisfies the demand for many, many small items generally made from the scrap cuttings left after making larger items. These include watch bands, especially the wide ones in fashion today, hair clips for women, bracelets, cigarette cases, even rings and brooches of carved, stamped, and dyed leather.

Of course, the main activity in leatherworking in olden times was harness making; every town had a harness shop, and many farmers made and repaired harnesses for their own use. Harness making, however, while now satisfying a growing demand for bridles, saddles, and other bits of horse furniture, has largely been taken over by factories. There are still a few handcraftsmen in this venerable area of leathercraft, found mostly in the Southwest and Mexico, but it no longer dominates the craft as it once did.

Those leatherworkers who operate in large cities have found a new market among television cameramen and technicians, who frequently need special lens cases and other small containers for the complicated equipment they carry with them. Leather cases that can be attached to the belt are ideal for this, and only a leatherworker can supply them.

Strangely for a craft so widely practiced in the United States, there are relatively few sources of training in leathercraft. Out of the hundreds of colleges and craft schools in the country no more than a dozen or so have leatherwork as a part of the formal curriculum. Several of these are found in the West, where a tradition of fine leatherwork has been inherited from Spain through Mexico, mostly in the form of fine carved saddles, bridles, and harnesses, and where leather clothing has always offered good protection against desert cactus thorns and the whip of sagebrush on the cattle range. The few others extend from the Middle West to New England and down the Appalachians in one or two colleges to South Carolina.

Leather has always been a favorite craft for teaching in summer camps and perhaps such training has been instrumental, certainly influential, in directing many of those who now make a living in leathercraft. Perhaps the summer camp flavor of leatherwork has also had an adverse influence on college curricula by making the craft seem unworthy of serious attention from the arts. If this is true the colleges are in error, for leather has great potential as a medium for artists.

Many leather craftsmen apparently are self-taught, learning techniques for a minimum of training, a great deal of reading, and long hours of actually working with leather. And this is as good a way as any to learn.

Others may have found more intensive formal training in the courses of municipal craft programs. There is no list available of these courses, for they change from period to period depending on the availability of instructors. People interested in formal training, however, should check with the recreational department of their local city or county government to learn if leatherwork is taught at any time during the year.

Another possible source of training is in the commercial craft centers which abound in every part of the country, though they are usually found in medium- to large-sized cities. Many of these stores will offer short courses in leathercraft from time to time as a means of merchandising their wares. Tandy's, the prime source of leather and leatherworking tools in the country, which operates a number of craft stores across the nation, might be consulted for local places of instruction. A list of the 200 or more Tandy Stores is found in the firm's handsome catalog which may be acquired merely by writing to headquarters in Dallas.

A list of those colleges known to teach leathercraft may be obtained by writing the American Crafts Council (see Appendix).

Consult as well the Bibliography, which includes instruction books.

But it should be emphasized that leathercraft is not entirely based on the techniques of working leather. The craftsman who wishes to make a living from this ancient occupation must also acquire a deep and broad background, an understanding, of fashion, jewelry design, and basic design if he is to succeed.

As with so many of the crafts, the equipment needed to work leather varies with the type of production planned by the leather-worker. If belts and other simple items are to be the only, or perhaps the initial, stock-in-trade, then little more is needed than a sturdy work table, a sharp knife, a punch, some assorted stamps or embossing wheels, and a modeler. The materials needed for such a simple operation include belt leather, some rivets or snaps, and, of course, buckles of a suitable size for belts and watch bands. Special equipment is helpful for setting brads and snaps.

Making belts and watch bands, then, requires a minimum of capital. A cutting knife can be purchased from the firms listed at the end of this chapter for from $2 to $5, while the traditional half-moon or head knife costs about $4.

Punches come in a variety of types and sizes from Saddlers punches, which cost from $3 to $5 each depending on size, to single or multi-headed spring punches, similar to a pair of pliers, which cost from $2.50 to about $16 each. Punches can also be easily impro-vised by cutting a tenpenny nail or short steel rods off square and hammering them through the leather over a wooden block to cut a clean hole of any size up to about ⅜ inch. The material for impro-vised punches will cost only pennies for each punch.

Leather stamps can be bought in a variety of designs for about $1 each. Easier than stamping for a series of designs, however, is an embossing wheel which consists of a carriage into which inter-changeable wheels of almost limitless designs may be fitted. The carriage sells for about $2 and the wheels for about 15¢ each. Stamps may also be made from tenpenny nails, by filing a design on the head.

Modelers, a form of stylus for embossing wet leather, sell for only $1 each and creasers which serve the same function sell for less than $2.

Rivets, snaps, and buckles are quite inexpensive. Rivets, for in-stance, bought in dozen or hundred lots cost less than 2¢ apiece and

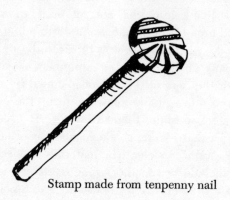

Stamp made from tenpenny nail

snap fasteners are about the same price. Buckles for a 1½-inch belt can cost from $1 to $3 a dozen, while small ½-inch buckles for watch bands cost but 3¢ each. Heavy brass belt buckles, however, might cost up to $3 each.

Riveting equipment and snap-fastener sets sell for from $2.50 for hand sets to $8 for a durable levered riveter which may be mounted on the worktable.

Considering the cost of leather, which will be treated more fully later in the chapter, the craftsman who wishes to start in this art, perhaps part time, by making belts in lots of two dozen can buy his equipment and material for about $50. He might expect to sell the lot for from $175 to $200.

Many leatherworkers, however, have advanced far beyond making simple belts, and as a consequence require more sophisticated equipment and types of leather, all of which requires more capital. Women's handbags are popular items which, when well designed and properly exposed to the market, can become most profitable to the leatherworker. But saleable handbags, unlike belts, are each of unique design and shape for the most part and the components cannot be bought individually. A whole hide must be purchased, patterns must be made, and the leather then cut so that each element of the handbag, including straps, matches to make an harmonious whole. Decoration may be stamped, embossed, carved, or colored. Lining must be provided from a good quality cloth or thin, supple leather. Usually the parts must be stitched together, though sometimes they may be laced.

Some of the equipment needed to make handbags, then, the skiving knife, the stamps, the modelers, are exactly the same as those used by the beltmaker, but stitching poses a different problem.

There is, and has been for ages, a sewing awl with which the handworker can do very professional stitching and this device can be bought with several different needles for less than $3. But with a sewing awl the fine stitching of one handbag may take an hour or two, rather slow work. The answer, of course, is a sewing machine, which is expensive.

Sewing machines suitable for stitching heavy leather sell for around $1,000 new and sometimes can be found second-hand for from $500 to $600, quite an outlay of capital. But with a machine the craftsman can stitch from 10 to 20 handbags an hour without essentially affecting the handmade quality of his production. Goodbye sewing awl, then, for the craftsman trying to make a living with his craft. Time is as valuable as talent and equipment in terms of livelihood.

Sewing machines also open up new areas of design and production. Once the machines are installed the leatherworker can use them to make sandals, leather coats, slacks, skirts, and even luggage. By expanding his line of production he also widens his market, for the customer who comes to the shop in search of a handbag is exposed to the availability of clothing and sandals and belts. And that's the way a business grows.

As has happened in actual circumstances, the purchase and use of the sewing machine to save the time of labor can easily lead to such expanded business that additional help will be needed as well as additional shop and display space.

Shop space for leatherworking is not nearly so critical a factor as one finds in blacksmithing or glassblowing. One man working with hand tools on relatively small items can operate quite efficiently in a booth 6 feet square with a 12-inch board as his workbench and pegs in the wall on which to hang his material.

Such tiny shops are quite traditional in Morocco and other parts of the world, but they are not ideal. A starting craftsman in leather should try to acquire space at least 10 by 15 feet, equipped with a bench with a top 3 by 5 feet and with shelves handy to the bench on which to keep his hand tools. If he is able to purchase a sewing machine, there is still room for this in a 10- by 15-foot shop. If, however, he hires a helper he will perhaps need another 25 square feet for this in order to avoid interference between two workers.

Leather craft shops, the working portion, can be set up almost anywhere including the home. Leather is a very clean material, free of dust and water, and working it does not require heat, acid, or any extraneous material other than dye, which is easily handled and controlled. Neighbors, in a residential or commercial neighborhood, will have no cause for complaint about smoke, noise, odor, or danger of fire from a leatherworking operation. Insurance rates are not affected by leather; nor are expensive remodeling or special facilities required.

The one factor which is important for sales is display space, and if this can be connected with the workshop, so much the better. Display, however, can be detached. A small retail shop can be located in a popular shopping center, or downtown perhaps in smaller cities, for from $100 to $300 a month rent, depending on location and size. Before committing himself to such an expenditure the leatherworker should borrow an effective tool of business, the market study. He should survey the location by asking questions of shoppers, nearby shop owners and shopping center managers to determine as nearly as possible if the character and taste of the patrons of the area make them likely customers for leather goods. It should be determined whether or not they might purchase handbags, belts, or sandals, and whether or not they will pay a price that will yield a profit to the leatherworker after he has paid rent and hired someone to run the retail operation. If some perspicacity is applied to the problem, there is a good chance that the rental of display space will become a profitable venture.

Hides sell at widely varying prices, ranging from about $3 a pound for scraps to $2 a square foot for whole hides of exceptional quality. Snake and lizard skins cost considerably more.

Leather may be bought from retail stores, from wholesalers if as many as 10 whole hides are bought at once, and by mail order. Chief among these sources is Tandy's, which sells wholesale and retail. Others, such as Brodhead-Garrett, sell by mail order. Most large cities have at least one leather wholesaler, and shoe and saddle manufacturers usually sell whole hides, especially if the operations include a tannery. Both Tandy's and Brodhead-Garrett have catalogs which may be ordered by mail. Both of these firms, incidentally, also sell leatherworking tools.

Rawhide, which is used traditionally for chair seats and Indian moccasin soles as well as lacing, may be bought for about $1.50 a square foot.

If one is in a town that has a slaughterhouse, he might be able to acquire green calf and cowhides for less. The hides must be scraped and dried by the purchaser, however, when bought from these sources, so it is really cheaper in the long run to pay the extra couple of dollars and buy dried hides.

Tanned hides are sold by type and weight with ounces designating thickness. For instance, a 1-ounce hide is approximately $\frac{1}{64}$ of an inch thick, while a 6-ounce hide is about $\frac{1}{8}$ inch. Some hides are split to yield a piece of leather of paper thinness suitable for lining handbags, belts, or other articles. Split sheepskin is less than 1 ounce, while split cowhide may be up to 2½ ounces, suitable for tooling and of very even thickness. Prices vary according to the type and quality of hides.

Special terms are used to designate different types of leather and these must be understood by the leatherworker so that he will know how to order and what to expect when he purchases leather. A *hide* is exactly what one expects, a whole hide from a sheep, goat, cow, or whatever. A *side* is half a hide, split down the middle. *Splits* are the flesh side of any type hide after the skin side has been split off, a thin flexible leather with a rough nap on both surfaces. *Suede leather* is another name for splits which have had one surface dressed to a velvety texture. A *skiver*, on the other hand, is the hair side of a split hide, with hair removed of course, and with one of its surfaces smooth and grained while the other has a nap as the result of being sliced with a skiving knife.

The variety of leathers are legion and must be learned as they are used since they must be identified by touch as well as by sight. They include *suede, chrome, backs, pigskin, lamb, goat, calf, turtle grain, ostrich on cow,* and a host of other terms designating grain and type. All can best be learned by spending time in a place like Tandy's just to observe and examine.

Blacksmith sides are of a brownish or black color with a sleek finish. The weight is around 5 ounces. One side consists of from 15 to 20 square feet, about 30 inches wide and 8 feet long—enough to make perhaps 2 dozen pairs of moccasins, 18 to 20 belts, a dozen handbags, up to 18 pairs of sandal soles. This type of leather sells for about $1.30 a square foot with slight reductions in price if more than one side is bought at a time.

Moccasin cow sides are almost identical to blacksmith sides except that they come in a range of colors from white to turquoise. They sell for $1.30 a square foot.

Sides of brown and yellow latigo, with a slightly better finish on the dark brown hair side and with the flesh side colored yellow, may be used for bags, moccasins, or belts, but it costs more than blacksmith or moccasin leather: from $1.90 to $2.10 a square foot. It is heavier, however, going up to 10 ounces, and the sides are larger, going up to 25 square feet.

Softer leathers suitable for various types of clothing are available in a number of sizes and types.

Sueded cowhide, which consists of splits that are chrome tanned and dyed in six colors, sells for only 75¢ a square foot. Usually these split skins consist of from 7 to 9 square feet, enough to make perhaps three vests. Two of them are necessary to make a coat.

Splits to simulate alligator and ostrich skin, used for light belts and billfolds, sell for as little as 60¢ a square foot. On the other hand, sharkskin used for the same purposes sells for $4.50 a square foot.

Soft, tanned calf hides with the hair on, in skins of from 6 to 8 square feet, are available for around $4 a square foot, and such skins dyed to simulate tiger and leopard skin, of the same size, cost about $30 apiece.

Almost every type of leather can be found in any of the catalogs of leathercraft suppliers. If a tannery is near, one can sometimes pick up the same leathers for about 25 percent less.

Since a great many types of relatively inexpensive leather are available, it might behoove the beginning cordwainer to specialize in items made of such leather to minimize capital expenditure.

Other materials besides the buckles and brads already mentioned, such as the hardware for handbags and carrying bags, different-sized needles, iron and brass rings, thread and such, can be purchased for a nominal cost from the leathercraft suppliers. A leathercraftsman should stock these small items before he opens his shop.

Leathercrafters in some instances make a very good living indeed. Take as an example a widely recognized shop in a Southeastern city run by two enterprising young men who have not yet reached their thirtieth birthdays. Some 4 years ago these young men, both dedicated to producing fine art in leather functional goods, raised about $600 and with it bought six hides. From these they made by hand a number of belts, handbags, sandals, wristwatch straps, hats, and other articles which appealed to the youth market. Now they have a well-located display room in an affluent part of the city with a workshop adjoining. In addition they now have six sales representatives selling nationally to better department stores and a full-time New York showroom.

The last year's sales volume was better than $1 million, and the net profit was between 25 and 30 percent on this volume, truly a handsome return on the original $600 investment. Business is still growing. The shop now has about 10 employees and 8 sewing machines turning out high-quality handbags for the national market and everything from coin purses and sandals to expensive slack suits for the local showroom.

Both of the owners still make leather goods with their hands, which is all they have ever wanted to do. They point out, quite logically, that applying business principles to their craft has allowed them to hire business managers, salesmen, retail clerks, and assistants, leaving them to be almost full-time artists. They must, of course, supervise assistants and keep abreast of finances. Their attitude should serve as a sterling example to any craftsman who wishes to devote a major part of his time to his art. It is no different from the numbers of Renaissance craftsmen and artists, Cellini being an excellent example, who followed the same principle and reached both fame and fortune without losing their integrity as dedicated artists.

Luck and circumstances play a part in anyone's life, however, and not every aspiring craftsman can anticipate such rapid success. But one must begin, and there are several starting points for leather-workers.

If capital is available, any craftsman should if possible, set up a display room and workshop where he will find customers. In addition to this, though, he will discover that working and displaying at craft fairs is an excellent medium for showing his skill and exposing his work to quite a large market. Since the cordwainer makes articles of everyday functional value he can expect to sell higher priced items at craft fairs than such craftsmen as the jewelry maker, the blacksmith, and the potter. He must also take pains to have each piece signed with stamp or metal tag and have sufficient business cards printed to distribute to customers and interested spectators.

A list of craft fairs in each state may be acquired by writing to the state Chamber of Commerce or the tourist development department in the various state governments.

Other places at which to seek display and sales for leather goods are clothing and gift shops which are found in or near almost any town in the country. Men's clothing stores are certainly good prospects for belts, billfolds, and sandals. The handcraftsman in offering his production must, however, offer unique design and superb craftsmanship in order to compete with articles which are mass-produced and in some cases widely exposed to the market through national advertising. Handcrafted items, properly made, can sell for higher prices than the usually handsome, but certainly not unique, products of the factory. The craftsman can only gain the highest price by negotiating with the manager or the owner of such stores as to price. Sometimes he must design items which can be sold at a certain price after the retail margin is added. Sometimes he and the store manager will not agree on the price of certain items and these must be forgotten.

One must show some discrimination in approaching stores. Handcrafted items of good design and quality must of necessity sell for more money than even the most handsome mass-produced items. They will not be sold if the clientele of the store is not affluent enough to pay the price. Go, therefore, only to the higher-priced stores.

Many items of leather can be sold to women's clothing shops, not only belts and sandals but also handbags, skirts, coats, slacks, coin purses, hair buckles, clogs, and a host of other things. The same discrimination and the same attitude toward prices must be exercised with women's shops as with men's. In dealing with women's shops, particularly, the leathercraftsman must develop a sense of fashion and keep up constantly with new fashions if he is to build a dependable trade with these retail establishments.

On soliciting the business of gift shops one should be fully as careful in picking prospects with proper clientele as with clothing shops. Gift shops will perhaps be interested in such items as leather coasters, barbecue aprons, book covers, and writing cases. It is well to visit these places before submitting any items to see what sort of merchandise might best fit in with what the shop offers.

Still, all in all, the leatherworker who has his own display space and retail operation in a shopping center or other carefully picked location will likely make a better living once he becomes established.

Leatherworkers starting out may expect to get paid about $3 an hour for labor. Of course, the man running his own operation must add to this the cost of material, plus a 15 to 20 percent markup for handling, and the cost of rent, salaries, and other elements of overhead. The experienced craftsman should be able to work faster, producing more per hour and consequently being worth more per hour. Some leatherworkers with experience should eventually be able to charge from $5 to $10 per hour for labor.

It is not likely that interest in leather goods will wane or that the opportunity for making a good livelihood from handcrafting leather will fade away. Success and the satisfying life from this ancient craft will, however, depend on good design, excellent craftsmanship, and willingness to maintain the craft as a modern source of functional items. The success of leathercraft has always depended upon these qualities. It must remain alive and attuned to the present now and always.

SOURCES OF SUPPLY

CCM Arts & Crafts, Inc.
9520 Baltimore Avenue
College Park, Maryland 20740

Dick Blick Company
P.O. Box 1267
Galesburg, Illinois 61410

California Crafts Supply
1419 North Central Park Avenue
Anaheim, California 92802

Crafttool Company, Inc.
1421 West 240th Street
Harbor City, California 90710

Crafts of Cleveland Leather
  Company
2824 Lorain Avenue
Cleveland, Ohio 44113

Fibrec Dye Center
2795 16th Street
San Francisco, California 94103

Herman Oak Leather Company
4050 North First Street
St. Louis, Missouri 63147

Tandy Leather Company
8117 Highway 80 West
Fort Worth, Texas 76116

6
Wood

CHAPTER XX

The Furniture Maker

THERE are many different types of furniture in our modern times. Some of it is made of plastic and shaped in ways that the eye would have considered weird in the days before plastics. Some of it is made of metal and some of cloth and leather, such as Arabic poufs and the overstuffed armed-sitting-cushions and even beds turned out by artistic stitchers. But most of it is made of wood as it has been for thousands of years, and this chapter will deal mostly with the men who work wood to create shapes that accommodate the needs of the human form for one purpose or another.

Furniture of one sort or another has been needed in human habitations since man first began to live in one place for more than a night or so. Even nomadic tribes, Tuaregs and Blue people, Blackfoot and Sioux have had beds which could be rolled into a bundle and carried from one hunting site to another. Such people also had ingenious portable backrests, primitive chairs as it were, and simple racks on which to hang pipe bags, bows, and other personal possessions.

Even the primitive furniture of long ago served as an art medium, being decorated with paint and beads and particularly carving to add pleasure to the eye as well as comfort to the body. And if good and lasting art is truly a reflection of nature, then furniture must be ranked among the foremost arts. Its only purpose is to reflect the natural positions of the human body in repose, at work and at play. Its very form is of necessity artistic.

Since ancient times some woodworkers have specialized in making chairs, tables, and beds, and since about the fourteenth or fifteenth centuries special furniture makers have existed among the community of craftsmen. The chairmaker, who is still found in very limited numbers in the Southern Appalachians and who was a recognized specialist in Britain until World War II, is a remnant of the medieval beginnings of the special furniture-maker's craft.

This special activity developed rapidly through the sixteenth and seventeenth centuries in Europe, perhaps reflecting the growing affluence brought by the new-found resources of the New World. It reached its peak perhaps in the eighteenth and early nineteenth centuries with the advent in England of Chippendale and Adam, with Goddard of Newport in New England, and with the consummate artists in wood who created and executed the rich furniture styles of France and Italy.

But Eli Whitney and his concept of mass production, and other circumstances, intervened in the early nineteenth century to halt the evolution of the handcraftsman making furniture, and cast him almost into the limbo which had already enveloped the flint chipper. For furniture began to be turned out in factories. Mortise and tenon joints gave way to dowel joints which could easily be handled by machine, and the need of consummate craftsmanship disappeared in such an atmosphere. So did the true furniture maker disappear almost entirely from the Western world with the exception of woodworkers in Scandinavia, where the industrial revolution was slow in coming.

And so the Western world to a large degree adopted the deadly dullness of the Grand Rapids School, and Chippendale became a rarity sought by collectors.

Thankfully, a reaction, or perhaps a rebellion, began to set in after World War I, largely in Denmark where a few artist-craftsmen created new styles of handmade furniture designated by a grateful world as Danish Modern. This style became most popular among limited groups and it inspired a few other craftsmen in other countries to follow suit and, behold, another facet of the renaissance of crafts was established.

Furniture making by hand has seen a comeback in America, too, largely since World War II. It had never quite waned to nothingness, but the market for such expensive work has been limited, indeed, and the situation was exacerbated by the general penury of the depression in the 1930s and the need for austerity during World War II and the Korean War. The new affluence of industrial America which followed the 1940s has been responsible more than anything for the rebirth of handmade furniture.

There are still only a few men in the 1970s who make a living by designing and making furniture by hand. They seem to be concentrated for the most part in California, with a few in New York, New England, and the Middle Atlantic States. They are not to be confused with the host of very competent cabinetmakers who turn out kitchen cabinets, specially designed mantels, molding, and paneling for costly homes and extravagant offices. The furniture makers of the modern world find the same markets for their work as the cabinetmakers, but their work is quite different. For the furniture makers are artists and designers as well as craftsmen, well aware of the needs of modern times and most capable in the use of machine tools as well as with certain irreplaceable functions of hand tools. They design and make all manner of furniture just as Chippendale and Goddard did, executing beautiful, expensive pieces in the modern mode to fit exactly into the decor of homes and offices. Not only do they make chairs and tables but they also produce bookcases, desks, china cabinets, beds, coffee tables, stools, and sofas and all kinds of small cases which sit on tables.

Another group of furniture makers, also small in number and found mostly in the East Coast regions from New England to North Carolina, specializes in making reproductions of traditional styles. There is quite a market for the work of these craftsmen, too, mostly made up of householders who find comfort in the solid, familiar styles of the past. Some of these traditionalists also design, but their designs are traditional and are executed to fit into traditional settings. But, as with their modernist colleagues, there are not enough of them to fill the constant demand for what they make.

And then there are a minuscule number of furniture makers who seem to love working with wood more than they love any particular style of furniture and who are proficient in designing and making both modern and traditional pieces. Most of these are known to architects and interior designers only, for these professionals can absorb the full capacity of almost any shop which turns out the sort of furniture they need.

Training in fine furniture making is not easy to come by. A number of colleges and universities across the nation have classes in woodworking, mostly furniture, but these classes constitute a very small proportion of the total number of craft classes offered and are probably next only to blacksmithing in the scarcity of instruction. As might be expected, most of the courses offered in the subject are found in California schools which offer more craft curricula than the schools of any other state. There are others, however, in Utah, Nebraska, Minnesota, Wisconsin, West Virginia, New York, North Carolina, and Kentucky, plus a few more. The American Crafts Council offers a list of schools teaching woodworking in return for a small fee. See the appendix on Training for further information on the American Crafts Council.

Possibly the best training available is through apprenticeship with a recognized furniture craftsman such as Arthur Espenet Carpenter in Bolinas, California, or in the cabinetmaker's shop in Colonial Williamsburg. All such places as these, though, are producing shops and most of them have applications from more apprentices than they can use.

As a consquence, the person who is seriously interested in becoming a furniture maker should try to enter one of the colleges or universities in which the subject is taught. There are great advantages to the university courses, for the aspiring craftsman can learn basic design, art history, and basic engineering as well as being exposed to other craft training. And, of course, he has all the other advantages of universities: libraries, guest artists, lecturers, rap sessions with other students and professors, good shops, all of which are important parts of the learning process.

It is possible, though difficult, for one who wishes to make furniture to teach himself, but this is the hard and uncertain way. To do so he must first of all learn his material so thoroughly that it becomes instinctive. He must know almost all the types of wood available in the world, where each type comes from, the special qualities and special uses of each, the ease or difficulty of working each, which type will bend, which will break, and which will split if not used properly. He must know which woods will fit together to become really a living construction.

In addition to his material he must know his tools, which he needs to make a living making furniture, and how to use them and maintain them. Some machine tools will certainly be needed by the professional but he must also know hand tools, where to get good ones from all over the world, and in some cases how to make his own in the tradition of older furniture makers.

Also he must know the engineering of joints, whether to use a mortise and tenon or a dowel joint for certain purposes, whether to use a butt joint, a ship lap, or a tongue and groove for table and desk tops.

All of this may be learned without instruction, but it takes a long, long time. The main advantage of teaching oneself is in gaining invaluable experience that is an essential complement to the very best instruction. Self-teaching is not advised unless one has had a large degree of dedication to woodworking from an early age. Even then the woodworker should seek additional instruction. No man, no matter how skilled, can know everything, especially about woodworking. Instruction can expose a master woodworker to new ideas, which might take years to develop by himself, and thus widen his horizons and stimulate his imagination.

The equipment of a master woodworker's shop will never be complete. He is utterly dependent, certainly, on basic tools and machinery and must always have equipment adequate to execute his designs and realize his visions, but as he adds variety to his work or tries new directions he must continually buy or make new tools.

Basic among his equipment are the essential hand tools that any craftsman in wood must have regardless of his wealth of mechanized equipment. He needs several types and sizes of hammers and mallets, for instance; several high-quality panel saws and a turning saw; a keyhole saw or two and a dovetail saw. Several sizes and types of both firmer and paring chisels will be needed from time to time. Holes may be bored quickly and easily with no sacrifice of craftsmanship by using a power drill equipped with twist bits from $\frac{1}{16}$ inch up to $\frac{1}{2}$ inch and with power wood bits from $\frac{1}{4}$ inch up to perhaps 2 inches. This should be complemented, however, with a modern ratchet brace with twist bits sized from $\frac{1}{4}$ inch to 1 inch. Also a small hand drill will be needed for special uses.

A set of screwdrivers, two or three gimlets, a nail set, and a nail puller will find uses when working special pieces. Squares and bevels are also needed.

There are a host of small additional tools without which the most mechanized artist cannot exercise his versatility. These include clamps, rules, calipers, marking gauges, a drawing knife, a spokeshave and, of course, several sharpening stones of different grades and shapes. A hatchet of good quality, while not essential, can sometimes save a great deal of time.

And, regardless of the sophistication of his machine, a professional woodworker will need a hand jack plane, a small smoothing plane and perhaps an even smaller finger plane. A combination plane with an assortment of plough, hollow, and round blades, while not necessary, will provide a great deal more versatility than can be furnished by molding cutter blades on a planer.

It is perhaps too bad that all modern furniture making cannot be done with the simple hand tools mentioned here. Compared with machines these tools cost very little, although in the aggregate the cost of all of them will well equal the cost of a sophisticated machine.

For example, a good-quality hammer costs from $4 to $9, depending on size. Mallets, both headed and turned, cost from $3 to $7.50.

Even with machines the furniture maker finds it necessary to have at least three crosscut panel saws of good quality, and at least one ripsaw. Good saws made either in the United States or Europe, with from 5 to 12 teeth per inch, cost from $10 to $15 each. Backsaws, with 15 teeth to the inch, used in miter boxes and for delicate cuts in certain elements of a piece of furniture, sell for around $12 each. Dovetail saws with 20 teeth to the inch and sometimes essential for fitting two pieces of wood together, sell for about the same price. Turning saws, made in Europe, cost about $12 and keyhole saws about $6.

Chisels for professional work must be of the very highest quality and workmanship, particularly in regard to tempering. These sell for from $2.50 to $7 depending on size. They can be bought in sets of four to six at a slight discount per chisel.

Electric drills cost from $40 for one powerful enough to bore a ½-inch hole in wood and up to $225 for one with power enough to bore a 2-inch hole. Hand braces are sold for from about $12 to $25. Drill points and twist bits sell for from 50¢ to $5 each, with expanding bits selling for up to $18. Hand drills cost from $10 to $15.

Smoothing planes, either with wooden stocks as made in Europe or with metal stocks, sell for about $15, while jack planes of good quality sell for around $25. Combination planes cost from $50 to $100, including a set of blades.

All the other small tools, such as rules and squares, can probably be purchased for an aggregate of $50 to $60.

Altogether, then, the starting woodworker requires capital of from $400 to $500 just for basic hand tools, not counting his workbench or the cabinets and shelves needed properly to store his tools.

Many of the hand tools needed by the furniture maker may be bought at any good hardware store, retail lumber dealer, or Sears and other reputable mail order houses. One of the best of the mail order houses for woodworking tools is the Woodcraft Supply Company in Woburn, Massachusetts, the address of which is listed at the end of this chapter.

The cost of hand tools, however, pales into insignificance when compared to the cost of machine tools which often, because of the time they save, make the difference between competing or not competing; being able to produce fine furniture for sale or working at the craft purely as a hobby. As an example, one young furniture maker in California tells of making a piece of furniture which took untold hours to finish simply because he could not afford to pay $50 for a special tool. When he finished the piece he had to charge the customer $4,000 to pay for his labor. Although the work was beautiful the customer refused the piece at this price. A $50 expenditure could have cut the cost of time to the point that the piece could have been sold for considerably less at a profit for the furniture maker. And the craftsman would have had more time for creative activity.

Of course, the beginning furniture maker may not need all available machine tools. The hand drill can almost do the work of a drill press, though it takes longer, and perhaps furniture may be designed at first that does not require turned elements, thus dispensing with the need for a lathe. But even the beginner should have a bench saw, a planer, and perhaps a band saw. Without these it will be awfully difficult to compete in pricing with mass-produced furniture, much of which is pretty and well made, or with custom-made furniture produced in a modern shop. Certainly he will need a belt sander although he might be able to get by with an electric hand sander.

Bench (or arbor) saws, some of which may be converted into planers and lathes with minor adjustment, sell for from $150 for a tilting saw up to $2,200 for one capable of heavy work. Planers and router-shapers of good professional quality cost from $500 to $700 each.

Belt sanders sell for as little as $150 and as much as $1,000, while an electric hand sander can be bought for around $50. Sanders are perhaps the finest time-savers of all the furniture maker's machine tools.

Drill presses suitable for furniture making cost from around $75 to $200. Lathes cost from $250 to $1,000.

If a lathe is acquired, the furniture maker will also require about 10 turning chisels, which sell usually for about $4 each.

Workbenches, which are quite necessary, may be made of heavy lumber bought locally for $50 to $75 or may be bought ready-made at a cost of about $250 to $400. The bought benches, most of which are made in Europe complete with vises, are of very good quality. An accomplished furniture maker, however, is surely qualified to make his own workbench of exactly the proper size to fit his requirements and physique and can thus save money in the beginning of his career.

So, with a bit of ingenuity in design, a tolerant attitude toward machines, and a realistic understanding of the market, a furniture maker can buy basic equipment for a total of from $3,000 to $5,000. He will need additional capital, of course, to rent shop and display space and to feed and shelter himself and his family until income starts coming in.

Shop space is no great problem for the woodworker insofar as location is concerned. What he needs more than anything is space—enough space to set up his machines, to store his wood, and to assemble his pieces. No serious furniture maker should consider less than about 1,000 square feet if he is working by himself, and ideally he should add about 200 additional square feet for any helpers he may hire. He will need, too, adequate electrical outlets, good lighting, and easy entrance next to a roadway to facilitate unloading of his raw material and loading of his finished products for delivery. Some modern furniture makers are commissioned to make quite large pieces requiring large doors to get them out of the shop without marring or denting a meticulously finished surface.

The shop space should be such that finishing materials, varnish, waxes, oil, shellac, and stains can be stored away from heat sources and near a special finishing area so that this final stage of furniture making will not interfere with pieces in the process of shaping or assembly.

Also, there should be a relatively quiet corner fitted with desk or drawing table and good lighting, where the artist can conceive his work with pencil and paper, draw up his designs for submission to his customers, and sit looking out of a window at times as he ruminates and stimulates the springs of imagination.

Woodworking shops may be located almost anywhere, within a city or out in the country, a chief objective being low rent. Display for furniture is not nearly so important as with some other crafts; furniture, which is relatively expensive, falls into the category that marketing men call *considered purchases* rather than *impulse purchases*. Custom-made furniture is of necessity expensive and consequently has a somewhat limited market. Those who want and can afford it will gladly visit the craftsman's shop regardless of its location. If display is deemed important, it may be procured in a heavily trafficked shopping area quite detached from the working area.

Some furniture makers who design and make original pieces for the general market rather than a custom market may find display space important, but it is cheaper and easier to sell such pieces on consignment in a regular furniture store that already has ample display space with no rent attached to it insofar as the craftsman is concerned. An additional advantage of selling on consignment, or perhaps directly to the store, is that the only prospective customers who will see the pieces displayed are people actively looking for furniture.

Selling through stores is advised only as a means of generating income and becoming known for a beginning custom furniture maker, or for the original designer who must display his work but cannot at first afford effective display space in a good location. Store displays offer a way to become known without a great deal of capital investment.

A basic part of training in furniture making and woodworking generally is to know the characteristics of the myriad of woods suitable for furniture in terms of beauty, strength, and workability. After training is over it is just as important to know where these woods may be acquired in the United States. They include traditional American woods as well as some woods so exotic that most people have never heard of them.

Unfortunately, the fine American furniture woods have suffered so much demand in the last generation that they have become very scarce in many cases and most expensive. Walnut, with its fine grain, its durability, and rich dark color, has been squandered for many years on luxurious paneling for fine offices and to an even greater degree on veneer for less expensive paneling and for television cabinets. Just a generation ago one found an abundant supply of big walnut timber in the sawmills of the Appalachian regions, but nowadays most of the trees being cut yield boards no more than 6 inches wide. Even small pieces used for gunstocks are now largely unavailable.

Cherry, once known as American mahogany, is practically nonexistent now in boards of more than 3 or 4 inches wide, a fact which fills one with frustration when he sees 15-inch to 18-inch planks of solid cherry in furniture made before 1875. The few wide cherry planks now available are cut from trees found individually by a furniture maker, bought individually, and sawn and dried to his order. And there's not much of it available even under these circumstances.

Oak, of course, is plentiful. So are poplar, birch, and maple, all of which are easy to work and which hold up well, but which simply lack the deep beauty of cherry and walnut.

Pecan wood, abundant in the forests of the Gulf Coast states, became suddenly popular during the 1960s, but one presumes that its passing popularity was based more on availability and promotion, in face of the scarcity of walnut, than on its innate qualities. Pecan, however, is strong, close grained and very light colored so that it will take stain and a good polish nicely.

The commoner, low-priced woods such as pine, fir, and gum are common enough in the woods but in the 1970s sometimes cost as much as walnut did 30 years before. Such woods, however, can be used in certain pieces of furniture for elements that do not show. The fine furniture makers of old often used the common, cheap woods for drawer rails, corner blocks and other pieces that were well hidden by fine wood. And pine does have a certain beauty for less expensive furniture as well as a reputation for being early American since it was used for the more functional furniture of the frontier.

Since the eighteenth century at least, most fine furniture has been made of mahogany, that splendid, close-grained, easily worked wood of the Caribbean areas. Once abundant, even this material is now somewhat scarce and certainly expensive. Other subspecies, such as Philippine and African mahogany, have become fairly popular in less expensive furniture, but these woods can never quite match the beauty, durability, or workability of the Dominican tree.

Teak, rosewood, ebony, and a host of other trees exotic to the Western world also make splendid pieces of furniture when they can be found, and all are imported into the United States. They are sold, usually on a wholesale basis and in large quantity, along with mahogany and sometimes American furniture woods by dealers who do business mostly with furniture mills and well-established fine furniture handcraftsmen.

Most seaport towns of any size have several lumber dealers who buy and sell exotic woods. They ship their wares by rail car and truckload to furniture mills and in small quantities to handcraftsmen and amateurs. Inland cities often have hardwood companies which stock and sell both domestic and exotic woods. Sometimes these inland dealers have unexpected designations such as oak flooring dealers. A partial list of sources for furniture woods is listed at the end of this chapter. Additional sources for walnut and cherry and other domestic woods are a few sawmills in Appalachia, north and south, and in the rural areas of such states as Indiana, Ohio, Arkansas, Missouri, New York, Pennsylvania, Virginia, and the states of the Southeast. A check with state forestry departments can often locate these mills.

Also, there is usually a degree of camaraderie among craftsmen which allows a beginner to ask an established furniture maker about sources of supply. Unless great scarcity of the supply is a factor, the beginner can almost always count on help from a senior craftsman, and can repay in kind at a later date.

The markets for handcrafted furniture can be designated in three main categories: individuals, architects, and interior designers. Individuals comprise the major market for those craftsmen who specialize in traditional design, the reproductions, or new designs based on traditional concepts. This market reflects the vast interest in antiques and the consequent plethora of antique shops in virtually every section of the United States, particularly in the East and South. It pays more for items of excellent design and workmanship and sometimes, through ignorance, pays well for items of poor design and workmanship.

It is only logical that a traditional craftsman, when possible, locate his shop near a collection of antique shops, using the antique shops as a drawing card for his own operation, and to some extent being used by them in the same manner. Once established he need not worry too much about display, for working mostly by hand he cannot aim at a huge volume; his first few customers, if satisfied, will continue to patronize him and will send others who have seen the craftsman's work displayed in the appealing setting of a home.

But in the beginning the reproduction furniture maker may need to stimulate traffic and trade. This can be done with relatively inexpensive advertising placed in magazines such as *Early American Life* for around $400 a page or less for smaller ads, or, if capital is available, in more expensive magazines such as the *New Yorker* or *House Beautiful*. A small ad one column wide and 3 inches deep might cost from $600 to $1,500 in these magazines depending on the size of the audience, since the magazines with larger circulation charge relatively more than those with small circulation. It would seem advisable for the average crafts entrepreneur to use the magazine of small affluent circulation since production by hand of any item will be limited at best to a small market. On the other hand, if a shop is located in a spot with considerable traffic, the furniture maker might best expose himself to his market through means of an attractive sign which lets people know where he is and what he does.

Designers and makers of original furniture may have quite a few individual customers, particularly in larger cities, but the main market for these latter-day Chippendales and Goddards is composed of architects and interior designers. These two groups are flourishing in contemporary America and the principal commodity in which they deal is originality. Much of their clientele is made up of businessmen who can afford very special offices furnished with original pieces; sometimes clients go so far as to request original designs for alabaster toilet bowls in private office washrooms. It should not be inferred that contemporary furniture makers do no work for residences; but the office market is much more affluent, and architects and interior designers are easier to find and often easier to work with than individual home owners.

Nor should it be inferred that the business office designer will impose his own taste on the furniture maker. The two can work together very comfortably. Frequently, the architect or designer creates a general concept and allows the furniture maker to create pieces which give substance to the concept.

Of course, the modern designer–furniture maker should succumb from time to time to the creative visions which beset any artist; if he sees a piece of wood and has an idea how to use the wood in a table, chair, or desk, he should get to work on the piece at the first opportunity. Sometimes it will work out and sometimes not. If it does work out the craftsman will then have to find a market for it. This should not be difficult if he is established and has already developed a clientele. If he does not have this enviable advantage, then he must advertise what he has to offer, through display at his shop or at some furniture store which will buy the piece or perhaps display it on a consignment basis.

Other methods of merchandising (a term and activity abhorrent to many modern craftsmen, but descriptive and necessary in the modern age) must include cultivating a rapport with architects and interior designers by any or all of a number of means.

These means might include personal visits, personal letters, and advertising. Most architects and interior designers will gladly see original furniture makers since it is to their advantage to find sources of supply which can help them realize their own creative thinking. When making calls, the furniture maker should show photographs of pieces he has made, and/or perhaps sketches of pieces he has in mind, using different woods. Most of all he should find out from the architect or interior designer what his own ideas are or what he thinks furniture should do or reflect. Perhaps he will find that he could not possibly be compatible with some of the people he calls on, but this is to his advantage. He can forget those and concentrate on others with whom he thinks he can work in harmony.

It is difficult to determine just how much a beginning furniture maker can earn per hour, or per month or year. An industrial craftsman as well as an independent small businessman may expect fluctuation in his income from month to month. The objective, of course, is to make a living without compromising artistic standards if this is possible. It costs more to live in New York City or San Francisco than in Winston-Salem or Yonkers, or in some smaller community outside New York or San Francisco.

In finding a base for charging the furniture maker should first determine how much his labor is worth. Certainly, even in the beginning, it should be no less than $3 and possibly worth $5 an hour depending on experience and efficiency. For instance, an inexperienced craftsman cannot expect to be paid for the time spent wondering what the next step is; an experienced craftsman will produce more per hour and consequently earn more per hour. And if the volume of his production is further increased by machines for certain operations in which handwork has no particular value, then his time becomes worth more. It must be remembered, however, that if he reaches maximum production through exclusive use of machines, he will no longer be a craftsman and artist and might as well go to work in a furniture factory.

The hourly charge for one's labor attends to but one facet of charging for one's production. Other costs enter into the price for a piece of furniture, such as the proportion of capital invested in machinery, shop space, advertising, help, et al. A proportionate amount of each of these factors must be included in the price of the furniture one makes. Figuring the correct proportion requires a rather deep application of intellect, but it can and must be done.

Most businessmen use government tax standards for the life of a machine, generally four years. If a machine is bought for $1,000 it will depreciate in value about 25 percent a year. This should be divided into the number of working hours a year and the quotient applied to the hours needed to create and execute a piece. The same is done with all other costs, remembering, however, that monthly rents and pay checks are applied directly without depreciation.

Not every machine or every helper is used on every piece of furniture, but to avoid complications the craftsman should apply the aggregate costs per hour to the prices for his finished work and add 5 percent for profit. This allows some flexibility in his pricing so he can meet competitive prices if necessary, although fine craftsmanship is seldom bought or made strictly on the basis of competitive prices. Circumstances will dictate to a large extent the importance of competitive pricing. The established furniture maker should not have to give it a thought.

But what of the beginner? He must raise capital, set up shop, develop clientele, make his furniture to satisfy his clients, create a reputation, and also make a living, perhaps for a family. He can do all this with determination, imagination, ingenuity, and patience.

One way is to compromise a little on the *type* of pieces he makes in the beginning but never compromising on the quality of his workmanship and design. Perhaps he should specialize in small, relatively inexpensive pieces produced in limited editions which can find a ready market, support his family, and create the opportunity to moonlight in his own shop on the larger pieces which lie unborn in his imagination. He might need to take a regular job during the day and make furniture a couple of hours a night and on the weekend. Or he might be lucky enough to find a job in a factory or office which has the increasingly popular three-day work week which will give him three or four days each week to follow his ambitions.

Or, if he is lucky and well educated, he might find a job teaching woodworking in college or technical school which will give him opportunity to practice his art while he teaches and which might allow him time to create and execute his cherished designs after the classroom is closed.

It will be well, as with all the other crafts, for the furniture maker to put his mark upon each piece he makes, large or small. In other days this was sometimes done with a simple paper label glued in an inconspicuous spot such as the back of a drawer or the inside of a table rail. Sometimes it was marked merely with a pencil, including name and date and maybe the location of the shop. A few craftsmen carve initials or name and date. Today the craftsman might buy small metal tags containing his printed name and space to stamp a date, and then tack this to his piece. Paper or pencil or carving somehow seem to fit better the concept of hand-craftsmanship. But the signature will in no manner affect the design and workmanship, which are usually the most enduring signatures of all.

There are but few handcraftsmen among the furniture makers of modern America, and the potential markets found in the modern economy will not support many. The field and market, however, seem to be growing slightly, and furniture making, like other arts and crafts, if done diligently, with inspiration and imagination, and love of tools and material, will create its own markets.

Good craftsmanship, too, is much like good government. When the greatly loved fifteenth-century Duke of Urbino was asked the secret of his power to govern so well he replied simply, "Essere Umano," *to be human.* If the work of the craftsman reflects human needs, he will make his own place even in a highly mechanized society.

SOURCES OF SUPPLY

A. D. Alpine Inc.
353 Coral Circle
El Segundo, California 90245

Brodhead-Garrett Company
4560 East 71st Street
Cleveland, Ohio 44105

Milton Bradley Company
Springfield, Massachusetts 01101

Rapid Rack
610 Sir Francis Drake Boulevard
San Anselmo, California 94960

Special Education Programs, Inc.
414 Avon Place
Cambridge, Massachusetts 02140

Three Arts Materials Group, Inc.
375 Great Neck Road
Great Neck, New York 11021

Walker Systems, Inc.
520 South 21st Avenue
East Duluth, Minnesota 55812

H. Wilson Corporation
555 West Taft Drive
South Holland, Illinois 60473

Woodcraft Supply Corporation
313 Montvale Avenue
Woburn, Massachusetts 01801

Woods:

All Woods, Inc.
P. O. Box 5056
Houston, Texas 77012

American Hardwood Company
P. O. Box 2224
Terminal Annex Station
Los Angeles, California 90054

Beckemeier-Jansen Lumber
Company
P. O. Box 5511
Bremen Station
St. Louis, Missouri 63160

Craftsman Hardwood Lumber
Company
2201 Davis Street
Blue Island, Illinois 60406

Emerson Hardwood Company
2279 NW Front Avenue
Portland, Oregon 97209

Forster-Mueller Lumber Company
(Forest Lumber Division)
P. O. Box 8323
Milwaukee, Wisconsin 53225

Frost Hardwood Lumber Company
Market & State Street
P. O. Box 15
San Diego, California 92112

General Hardwood Company
7201 East McNichols Road
Detroit, Michigan 48212

Heidler Hardwood Lumber
Company
2559 South Damen Avenue
Chicago, Illinois 60608

Holt & Bugbee, Inc.
1600 Shawsheen Street
Tewksbury, Massachusetts 01876

Logan Lumber Company
P. O. Box 1608
Tampa, Florida 33601

MacBeath Hardwood Company
2150 Oakdale Avenue
San Francisco, California 94124

E. J. Maxwell Limited
5080 St. Ambroise Street
Montreal 208, Quebec (CANADA)

Mercury Hardwood Lumber
Company
14166 Nelson Avenue
City of Industry, California 91744

R. A. Miller Hardwood Company,
Inc.
501 North Forest Road
Buffalo, New York 14221

Monarch Hardwood Lumber
Company
3250 North Kedzie Avenue
Chicago, Illinois 60618

J. H. Monteah Company
2500 Park Avenue
Bronx, New York 10451

Reisen-Seidel Hardwood Company
1080 Morris Avenue
Union, New Jersey 07083

Simmons Hardwood Lumber
Company
1150 Mine Avenue
P. O. Box 368
Montebello, California 90640

Spellman Hardwoods, Inc.
2865 Grand Avenue
Phoenix, Arizona 85017

Chester B. Stem, Inc.
New Albany, Indiana 47150

Thompson Hardwood Lumber
Company, Inc.
9925 Logan Avenue, South
Minneapolis, Minnesota 55431

Tidewater Hardwood Lumber
Company
Harman, Maryland 21077

Local lumber yards and sawmills should also be investigated for various types of hardwood, domestic and imported. Some of the sources listed above may not sell furniture wood in small quantities, but each can direct inquiries to dealers who do.

CHAPTER XXI

The Woodcarver

THERE are two basic types of woodcarvers. Both seem to be disappearing from the face of the earth, or at least from the Western world. And one type is disappearing much faster than the other.

Architectural woodcarvers, the men who in the past carved the beautiful mantels of royal palaces, the breathtaking capitals of doorways in state reception rooms, and the intricate decorations on the crown molding of well-endowed university board rooms, have practically disappeared. One finds a few more survivors among the furniture carvers, but the field for this less complicated carving is small and growing smaller as furniture manufacturers adopt carving machines for mass production or substitute molded decorations which simulate carving for the delicate beauty once yielded only by a multitude of razor sharp carving chisels and a steady hand. Furniture factories still employ carvers to make original patterns for molds and machines, but, of course, the artist is somewhat inhibited by the limitations of mass-production technology. Neither molds nor machines can reproduce the sometimes necessary undercuts which provide beauty of dimension and detail in truly fine carving.

In between the architectural carver and the furniture carver is a subcategory of craftsmen which perhaps is more alive than the other two and which has some future. This consists of the relatively small group of carvers who carve, paint, and gild wall decorations such as plaques for fraternities and military groups, crests for private families, and similar decorations for business and law offices.

There are, too, a few skilled sculptors who work with wood and produce true art ranging in size from table sculpture to massive pieces for outdoor gardens. But the few members of this group consider themselves artists rather than craftsmen and generally use entirely different techniques and tools from those used by the true woodcarvers.

At one time Europe had a number of woodcarvers who worked regularly on carving ornate and beautiful picture frames, mirror frames, boxes, and small containers. Most of these were concentrated in Italy and Germany. Since World War II, however, the numbers of these craftsmen have dwindled due to a lack of interest in necessary apprenticeship by young men and women and also due to the adoption of more modern, more sterile forms of architecture and interior decoration.

A number of university art departments offer courses in woodcarving. The emphasis in these courses seems to be on design, a necessary and most important part of any craft. But what these courses cannot teach is the very special nature of wood. Wood does not go through the homogenizing process of wool, for instance, for which a few yards of yarn are derived from the fibers of possibly a hundred sheep, or alpacas, or yaks. Nor is it like silver or gold, of which the ore and scrap may represent 2,000 years of mined silver and gold. Each piece of metal has its subtle differences yet each can be worked essentially alike and with the same tools. Wood is not like these materials.

For every single piece of wood comes from a single tree. Each piece of wood represents generations of storms and droughts and violent winds, of sunshine and insects and arbitrary influences from surrounding trees and clinging vines. Wood, like woodcarvers, is processed from beginning to end by God, and only its outside form is altered by man. And all the pieces from a single tree are different from each other, with different challenges requiring different solutions. The variety of trees, each with its different carving characteristics, is overwhelming to the craftsman who does not understand this marvelous medium.

A wood sculptor can control his design to circumvent the problems inherent in his material. But the woodcarver, the craftsman in the old-time sense, must often execute an architect's design without the authority to change that design to fit a particular block of wood. If a cavity or a relief must be molded into a block of wood where a bit of aberrent grain lies hidden, then the wood-carver must know how to handle the situation to execute his design as planned. He must know which tool to use; and if he lacks the tool he must know how to make a tool to do the job. His skill allows him to cut across the grain as smoothly as cutting with the grain.

Making tools seems to be a skill most woodcarvers no longer learn. It is uncertain how much time is given in woodcarving courses in university art schools to shaping and tempering special, sometimes essential, chisels. One school, the Alexander Weygers School of Sculpture in Carmel Valley, California, has a number of forges and anvils set up and offers special instruction for making the tools needed to carve wood and stone. Let us hope that other schools offer the same advantage to students, for certainly the woodcarver can be no better than his tools, and the variety of carving tools offered by tool manufacturers is of necessity limited.

The recognized living masters of the dwindling company of classic woodcarvers all say that manufactured tools are not satisfactory and, above all, not of sufficient variety, to allow the best of carving. They say that no woodcarver can be great unless he makes his own chisels.

Perhaps colleges will someday add tool making to the curriculum of woodcarving. Until then the serious student of wood-carving must either enroll in Mr. Weygers's school or learn the mysteries of 75-point carbon steel, its forging, and particularly its tempering, on his own, by reading books and experimenting. One or two books on blacksmithing contain this information. They are listed in the bibliography to this chapter. Also, some colleges do offer separate courses in blacksmithing which might be audited by the woodcarving student in order to learn something about tempering steel.

Lest the intricacies of making woodcarving tools be discouraging, the student should consider the experience of one of the few true masters of the art. This man, who trained as an apprentice in England for 5 years and has followed his art for the last 65 years, heats his small pieces of steel over a gas burner and shapes them with a light hammer on a small block of scrap steel and with files. He uses the gas burner to heat the steel for hardening in a pan of water and draws the temper to its proper color with the flame of a candle. Thus, no complicated equipment is needed for making woodcarving tools. What is needed is the proper steel and knowledge of how to work it.

Of course, all this can be learned through an old-fashioned apprenticeship with a master carver if one willing to take an apprentice can be found. Some of the few masters left in England, Italy, Germany, or Scandinavia might be sought out and approached on the idea of an apprenticeship. The names of woodcarvers might be found by writing to the cultural attachés of the embassies of the countries mentioned.

It should not be overlooked that some of the finest woodcarving of all has been done in the Orient: in China, Japan, Thailand, and India. One suspects that arranging an apprenticeship in these countries might be a little more difficult than in Europe. Also, the language difficulties of the Orient might be insuperable. Again, however, the cultural attachés of Far Eastern embassies might provide guidance on the matter. There are also fine woodcarvers in Africa, but there, too, the language might well make it difficult to apply for an apprenticeship.

The woodcarver is fortunate in not needing a great deal of equipment and really needing no mechanical equipment, though some modern woodcarvers might wish to have a bench saw and a band saw for roughing out shapes. One must have a sturdy workbench equipped with a vise or two and up to 300 different carving chisels—maybe 10 firming chisels and 3 or 4 mallets of different weights. Of utmost importance, the woodcarver must have 10 or more sharpening stones, some coarse and some very fine and hard for honing; some flat bench stones; and a variety of hard slipstones, gouge stones, file sets, tapers and points for putting the ultimate edge on flat chisels, gouges, veiners, and other irregularly shaped edges.

A workbench may be made by the woodcarver of heavy 2-inch boards, preferably hardwood such as maple or beech, although pine will do. Material for making such a bench will cost from $25 to $50 depending on the type of wood available at the local building supply dealer. A wood vise, usually of steel with wooden jaws, may be bought at Sears, Roebuck, a local hardware store, or the sources of supply listed at the end of this chapter for from $15 to $50. Some woodcarvers prefer a quick action vise which sells for about $50. If the bench is homemade and does not have an end vise or screw box for clamping long stuff, an edge vise, which sells for about $25, may be purchased from the mail order suppliers listed at the end of this chapter.

Very fine workbenches imported from Europe or made in this country may be bought for around $400, equipped with vise and usually with a tool drawer.

Even master woodcarvers buy some carving chisels although they themselves make 50 percent of their own tools. The best mass-produced chisels available are made in England and Switzerland and sell for from $4 to $8 each. They may be ordered in matched sets or singly from the suppliers listed at the end of this chapter. Firmer chisels sell for about the same price.

Mallets of boxwood sell for from $2 to $5 depending on weight; lignum vitae mallets cost about $1 more.

Various types of sharpening stones

Stones are more expensive than one might imagine. For instance, fine Arkansas slipstones cost up to $8 apiece. A set of 8 or 10 stones in the variety needed by a woodcarver can cost up to $75, but without these the woodcarver's tools will never be adequate for his work.

Bench saws and band saws, when desired, cost from $150 to $350. The woodcarver should not need one that costs more than $150; he might possibly check woodworking equipment dealers in larger cities for a secondhand saw at perhaps half the price.

Additional hand tools for roughing out blocks to be carved consist of a coping saw, which may be bought at any hardware store for $3, a hatchet at about $5, and a drawknife, which can be ordered by mail or sometimes found in hardware stores for around $7.

It is a problem to find the proper type of carbon steel with which to make one's tools. Regular tool steel alloys are not usually suitable. What is needed is a carbon steel of 65- to 75-point carbon content. Sometimes, but not often, this can be found at steel supply houses in larger cities. The best sources are the Crucible Steel Company, the address of which is listed at the end of this chapter, or some of the English, German, and Swedish steel companies, such as Uddeholm, which have offices in a few large American cities. Enough steel in various sizes to make literally hundreds of small chisels should not cost more than $10 or $15.

Aside from equipment, the main requirement of a woodcarver's shop is good lighting. A master carver usually places the bench in front of a window which runs the length of the bench and is not shaded by trees or bushes. In addition, he has a good fluorescent light fixture mounted on the ceiling above the bench and perhaps a student lamp with at least a 100-watt bulb which he can place directly above his work when needed on dark days or at night. Lighting fixtures or lamps may be bought for from $5 to $10.

The woodcarving shop does not need to be especially large. Usually a space 12 feet by 20 feet will suffice. More space might be needed if a bench saw and band saw are installed. Since woodcarving is done on relatively small pieces of wood, storage space for material presents no special problem.

A variety of wood may be used for carving, the main requirement being that it be relatively close grained, particularly if the carving has small details. White pine, sugar pine, and basswood are all relatively soft and relatively close grained. These three might be called the common woods for carving. They are used for room decorations, capitals for doorways, picture and mirror frames, sconces and carved decorations for baroque style furniture, all of which are commonly painted, gilded, or lacquered.

Mahogany is a fine carving wood, as are black walnut, circassian walnut, ebony, teak, and rosewood. All of these are used for rare carved doors, ornate furniture, and on occasion carved moldings and framing. These woods are hardly ever painted, and though portions of a carving in any of them may be colored or gilded, the grain and rich color of the wood are allowed to enhance the beauty of the carved form.

Oak, though relatively coarse grained, is a traditional carving wood in the British Isles, in Spain, and in Portugal. For certain types of carving, not too detailed, its tawny color and rugged grain give a feeling of strength and design to carved work.

Some of these woods may be ordered from large lumber dealers in large cities or from special hardwood or exotic wood dealers who, though they generally sell wholesale to furniture manufacturers, will sometimes sell small pieces of white pine, sugar pine, or furniture woods, cut to dimensions specified by the carver. Prices, of course, vary greatly depending on the type and rarity of the wood. A piece of sugar pine, for instance, 4 inches thick, 8 inches wide, and 4 feet long normally sells for from $3 to $5, the price including special cuts. A piece of walnut, now very hard to find, of the same size might sell for $15. Mahogany of the same dimensions might sell for $8, while rosewood, also in scarce supply and almost impossible to buy in such large pieces, might cost $20. Basswood, possibly the most popular common wood for carving, will sell at about the same price as sugar pine.

Some sources for wood, domestic and exotic, which accept mail orders are listed at the end of this chapter. Other sources for small pieces of all the woods mentioned are the host of building supply retailers which have sprung up all over the country since World War II. Many of these operations offer wood for amateur furniture makers and some own sawmills in the United States and out of the

country from which the store manager can order pieces of special
dimensions.

Architectural woodcarvers, who deal almost exclusively with
architects and interior designers, often require that the client furnish
the wood properly rough sawn into suitable shapes for specified
carvings. This relieves the artist of the unproductive burdens of
finding sources for wood, dealing with bills of lading and invoices,
and the investment for mechanical saws. Furniture carvers generally
have adequate sources of supply for the wood they use. It is the
amateur or part-time carver who faces a problem in finding suitable
material.

There is not a great deal of demand in the United States at this
time for full-time woodcarvers either of furniture or architectural
designs. Of the two fields, the furniture carver undoubtedly has a
better opportunity, but only by hiring himself out to a large furniture manufacturer where he may eventually reach an income of
$12,000 to $15,000 a year. So little architectural carving is required,
and the background and experience for this true art must be so intensive that it is highly unlikely to survive after the few masters of
the art have retired or died. Perhaps one reason is that the ranks of
woodcarvers have not been replenished over the last two generations, thus limiting the supply, and architects don't specify woodcarving anymore because they can't find woodcarvers. Even the
architectural woodcarver, were he able to find constant commissions,
could not expect to make over $12,000 a year.

Should a carver of great skill appear, well steeped in modern
design and modern architectural and interior decorating methodol-
ogy, he might be able to generate full-time business by letting his
skill and sense of design be known to architectural and interior design firms all over the country. The process, however, in a nation as
large as ours, would be time-consuming, expensive, and probably
unprofitable as a result.

Possibly the best opportunity today for aspiring master woodcarvers is to concentrate on carving and selling small pieces, some
of which may be commissioned and some of which may be of the
carver's own design. Such pieces might be family crests, fraternity
plaques, carved trophies, lamp stands, hanging shelves, cigarette
boxes, and the like.

To find a market for plaques and trophies he must send photographs of his work or take samples to fraternal organizations and the firms in larger cities which supply trophies to legions of clubs and schools.

To sell other items he should take samples to furniture stores, gift shops, and interior decorating firms, talk to these people, find out what carved items might appeal to their customers and ask for an order of several pieces at a specified price.

Another outlet for good carvings will be the many craft fairs held in every part of the country every year. A list of these fairs may be acquired by writing the department of tourism in all state capitals. Craft fairs offer a good market for small items costing between $5 and $10.

It is difficult to say how much a woodcarver should charge for his work. He must, of course, charge for the wood he uses and for other costs of operation. He should expect to earn at least $3 an hour for his work. Once he becomes established and more skillful and can turn out his work faster he should expect to raise his labor rate to perhaps $5 or $6 an hour. If he designs a simple but attractive piece and produces limited editions of some pieces, he might be able to raise his prices based on demand. Only individual experience will finally give guidance as to how much a carver may charge for each piece.

Everything produced by a woodcarver should be signed with his name and address as a means of encouraging future orders and commissions.

All in all, woodcarving does not offer a very lucrative career at this time. It is a very satisfying craft, however, and it seems possible that dedicated woodcarvers can enjoy its satisfaction and use it as a source of supplementary income by holding down a regular job and devoting evenings, weekends, and holidays to woodcarving. Hopefully, enough part-time carvers will develop to keep this fine art and its techniques alive for future generations.

SOURCES OF SUPPLY

Art Consultants
97 St. Marks Place
New York, New York 10009

A.D. Alpine Inc.
353 Coral Circle
El Segundo, California 90245

Brodhead-Garrett Company
4560 East 71st Street
Cleveland, Ohio 44105

Crucible Steel Company
321 West 32nd Street
Charlotte, North Carolina 28206

Milton Bradley Company
Springfield, Massachusetts 01101

Rapid Rack
610 Sir Francis Drake Boulevard
San Anselmo, California 94960

Special Education Programs, Inc.
414 Avon Place
Cambridge, Massachusetts 02140

Three Arts Materials Group, Inc.
375 Great Neck Road
Great Neck, New York 11021

Walker Systems, Inc.
520 South 21st Avenue
East Duluth, Minnesota 55812

H. Wilson Corp.
555 West Taft Drive
South Holland, Illinois 60473

Woodcraft Supply Corporation
313 Montvale Avenue
Woburn, Massachusetts 01801

CHAPTER XXII

The Musical Instrument Maker

ONLY a few musical instruments will be treated, and those briefly, in this chapter. To describe the needs and tools of the makers of all the musical instruments made in the world would require a veritable encyclopedia. The task would be akin to that of an ancient craftsman of Imperial China who might spend a lifetime carving one lacquer box; the task is too great for one chapter of this volume.

There are, however, a very few men and women in the United States of the 1970s (some of whom earn a fairly decent living) who make musical instruments of a limited variety, mainly those evolved by the societies of the Western world. These include dulcimers, violins and the larger siblings of violins, guitars, lutes, banjos (originally an Afro-American instrument) and woodwinds, this latter category including both modern and ancient forms. Possibly the dulcimer makers, found mostly in the Southeast where the dulcimer was mainly used, enjoy the highest demand for work in the United States. More violins, cellos, clarinets, and flutes are sold than dulcimers, certainly, but these more common, more formal instruments are made mostly in Europe and the competition from European craftsmen in this field is rather difficult to overcome by an American craftsman. Some woodwinds are made individually by American craftsmen but most of those sold are semi-mass-producd with craftsmen giving only the final touches of precise tuning.

Strangely enough, several Americans on the West Coast have endured the 7-year apprenticeship required of Japanese bamboo flute makers; they produce these once-exotic instruments for what must be an extremely limited market on the West Coast. This instru-

ment will not be described in this book because of its general ob-
scurity, both to craftsmen and to writers. Pianos and harpsichords
will be ignored only because factories and teams of consummate
craftsmen are usually needed to produce them (although one or two
individuals make pianos or harpsichords, supplementing the income
from their crafts by acting as consultants in various fields of musi-
cology). Training in making any of the smaller instruments will be
of value to a craftsman seeking a job in a piano factory. The field is
limited, however, and the turnover of craftsmen rather slow.

Dulcimers are not only the simplest musical instruments to make
but they are made in more different forms than any other single instrument. They come in all sorts of shapes and sizes, some with three
strings and some with as many as eight strings. Unlike the more
complicated violins and lutes, dulcimer making has largely been a
home craft over the generations, the few specialists who made them
in the Appalachian regions being, for the most part, farmers supplementing their income. Nowadays, however, there are numbers of
dulcimer makers in the land, some part-time craftsmen but others
who make a living of sorts by making and selling the instruments
individually, through craft shops or at craft fairs. Some instrument
makers live in the country and others follow their craft in larger
cities.

Unlike the more classical instruments, dulcimers are often sold
for decoration, to serve as a small and unusual wall hanging rather
than for playing. This circumstance greatly expands the market and
might inspire otherwise indifferent musicians to learn to play the
simple instrument as accompaniment to folk singing.

There is no rigidly defined market for dulcimers. Young and old,
educated and uneducated are all attracted to the graceful shape of
the instrument and to its plaintive sound.

Insofar as is known to the author, there is no formal course anywhere in the making of dulcimers. Such training as the dulcimer
maker acquires, he must pick up on his own by studying dulcimers
old and new, by reading the few available books on the subject, by
observing other dulcimer makers, and by making dulcimers. Musical
training is also helpful in judging which woods and shapes offer the
best tones; however, dulcimers are traditionally made of almost any
type of domestic wood with walnut, beech, and cherry being the finest.

Any sort of training and experience in handcraft work, particularly woodworking, is also very helpful.

The wood is of necessity quite thin, no more than ⅛-inch in thickness. Such wood can be worked, and dulcimers have been made, with no more than a good-quality, carefully honed pocket-knife. A few additional tools of a simple nature, however, will make production easier and quicker so that the craftsman can be better paid for his time.

Such tools include a coping saw, which may be bought at any hardware store for about $2, and a carpenter's brace, which sells for around $10 at hardware stores, with several bits which cost about $2 to $3.50 each. Also needed is a woodworker's vise which can be bought for as little as $20 or as much as $50 at hardware stores, mail order houses such as Sears, or from the special suppliers listed at the end of this chapter. For making the neck the craftsmen will need a couple of firming chisels which cost from $3 to $5 each, a mallet which costs $3.50, and perhaps a set of five woodcarving chisels of good quality, preferably imported, which sell for around $20. Several rasps and files will be useful. These may be bought at hardware stores for from 75¢ to $2 each.

An 8-point panel crosscut saw and a 5½-point panel ripsaw, $10 each, will be needed to saw out fingerboards, and a 6-inch smoothing plane, available at most hardware stores or from mail order supply houses for about $5, will be needed to smooth the saw cuts.

Gluing the components of a dulcimer together requires from five to ten clamps, either small woodworking double screw clamps which are sold by woodworking equipment mail order suppliers for about $6 apiece, or metal C-clamps, usually found at hardware stores for about $1 each.

All the forms needed for bending and assembling dulcimers must be made by the craftsman himself based on his needs and his observation of other dulcimer makers. Forms can usually be made from scrap lumber which costs virtually nothing.

Production can be speeded up by substituting for the handsaws a small bench saw, available at some hardware stores or at Sears for about $50. A power jigsaw, to replace the coping saw, will cost from $25 to $35. And while a brace and bit can do certain jobs a power tool cannot do, a power drill, $15 to $20 from hardware stores or mail order suppliers, with wood cutting bits which cost about $1.50 each, will make holes much faster than the brace and bit and will save considerable time if volume warrants the capital expenditure.

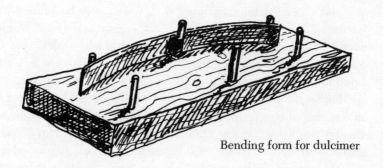

Bending form for dulcimer

Certainly a workbench will be needed, but it need not be so sophisticated as that of the furniture maker or the woodcarver. Generally a homemade bench 6 feet long and 3 feet wide, with well-broced legs of 2- by 4-inch stuff and a top of 2-inch-thick boards, is more than adequate. Lumber for such a bench will cost perhaps $10.

Tools, knowledge, and love of the work are more important to the dulcimer maker than formal shop space. Many a fine instrument has been made on a ramshackle hewn bench under a big oak tree beside a mountain cabin. Others have been turned out in quantity in a small basement workshop in the city. And many dulcimer makers set up temporary shop at craft fairs and demonstrate to an admiring crowd how the dulcimers they sell are put together. Certainly a craftsman should have enough space in which to store his wood, hang his tools, and keep his benchtop clear while working. If he has the advantage of a small bench saw and a mechanical jig- or band saw, then he needs additional space for these in order to allow long boards to be run through each without being stopped by a wall. Apart from these, there are no specifications for the dulcimer maker's workshop.

Materials consist of wood and glue. Any of the white glues, which sell for about $1 for a half-pint bottle, is suitable as is old-fashioned glue which must be mixed with water or new-fashioned epoxy glues which come in a tube that sells for slightly more than a dollar for enough to make a couple of dozen dulcimers. All these types of glue are easily available at hardware stores or even drug stores and grocery stores.

Getting the proper wood creates something of a difficulty. Thin boards are needed, no more than ⅛-inch thick and planed to satin smoothness; these must be from 1½ inches wide for ribs, and from 4 to 8 inches wide for fronts and backs (in the older parlance, *backs* and *bellies*). Four-inch boards are joined together with glue to provide sufficient width for front and back boards. Fingerboards are about ¾-inch thick and up to 30 inches long. Scrolls and the short neck of the dulcimer are carved from pieces of hardwood about 6 inches long and 1½ to 2 inches thick.

As mentioned, almost any type of hardwood, and some spruce, can be used for dulcimers. Black walnut and cherry are favorites because of the beauty of the grain. Walnut boards to make one dulcimer will cost from $7 to $8 from any of the several mail order suppliers who stock such wood. Yellow poplar, or tulip poplar, will cost only about $2.50 to $3 for the same amount of boards. Maple, which gives a fine tone, will cost about the same, or slightly more, than the poplar. Spruce, which is sometimes used for the front board, with a hardwood backboard, will cost about $1 to $1.50 for one board. Cherry is slightly more expensive than walnut.

Dulcimer makers who produce in quantity and have steady sales might install a large band or bench saw and a planer and rip their own boards at considerably less cost per board, but the capital expenditure for the equipment is often more than the profit on less expensive boards. Thin boards can be ripped by hand, but the time required raises the price of labor for each dulcimer enough to make it exorbitant for most prospective purchasers. Buying the boards from a regular supplier is by far the most practicable method of acquiring wood for amateurs, part-time dulcimer makers, or even most full-time professionals.

Included among materials is the small 10-gauge brass wire which is used to make frets under the melody string. This may be bought in rolls of 10 feet at most hardware stores for around $1. Old-time dulcimers usually had thin brass wire strings, sometimes available at hardware stores for about $2 for a roll 10 feet long. Most modern dulcimers, however, use metal or nylon first strings for guitars which can be bought from any musical instrument dealer for about 50¢ each.

Surprisingly, there is quite a dulcimer cult in the United States and most dulcimer makers, once established, develop enough word-of-mouth advertising to sell all the dulcimers they make. This is particularly true of city craftsmen who become established by working in craft fairs or selling their dulcimers through gift and craft shops in the cities. Craftsmen in rural areas at first sell through tourist shops or in front of their own workshops if located on a tourist traffic artery.

What builds the name of the dulcimer maker, however, is the small piece of paper with the craftsman's name and address pasted on the inside of the back where it can be read through one of the sound holes. Such identification has been used since the time of Stradivarius. It still works.

Most dulcimer makers can produce seven or eight instruments a month which sell for from $75 to $175 each. Of course, the price of each varies according to the type of wood used, the cost of which is included in the price, and the number of strings. A dulcimer with six strings, for instance, requires more labor than one with three strings.

More and more amateurs in the 1970s seem to be taking up the making of guitars, and a few fine guitars are made for sale in the United States by full-time musical instrument makers. Construction of guitars requires very much the same tools, materials, and shop space as dulcimers. Guitars, however, are usually embellished with various inlays which may be bought from suppliers of fine wood for furniture makers. Also, the making of guitars requires considerably more work than dulcimers and a greater knowledge of music as well as a good ear for tone. There are a few very good books on making the classic Spanish guitar, and this is possibly the best source of training for one who wishes to tackle guitar making.

No training courses other than regular woodworking courses are known to the author. An apprenticeship, in this country or in Spain, Portugal, Mexico, or South America, is the finest training one can find but difficult to arrange. Names of guitar makers in foreign lands may be requested from the appropriate embassies in Washington and the master craftsmen then written to asking about the possibility of apprenticeships. Also, one might apply to the Musical Instrument Maker's Shop at Colonial Williamsburg, Williamsburg, Virginia.

A fine guitar, which might take a week of steady labor to make and decorate, will sell for up to $250. Guitar making in the United States, however, is not likely to offer a good livelihood because of the competition of established guitar makers in other countries.

The same situation applies to the making of lutes, viola da gambas, violas, cellos, bass violins, violins, and other stringed instruments of traditional or exotic nature. Making all of these instruments requires much more knowledge, skill, and tools than either dulcimer or guitar making. As a consequence the instruments themselves are quite expensive and the market severely limited even in a nation of over 200 million people. Also, the competition of established instrument makers in Europe with its generally more experienced labor offers strong competition to the American craftsman.

There are perhaps five or six fine stringed instrument makers in the United States who develop a fair living from making various instruments. Most of them, however, are dedicated craftsmen with years of apprenticeship who are happy making beautiful-looking and beautiful-sounding musical instruments and are content with a limited income. After some years, an established master musical instrument maker might reach an income of maybe $20,000 a year if he is lucky (and if the national economy holds up). Unfortunately there is little replacement market for musical instruments and just not a big enough original market to support many of these fine craftsmen.

A small but growing number of amateurs seem to be taking up the making of woodwind instruments, but again, the competition of established European craftsmen makes it difficult for a professional trying to make a living by making recorders, clarinets, oboes, shawms, flutes, fifes, krumhorns, and racketts. The author knows of no formal training curricula for these instruments in the United States, and few apprenticeships are available. Some excellent training can be acquired by taking a job with one of the large musical instrument factories, but few jobs are open. Much can be learned from books if the student has a natural facility with his hands and some basic understanding of the properties of wood and of music. For all but a very few, however, making woodwinds should be approached as a fascinating hobby.

The tools for making woodwinds include a wood turning lathe, which will cost around $100 to $150 at large hardware stores, mail order stores such as Sears, and the suppliers listed at the end of this chapter. A few hand tools, such as brace and bits, rasps and reamers are needed. Costs range from $1.50 for bits to $10 for a good-quality carpenter's brace. Taper reamers available from machinist's supply houses can be quite expensive, up to $100 apiece for larger sizes. Special ones can be made to a simple design, described in the books listed in the bibliography to this chapter, at any

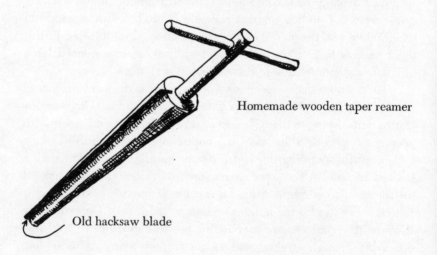

Homemade wooden taper reamer

Old hacksaw blade

machine shop at a cost that will vary from $10 to $50, depending on size and the location of the machine shop. Also, wooden taper reamers with an inset steel blade can be turned on a wood lathe for virtually no cost.

Except for the dulcimer maker, instrument makers might look for jobs repairing instruments for large retail music stores in metropolitan areas. The income will not be large, but the work will be steady and enjoyable without the risk of capital expenditure.

SOURCES OF SUPPLY

The Brookstone Company
14 Brookstone Building
Peterborough, New Hampshire
 03458

Albert Constantine and Son
2050 East Chester Road
Bronx, New York 10461

Craftsman Wood Service Company
2727 South Mary Street
Chicago, Illinois 60608

7
Wax

CHAPTER XXIII

The Candlemaker

WAX has probably been used for certain transitory forms of decoration since the first man robbed a bee tree and applied his imagination to the plastic wax which was left when the honey was eaten. For a long, long time, since he found that beeswax was combustible, he has been using the material for candles. He has supplemented beeswax with the wax from bayberries and other vegetable materials and, for the last hundred years or so, with paraffin, a derivative of oil. And while candles have been largely displaced for functional lighting during this same period by electric lights, they have never disappeared. The beauty of candle light has not and likely will not ever be completely displaced.

For many years now the source of candles has been factories where very elegant, and sometimes "cute," shapes have been turned out by machines and molds. The same processes as the hand dippers and molders of old are used, but machines replace the servant maids who formerly performed this necessary chore. In the last 20 years, however, candlemaking has joined the reborn handcrafts, and legions of candlemakers, amateur and professional, are once more seen in the land. Some make a living from the craft, but most do so because of the boundless imagination which has been applied to making candles of shapes and modern purposes quite unheard of in colonial days. In the last few years, wax has become an artistic medium, and its future as a craft will depend on the public's maintaining this attitude.

Of the 3,000 or so colleges listed by the American Crafts Council as having craft curricula, not one lists candlemaking as a formal course. There are probably reasons for this other than artistic snobbery. The very ease with which wax can be poured into limitless shapes hardly requires a long course of instruction in the basic techniques as is required in glass, iron, or fiber. The tools of the candlemaking trade are simplicity epitomized; neither trip-hammer nor expensive joining tools, nor $10,000 furnaces nor even $500 lathes are required. Anyone with a knowledge of the melting heat of wax (about 140°), a gas jet, a secondhand pot from Goodwill Industries, and a couple of discarded milk cartons can become a candlemaker. But all of these factors concern only tools and technique. They do not reflect the very real talent of a few candlemakers who are devoted to a craft producing rather transitory items, particularly when these items are burned for lighting. Perhaps the talent of a candlemaker can be compared with that of a performing artist who gives a brilliant stage performance that is immediately lost, except in the memories of the audience. And perhaps the successful candlemakers of the world have the perspicacity to recognize this reality and design and produce accordingly.

But candles should be artistic and those who buy candles respond, as with every craft, to design, to evidence of imagination, and to things different. The candlemaker, then, can derive much benefit from training in drawing, painting, and sculpture, for form and color and proportion are the factors that make a candle beautiful whether it is lit or unlit. Also one should experiment with his waxes, combining colors and waxes of different melting points. He should try different sized wicks with different waxes to learn the effect of larger and smaller melting pools in various waxes. And he should try forms of all sorts—traditional, rectangular, or sculptured—in solid or mixed colors to see what happens to this form and color when the wick is lit and the candle is slowly consumed. There is adventure as well as some waste in such experimentation, but the training is necessary if a candlemaker hopes to produce distinctive work. Eventually he should be able to create truly mobile, changeable sculpture, the constant differences being the result of the gentle flame that is the basic charm of a candle.

There are a number of books on candlemaking, some of them quite good. Most of these are listed in the bibliography to this chapter.

Also those who wish detailed instruction in the craft should check the recreation departments of cities or counties and inquire about courses of instruction in a local government-sponsored craft school.

As already mentioned, basic equipment for candlemaking is simplicity itself although the professionals in many cases have evolved slightly more sophisticated equipment.

A gas stove or burner is as good as anything for melting the wax, but it is inadvisable to use an electric stove because an electric heating coil stays hot for some length of time after being turned off; gas can be cut off immediately.

Containers for the wax can be any sort of cooking pot, including a double boiler which minimizes the danger of fire. Pots can be bought at any hardware, department, or variety store for a couple of dollars each. They can be found secondhand at a local Goodwill Store for considerably less. Most experienced candlemakers prefer enameled pots.

A cooking thermometer of some sort is necessary to help control the melting wax which, if it gets too hot after melting, may catch fire. Some candlemakers convert a secondhand gas hot water tank for melting since the thermostat on the gas burner can be used in place of a thermometer.

Candles may be molded or dipped, but virtually all modern candles are shaped either by being cast or by having blocks of wax stuck together with melted wax. Commercial molds are available from several manufacturers, but the craftsmen among candlemakers spurn them with a feeling akin to horror. This is well. Modern candlemakers have applied much imagination to the shapes of their molded products and have, as a consequence, produced sculpture from nothing much more substantial than a mass of wax.

Candles may be molded in all sorts of objects. Among the most popular are paper milk cartons which serve one time and are destroyed in the process. The same applies to mayonnaise jars, Coca-Cola bottles, tin cans and shoeboxes, all of which may be classified as candlemaking equipment.

The most popular and most versatile molding equipment is a sand box, constructed either from a cardboard carton, a grape crate, or a large box, on legs whereby it becomes a sand table similar to

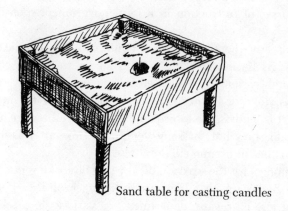

Sand table for casting candles

the sand tables of elementary school instruction. This table can be homemade out of ⅜-inch plywood or boards, with 2-by-2-inch legs, for less than $10. Its size may vary from 2 feet square to 3 feet by 5 feet, with sides from 8 inches to 10 inches high. One or two bags of sand to fill it may be bought for about $1.50 each at retail building supply houses. When the sand is dampened just enough to pack nicely, shapes are pressed into it or dug out, a wick put into position and molten wax poured into the cavity around the wick.

If one does not wish to make a sand table, he may pick up a corrugated cardboard carton from behind any grocery store, fill it with sand, and utilize it just as efficiently as a permanent table.

Assorted spoons and paddles, some of them homemade, and perhaps some potter's tools which may be found at art supply stores, are sometimes used to create special effects on already molded candles. The whole lot of this supplementary equipment can be purchased for from $5 to $10.

If the candlemaker wishes to produce traditional dipped candles for the table, he will require a large melting pot at least a foot wide and perhaps 2 feet deep. Such a pot should preferably be enameled although a galvanized pail, which sells for about $2 at any hardware and at most grocery stores, is quite suitable.

Certainly a work table is needed, on which to place a small sand box or other molding equipment, with a drawer in which to keep

Various homemade candlemaker's wooden paddles

wicking and spoons. A common kitchen table serves this purpose very well. One may be bought new for from $15 to $20, or second-hand for perhaps $7.50 to $10. A candlemaker with a few wood-working tools can make his own from 2 by 4s, 1 by 8s, and ½-inch plywood for from $5 to $10, if he obtains his material from a building supply dealer.

Shelves or a cabinet of some sort are needed for storage of wax. Shelves may be built from about $8 worth of 1-inch by 12-inch knotty pine shelving. A steel cabinet may be purchased new for about $20 or second-hand for from $5 to $10. Wooden fruit and vegetable crates, or even heavy corrugated cartons, may be stacked to substitute for shelves or cabinets.

No great amount of space is needed for a candle shop. Almost any kitchen, or a kitchenette, is large enough for most operations. Part of a basement may be set aside for candlemaking if a gas line, good lighting, and hot water are available. Candlemakers who operate retail shops may enclose, fully or partially, a space in the back of the display and sales space for a shop. The shop should be at least 10 feet by 10 feet and, of course, must have gas and water.

Only two basic materials are needed for candlemaking: wicking and wax. Both, however, are needed in great variety.

It is recommended that even the beginning candlemaker purchase regular braided wicking in various sizes for different-sized candles instead of mere string. Wicking in all sizes can be bought retail at most craft or hobby shops in packages of 7 feet for about 50¢. It may also be bought in spools from the suppliers listed at the end of this chapter for only a few cents per yard. Special wicking with a soft metal core, which keeps the wick upright, costs very little more.

Special candle wax with a rather high melting point can be bought at most craft and hobby shops in any city or ordered from the suppliers listed at the end of this chapter. It costs about 50¢ a pound retail or 35¢ a pound when bought in large quantities. A pound of wax will just about fill a pint milk carton, or it will make 5 or 6 dipped candles depending on length.

Beeswax, considered the elite material of the candlemaker, can be bought from beekeepers if one is in the neighborhood for around 75¢ a pound. When purchased from hobby shops, it costs from $1 to $2 a pound. Another elite material, bayberry wax, is also sometimes available in hobby shops or from mail order suppliers. Bayberry wax, too, is expensive, selling for about $2.50 a pound retail, or slightly less when bought in wholesale quantities. Often bayberry wax is used as the last dip or two, which coats a normal candle with the expensive wax and imparts both bayberry color and scent to the candle.

Regular canning wax, or paraffin, is suitable for candles but more expensive than regular candle wax. It may be found in most grocery stores and sells for about 85¢ a pound. Since it has a higher melting temperature than candle wax, it is sometimes blended with the candle wax to raise the melting temperature slightly.

There seems to be a fairly good market for candles and they may be sold by a number of methods. Some candlemakers sell on the sidewalk from a cardtable which displays their work. The location for this type of sales should be picked carefully; some good locations might be near buildings with large numbers of office workers in a city, at a shopping center, or in the antique store section in smaller towns.

Craft fairs and sidewalk art shows also offer a good marketing situation for candles. Sometimes a small temporary shop can be set up at craft fairs, the actual work being a drawing card to the finished products which are displayed on shelves or tables. LP gas must be used in temporary shops.

Gift shops provide quite a good market for artistic and traditional candles, although the traditional candles, even the dipped ones, are mass-produced and sold for considerably less than handmade candles. Samples of one's work should be taken to gift shop proprietors, and the candlemaker should attempt to obtain an order for at least a dozen candles, all different or in a limited edition, from the proprietor or manager.

In some cities and towns which, for historical or other reasons, attract a number of tourists, candlemakers have found it worthwhile to set up regular retail operations in a neighborhood of craft and gift shops. Such an operation, of course, requires at least $5,000 capital for the rent and the purchase of items other than candles which are sold to widen the attraction of the shop and to help take care of overhead. If such an operation is attempted, and if sufficient capital has not been accumulated, the entrepreneur should talk to a local banker about a loan. Cost of store space, renovation, telephone, utilities, and other facets of the operation should be checked out carefully. Also, a survey of neighboring shops should be made to try to anticipate if there is enough market to support a shop and its owner, and what type and price goods sell best.

Candlemaking should not be considered the most lucrative calling one can find. Its satisfaction comes more from the achievement of shapes, smells, and colors than from the money it makes. Unless the candlemaker runs a successful retail operation, he cannot expect to make more than $1.50 to $2.50 an hour in most cases. Also, there is not a big enough market for candles to support many people in the craft.

When the candlemaker sells his products, he must be sure to charge for his material after adding 20 percent of its cost for handling, and on top of this he should add the estimated cost of gas and equipment. Cost of time is the last factor to be considered, and this will have to be figured to some extent by whether it raises the price of the candles too high to sell.

Many candlemakers hold down a regular job and on the weekends make candles which they sell as a source of supplementary income. This is advised for most.

SOURCES OF SUPPLY

Acto, Inc.
48-41 Van Dam Street
Long Island, New York 11101

Borsteo's Hobby Craft, Inc.
Box 40
Monmouth, Illinois 61462

The Candle Shop
Goode, Virginia 24536

CCM Arts & Crafts, Inc.
9520 Baltimore Avenue
College Park, Maryland 20740

Crafts of Cleveland
2824 Lorain Avenue
Cleveland, Ohio 44113

Dremel Manufacturing Company
4915 21st Street
Racine, Wisconsin 53406

Economy Handicrafts
47-11 Francis Lewis Boulevard
Flushing, New York 11361

Graphic Chemical & Ink Company
728 North Yale Avenue
Villa Park, Illinois 60181

Hunt Manufacturing Company
1405 Locust Street
Philadelphia, Pennsylvania 19102

The Morilla Company
43-01 21st Street
Long Island, New York 11101

Sander Wood Engraving, Inc.
117 West Harriston Street
Chicago, Illinois 60605

Shelby School Supply Company
Route 6, Box 493
Shelbyville, Kentucky 40065

Stewart Industries
6520 North Hoyne Avenue
Chicago, Illinois 60645

Vanguard Crafts, Inc.
2915 Avenue J
Brooklyn, New York 11210

8
Future Crafts

CHAPTER XXIV

Applying the Artistic Mind to New Materials in the Future

THIS chapter cannot be completed now, but only outlined. It can only speculate on how the reborn crafts might develop in a future none of us yet understands. All we know about the future, really, is that man will still be here; that man's imagination and manual dexterity, the qualities which changed him from a club-carrying ape to a sometimes blundering master of his universe, will still be here to apply to the now unknown qualities of our future environment.

If the crafts are truly being reborn in the twentieth century, and if man has basically the same character he has had since crafts began, then the crafts will grow and embrace the new materials and technology of our future. New materials and new technology will not displace the beauty and function of the natural materials the craftsman has always used; they will merely expand the numbers of craftsmen and perhaps develop ideas which can be adapted by the established crafts to give them strength in future generations.

There has been some beginning in the use of new type materials for crafts. As usual, the origins of some of these appeared far longer ago than we imagine. Plastics, for example, may be said to have originated in the 1860s or 1870s when a composition material to make billiard balls was first invented in a laboratory. Bakelite was used at the beginning of the twentieth century, long before the appearance of the multiplicity of non-biodegradable substances which now grace our grocery store shelves and iceboxes as containers for food and other products and which embellish our space-age middens.

Rayon was an acceptable fiber for clothing in the nineteenth century, two generations or more ago, an unrecognized harbinger of the host of synthetic fibers such as nylon and polyester which have to a great extent replaced the natural fibers of olden days.

Plastic substances, all manmade and all requiring vast factories to produce, are only a few manifestations of possible craft materials. Since World War II additional materials, some quite insubstantial and others more solid than anything found on earth, have been discovered and in some cases used by artist and craftsman.

The most obvious of what might be called the *neo-new materials* are moon rocks. What can be done with these to make our world and our individual lives more beautiful? Undoubtedly, in years to come, when the supply of cosmic materials may become relatively abundant, craftsmen will learn to work these minerals and discover beneath the surface a beauty similar to that of the first cut diamond in an age when the moon was a goddess.

Then there are other matters, not substances exactly, but certainly entities that are the result of modern science. Is there potential beauty, in one form or another, for the craftsman who seeks beauty in the tactile, visual, and audial sensations of electricity and electronics?

That consummate silversmith, Mary Ann Scheer, of Kent State University, has already used a radiation detection device as a quasi-jeweled setting in a silver belt. It does not gleam like a jewel, but leads one indirectly to the natural beauty of unpolluted air. No traditional jewel could be more exquisite.

And there might be potential for some scientific-minded craftsman to devise a system of electronic impulses and electrical switches which would replace the traditional loom or potter's wheel and allow him to conceive and create a new indescribable sensation that might equal the visual, audial, and tactile sensations brought to us by ancient, traditional crafts.

Of course, one might expect a reaction of horror from the traditional craftsman against the injection of science and manmade materials into the ancient arts and skills of the handworker, but such a view is on examination quite illogical. After all, no man can make iron or wood or clay, yet he uses them to create beauty. The same attitude can be applied to other materials which are made in factories. The new materials often are different from the old only in degree. Every plastic must be made from the materials found in the natural world, just as iron must be smelted, wool shorn and spun, and wood sawn. Electricity and the sensations of electronics are, after all, a part of our natural universe regardless of insubstantiality.

All these new materials and ideas should be examined by the craftsman even if they are discarded on the basis of personal taste. For examination and, in some cases, experimentation reflect the true, elemental attitude of the craftsman, old and new.

Without a questing attitude by craftsmen of the past our crafts might well have stopped with the prehistoric flint chipper.

SOURCES OF SUPPLY

Adhesive Products
1660 Boone Avenue
Bronx, New York 10460

Arthur Brown & Bros.
2 West 46th Street
New York, New York 10036

California Titon Products
2501 Birch Street
Santa Ana, California 92707

Dow Chemical
2020 Dow Center
Midland, Michigan 48640

J. R. Educational Aides
25600 Ekna Road
Los Altos Hills, California 94022

M. Grumbacher, Inc.
460 West 34th Street
New York, New York 10001

Polyproducts Corporation
13810 Nelson Avenue
Detroit, Michigan 48227

Sculp-Metal Company
701 Investment Building
Pittsburgh, Pennsylvania 15222

Appendix: Training

THE most complete list of craft courses, including those offered by the art departments of universities, is compiled each year by the American Crafts Council and furnished to interested persons for a small fee.

This list, called the *Craft Courses Directory*, provides the courses available at each school, tuition, the instructors' names for each, and the degree offered. It may be acquired by writing:

> The American Crafts Council
> Publication Sales
> 44 West 53rd Street
> New York, New York 10019

Cost of the list is $2.50 for members of the American Crafts Council, $3 for non-members.

ACC also publishes annually a *Directory of Summer Crafts Courses*, which lists a number of private schools, many of them teaching only one or two crafts to a limited enrollment in almost every section of the country.

It is reiterated that sometimes excellent training can be acquired at craft schools which are operated by many municipal governments. Information on these courses may be obtained by telephoning the recreation and parks department of any city.

Also, informal basic training in some crafts is available for a small fee from certain craft and hobby shops in many cities.

Note: The author knows of no formal instruction offered for either macrame or candlemaking.

Bibliography

CHAPTER I—THE WEAVER

Albers, Anni, *On Weaving*, Wesleyan University Press, 1965.

Atwater, Mary, *The Shuttle-Craft Book of American Hand-Weaving*, Macmillan Co., 1951.

Atwater, Mary, *Shuttle-Craft Course in Hand Weaving*, Shuttle-Craft Co., 1923.

Black, Mary E., *Key to Weaving: A Textbook of Hand-weaving Techniques and Pattern Drafts for the Beginner*, Bruce Publishing Co., 1949.

Blumenau, Lilli, *The Art & Craft of Hand Weaving*, Crown Publishers, 1955.

Davison, Marguerite Porter, *A Handweaver's Pattern Book*, Swarthmore, Pa., 1950. (Privately published)

Fred, Berta, *Designing and Drafting for Handweavers*, Macmillan Co., 1961.

Hart, Robert, *How to Sell Your Handicrafts*, David McKay Co., Inc., 1953.

Kirby, Mary, *Designing on the Loom*, Studio Publications, 1955.

Nelson, Norbert, *Selling Your Crafts*, Van Nostrand Reinhold Co., 1967.

Oelsner, Gustaf Hermann, *A Handbook of Weaves*, Dover Publications, 1951.

Pritchard, Miriam Eleanor, *A Short Dictionary of Weaving*, Allen & Unwin, 1954.

Tidball, Harriet, *The Weaver's Book*, Macmillan Co., 1961.

Tovey, John, *Weaves and Pattern Drafting*, Reinhold Book Corporation, 1969.

CHAPTER II—THE TAPESTRY MAKER

Beutlich, Tadek, *The Technique of Woven Tapestry*, Watson-Guptill, 1967.

Hart, Robert, *How To Sell Your Handicrafts*, David McKay Co., Inc., 1953.

Ingers, Gertrud, *Flemish Weaving: A Guide to Tapestry Technique*, Van Nostrand Reinhold, 1971.

Ljsselsteyn, Gerardina Tjebberta Von, *Tapestry*, Brussels, Von Goor, 1969.

Lurcat, Jean, *Designing Tapestry*, London, Rockliff, 1950.

Nelson, Norbert, *Selling Your Crafts*, Van Nostrand Reinhold Co., 1967.

Tidball, Harriet, *Contemporary Tapestry*, Craft & Hobby Book Service, 1964.

CHAPTER III—THE EMBROIDERER AND NEEDLEPOINTER

Beilter, Ethel Jane, *Create with Yarn: Hooking, Stitchery*, International Textbook Co., 1964.

Bennett, Maggi, *Stitchery*, Dukane Press, 1970.

Butler, Anne, *Embroidery Stitches*, Praeger, 1968.

Christopher, Catherine, *The Complete Book of Embroidery & Embroidery Stitches*, Greystone Press, 1948.

de Dillmart, Th., *The Complete Encyclopedia of Needlework*, Running Press, 1972.

Drew, Joan H., *Embroidery & Design*, Sir Isaac Pitman & Sons, Ltd., 1929.

Guild, Vera P., *Creative Use of Stitches*, Davis Publications, 1964.

Hart, Robert, *How To Sell Your Handicrafts*, David McKay Co., Inc., 1953.

Karasz, Marista, *Adventures in Stitches*, Funk & Wagnalls, 1959.

Krevitsky, Nik, *Stitchery: Art & Craft*, Reinhold, 1966.

Lane, Maggie, *Needlepoint by Design*, Scribner, 1970.

Nelson, Norbert, *Selling Your Crafts*, Van Nostrand Reinhold Co., 1967.

Picken, Mary Brooks, *Needlepoint for Everyone*, Harper & Row, 1970.

Sidney, Sylvia, *Sylvia Sidney Needlepoint Book*, Reinhold Book Corp., 1968.

Wilson, Erica, *Crewel Embroidery*, Scribner, 1962.

CHAPTER IV—THE MACRAME WORKER

Graumont, Raoul, *Square Knot Handicraft Guide*, Cornell Maritime Press, 1949.

Hart, Robert, *How To Sell Your Handicrafts*, David McKay Co., Inc., 1953.

Harvey, Virginia, *Color & Design in Macrame*, Van Nostrand Reinhold, 1971.

Meilach, Dona Z., *Macrame: Creative Design in Knotting*, Crown Publishers, 1971.

Nelson, Norbert, *Selling Your Crafts*, Van Nostrand Reinhold Co., 1967.
Short, Eirian, *Introducing Macrame*, Batsford, 1970.
See also Bibliography for the Knitter and Crocheter.

CHAPTER V—THE STITCHER AND SEAMSTRESS

See Bibliography for The Embroiderer and Needlepointer.

CHAPTER VI—THE LACEMAKER

Brooke, Margaret L., *Lace in the Making, with Bobbins and Needle*, G. Routledge, 1923.
Capin, Jessie Florence, *The Lace Book*, Macmillan Co., 1932.
Gubser, Elsie H., *Bobbin Lace*, Robin & Russ Handweavers, 1949.
Hart, Robert, *How To Sell Your Handicrafts*, David McKay Co., Inc., 1953.
Henneberg, Alfred Freiherruon, *The Art & Craft of Old Lace*, E. Weyhe, 1931.
Kinmond, Jean, *Anchor Book of Lace Crafts*, Batsford, 1961.
Kinzel, Marianne, *Second Book of Modern Lace Knitting,* Mills & Boon, 1961.
Milroy, Mary Elizabeth Wallace, *Home Lace-Making*, P. Van Nostrand, 1906.
Nelson, Norbert, *Selling Your Crafts*, Van Nostrand Reinhold Co., 1967.
Powys, Marian, *Lace & Lace-Making*, C. T. Bronford Co., 1953.

CHAPTER VII—THE BATIK PRINTER

Belfer, Nancy, *Designing in Batik and Tie Dye*, Davis Publications, 1972.
Hart, Robert, *How To Sell Your Handicrafts*, David McKay Co., Inc., 1953.
Keller, Ila, *Batik: The Art & Craft*, C. E. Tuttle Co., 1966.
Krevitsky, Nik, *Batik Art & Craft*, Reinhold Publishers Corp., 1964.
Maile, Anne, *Tie-and-Dye as a Present Day Craft*, Mills & Boon, 1965.
Nelson, Norbert, *Selling Your Crafts*, Van Nostrand Reinhold Co., 1967.
Samuel, Evelyn, *Introducing Batik*, Watson-Guptill, 1968.
Steinmann, Alfred, *Batik, A Survey of Batik Design*, F. Lewis, 1958.

CHAPTER VIII—THE TIE DYER

See Bibliography for The Batik Printer.

CHAPTER IX—THE SILK SCREEN AND BLOCK PRINTER

Agoos, Sharilyn, *Serigraphy as a Discipline*, University of Georgia Press, 1965.

Auvil, Kenneth W., *Serigraphy: Silk Screen Techniques for the Artist*, Prentice-Hall, 1965.

Biegeleisen, Jacob Israel, *Silk Screen Printing as a Fine Art*, McGraw-Hill, 1942.

Chieffo, Clifford T., *Silk-Screen as a Fine Art*, Reinhold, 1967.

Eisenberg, James, *Silk Screen Printing*, McKnight & McKnight Publishing Co., 1957.

Hart, Robert, *How To Sell Your Handicrafts*, David McKay Co., Inc., 1953.

Nelson, Norbert, *Selling Your Crafts*, Van Nostrand Reinhold Co., 1967.

Shokler, Harry, *Artist's Manual For Silk Screen Print Making*, American Artists Group, 1946.

Sternberg, Harry, *Silk Screen Color Printing*, McGraw-Hill, 1942.

Thomas, Larry Beck, *An Introduction to Photographic Silk Screen*, University of Georgia Press, 1969.

CHAPTER X—THE KNITTER AND CROCHETER

Caplin, Jessie Eflorence, *Knit Fabrics*, Riverside Press, Inc., 1940.

Boehm, Peggy, *Macrame and Other Projects for Knitting Without Needles*, Gramercy, 1963.

Hart, Robert, *How To Sell Your Handicrafts*, David McKay Co., Inc., 1953.

Nelson, Norbert, *Selling Your Crafts*, Van Nostrand Reinhold Co., 1967.

Norbury, James, *Odhams Encyclopedia of Knitting*, Odhams Press, 1957.

Norbury, James, *Traditional Knitting Patterns*, B. T. Batsford, 1962.

Peake, Miriam Morrison, *The Wise Handbook of Knitting & Crocheting*, W. H. Wise, 1953.

Ray, Juliana, *Crochet Designs From Hungary*, B. T. Batsford, 1959.

Thomas, Mary, *Mary Thomas's Book of Knitting Patterns*, Hodder & Stoughton, Ltd., 1943.

Tillotson, Marjory, *The Complete Knitting Book*, Sir Isaac Pitman, 1947.

CHAPTER XI—THE BASKETMAKER

Brigham, William Tufts, *Mat Basket Weaving of the Ancient Hawaiians*, Bishop Museum Press, 1906.

Crampton, Charles, *The Junior Basketmaker*, Dryad Press, 1953.

Gallinger, Osma Couch, *Hand Weaving with Reeds and Fibers*, Pitman Publishers Corporation, 1948.

Hart, Robert, *How To Sell Your Handicrafts*, David McKay Co., Inc., 1953.

James, George Whaston, *Indian Basketry and How to Make Indian and Other Baskets*, Milton Bradley Co., 1903.

Knapp, Elizabeth Sanborn, *Raphia and Reed Weaving*, M. Bradley, 1901.

Knock, A., *Willow Basketry*, Manual Arts Press, 1949.

Kroncke, Grete, *Weaving with Cane and Reed*, Reinhold Book Corp., 1968.

Lee, Martha L., *Basketry and Related Arts*, D. Van Nostrand Co., 1948.

Nelson, Norbert, *Selling Your Crafts*, Van Nostrand Reinhold Co., 1967.

White, Mary, *How to Make Baskets*, Doubleday, Page, & Co., 1901.

Wright, Dorothy, *Baskets and Basketry*, B. T. Batsford, 1959.

CHAPTER XII—THE POTTER

Dougherty, John Wolfe, *Pottery Made Easy*, The Bruce Publishing Co., 1939.

Duncan, Julia Hamlin, *How to Make Pottery and Ceramic Sculpture*, Simon & Schuster, 1947.

Hart, Robert, *How To Sell Your Handicrafts*, David McKay Co., Inc., 1953.

Honore, York, *Pottery Making From the Ground Up*, Viking Press, 1950.

Jenkins, Roy Horace, *Practical Pottery for Craftsmen and Students*, The Bruce Publishing Co., 1941.

Kenny, John B., *The Complete Book of Pottery Making*, Greenberg, 1952.

Leach, Bernard Howell, *The Unknown Craftsman*, Faber & Faber, Ltd., 1946.

Nelson, Norbert, *Selling Your Crafts*, Van Nostrand Reinhold Co., 1967.

Norton, Frederick Harwood, *Ceramics for the Artist Potter*, Addison-Wesley Publishing Co., 1956.

Roy, Vincent A., *Ceramics: An Illustrated Guide to Creating and Enjoying Pottery*, McGraw-Hill, 1959.

Wren, Henry Douglas, *Hand Craft Pottery for Workshop and School*, Sir Isaac Pitman & Sons, Ltd., 1933.

CHAPTER XIII—THE ENAMELER

Bates, Kenneth Francis, *Enameling: Principles and Practice*, World Publishing Co., 1951.

Bates, Kenneth Francis, *The Enamelist*, World Publishing Co., 1967.

Clarke, Geoffrey, *The Technique of Enameling*, Reinhold, 1967.

Hart, Robert, *How To Sell Your Handicrafts*, David McKay Co., Inc., 1953.

Maryon, Herbert, *Metalwork and Enameling*, Dover Publications, 1971.

Millchet. Louis Elie, *Enameling on Metal*, D. Van Nostrand Co., 1947.

Nelson, Norbert, *Selling Your Crafts*, Van Nostrand Reinhold Co., 1967.

CHAPTER XIV—THE CERAMIC MURALIST

See Bibliography for The Potter.

CHAPTER XV—THE SILVERSMITH AND COPPERSMITH

Abbey, Staton, *The Goldsmith's and Silversmith's Handbook,* Technical Press, 1952.

Bovin, Murray, *Silversmithing and Art Metal for Schools, Tradesmen, and Craftsmen,* Forest Hills, 1963.

Choate, Sharr, *Creative Casting,* Crown Publishers, 1966.

Cuzner, Bernard, *A Silversmith's Manual,* N.A.G. Press, 1949.

Hart, Robert, *How To Sell Your Handicrafts,* David McKay Co., Inc., 1953.

Lukowitz, Joseph J., *Interesting Art-Metal Work,* The Bruce Publishing Co., 1947.

Maryon, Herbert, *Metalwork & Enamelling,* Dover Publications, 1971.

Nelson, Norbert, *Selling Your Crafts,* Van Nostrand Reinhold Co., 1967.

Wilson, H., *Silverwork & Jewelry,* Pitman Publications Corp., 1948.

CHAPTER XVI—THE JEWELRY MAKER

Baxter, William Thomas, *Jewelry, Gem Cutting, and Metal Craft,* McGraw-Hill, 1966.

Clegg, Helen, *Jewelry Making for Fun and Profit,* McKay, 1951.

Hart, Robert, *How to Sell Your Handicrafts,* David McKay Co., Inc., 1953.

Lukowitz, Joseph J., *Interesting Art-Metal Work,* The Bruce Publishing Co., 1947.

Martin, Charles James, *How to Make Modern Jewelry,* Doubleday, 1960.

Morton, Philip, *Contemporary Jewelry,* Holt, Rinehart and Winston, 1970.

Nelson, Norbert, *Selling Your Crafts,* Van Nostrand Reinhold Co., 1967.

Pack, Greta, *Jewelry and Enameling,* D. Van Nostrand Co., 1947.

Rose, Augustus Foster, *Jewelry Making and Design,* Dover, 1967.

Shoenfelt, Joseph F., *Designing and Making Handwrought Jewelry,* McGraw-Hill, 1963.

Von Newmann, Robert, *The Design and Creation of Jewelry,* Chilton Co., 1961.

Wiener, Louis, *Hand Made Jewelry, A Manual of Techniques,* D. Van Nostrand Co., 1948.

Wilson, H., *Silverwork and Jewelry,* Pitman Publishing Corp., 1948.

CHAPTER XVII–THE BLACKSMITH

Art in Iron: The American Ironsmith Magazine, 1932–1934.

Bacon, John Lord, *Forge Practice,* Braunworth and Co., 1919.

Bealer, Alex W., *The Art of Blacksmithing,* Funk & Wagnalls, 1969.

The Blacksmith, London, Rural Industries Bureau, 1959.

Bollinger, Thomas Walter, *Elemental Wrought Iron,* The Bruce Publishing Co., 1930.

D'Allemagne, Henry Rene, *Decorative Antique Ironwork,* Dover Publications, Inc. 1968, from the 1924 French catalogue of the Secq des Tournelles Museum of Rouen.

Decorative Iron Work, London: Rural Industries Bureau, 1964.

Encyclopaedia Britannica, "Forging" and "Iron and Steel," 1910.

Encyclopedia of Iron Work, Weyhe, 1927.

Examples of Metal Work, Boston Architectural Club, 1930.

Hart, Robert, *How to Sell Your Handicrafts,* David McKay Co., Inc., 1953.

Holmstrom, J. G., *Modern Blacksmithing,* Fred J. Drake and Co., 1904.

Hughes, Thomas P., *Forging and Heat Treatment of Steel,* Burgess-Roseberry Co., 1930.

Jenkins, J. Geraint, *Traditional Country Craftsmen,* Frederick A. Praeger, 1966.

Jones, Lynn C., *Forging and Smithing,* The Century Co., 1924.

Naujohs, Waldemar, *Forging Handbook,* The American Society for Metals, 1939.

Nelson, Norbert, *Selling Your Crafts,* Van Nostrand Reinhold Co., 1967.

Pehoski, Joe, *Blacksmithing for the Home Craftsman,* Grand Island, Nebraska, 1973 (privately printed).

Richardson, M. T., *Practical Blacksmithing,* 4 vols., M. T. Richardson Co., 1901.

Schwarzkopf, Ernest, *Plain and Ornamental Forging,* M. T. Richardson Co., 1919.

Selvidge, Robert Washington, *Blacksmithing: A Manual for Use in School and Shop,* The Manual Arts Press, 1925.

Selvidge, Robert Washington, and Allton, J. M., *Blacksmithing,* Manual Arts Press, 1925.

Smith, J. R. Bradley, *Blacksmith's and Farrier's Tools at Shelburne Museum,* Shelburne, Vt., The Shelburne Museum, Inc., 1966.

Stribling, Thomas Sigismund, *The Forge,* Sun Dial Press, 1938.

United States Army, *The Blacksmith and Welder,* War Department, 1941.

Weygers, Alexander G., *The Making of Tools,* Van Nostrand Reinhold Co., 1973.

Weygers, Alexander G., *The Modern Blacksmith,* Van Nostrand Reinhold Co., 1974.
Wrought Iron Railings, Doors and Gates, London, Iliffe, 1966.
Wrought Iron Work, London, Rural Industries Bureau, 1961.

CHAPTER XVIII—THE GLASSBLOWER AND LAMPWORKER

Burton, John, *Glass: Philosophy and Method,* Chilton Book Co., 1967.
Hammesfahr, James E., *Creative Glass Blowing,* W. H. Freeman, 1968.
Hart, Robert, *How To Sell Your Handicrafts,* David McKay Co., Inc., 1953.
Johnson, William Harding, *The Ceramic Arts,* The Macmillan Co., 1942.
Kinney, Kay, *Glasscraft,* Chilton Co., 1962.
Nelson, Norbert, *Selling Your Crafts,* Van Nostrand Reinhold Co., 1967.
Schuler, Frederic, *Glassforming,* Chilton Book Co., 1970.

CHAPTER XIX—THE LEATHERWORKER

Cox, Charles W., *Adventures in Leathercraft,* J. W. Walch, 1959.
Groneman, Chris Harold, *Applied Leathercraft,* The Manual Arts Press, 1942.
Hart, Robert, *How To Sell Your Handicrafts,* David McKay Co., Inc., 1953.
Nelson, Norbert, *Selling Your Crafts,* Van Nostrand Reinhold Co., 1967.
Thompson, Robert Long, *Leathercraft,* D. Van Nostrand Co., 1948.
Waterer, John William, *Leather Craftsmanship,* Praeger, 1968.

CHAPTER XX—THE FURNITURE MAKER

Cherner, Norman, *How to Build Children's Toys and Furniture,* McGraw-Hill, 1954.
Feirzr, John Louis, *Advanced Woodwork and Furniture Making,* C. A. Bennett Co., 1954.
Gottshall, Franklin H., *How to Make Colonial Furniture,* Bruce Publishing Co., 1971.
Hart, Robert, *How to Sell Your Handicrafts,* David McKay Co., Inc., 1953.
Honour, Hugh, *Cabinet Makers and Furniture Designs,* Putnam, 1969.
Hooper, Rodney, *Modern Furniture Making and Design,* The Manual Arts Press, 1939.
Joyce, Ernest, *Encyclopedia of Furniture Making,* Drake Publications, 1970.
Katz, Laszlo, *The Art of Woodworking and Furniture Appreciation,* New York, P. F. C. Woodworking, Inc., 1971.
Nelson, Norbert, *Selling Your Crafts,* Van Nostrand Reinhold Co., 1967.

O'Hare, Eugene, *How to Make Your Own Furniture,* Harper & Brothers, 1941.

Pelton, B., *Furniture Making and Cabinet Work,* 1949.

Schutge, Rolf, *Making Modern Furniture,* Reinhold, 1967.

CHAPTER XXI—THE WOODCARVER

Carstenson, Cecil C., *The Craft and Creation of Wood Sculpture,* Scribner, 1971.

Cox, Charles W., *Adventures in Woodcraft,* Walch, 1959.

Dank, Michael Carlton, *Creative Crafts in Wood,* The Manual Arts Press, 1945.

Durst, Alan Lydiate, *Woodcarving,* Studio Publications, 1959.

Fawlkner, Herbert Waldron, *Woodcarving as a Hobby,* Harper, 1934.

Gross, Chaim, *The Technique of Wood Sculpture,* ARCO Publishing Co., 1957.

Hanover, Elsie U., *Handbook of Woodcarving & Whittling,* A. S. Barnes, 1967.

Hart, Robert, *How to Sell Your Handicrafts,* David McKay Co., Inc., 1953.

Hunt, Walter Bernard, *Contemporary Carving & Whittling,* Bruce Publishing Co., 1967.

Jack, George, *Woodcarving: Design & Workmanship,* A. S. Barnes & Co., 1934.

Manning, Frank, *Creative Chip Carving,* Carlton Press, 1967.

Mason, Bernard Sterling, *Woodcraft,* A. S. Barnes & Co., 1939.

Meilach, Dona Z., *Contemporary Art with Wood,* Crown Publishers, 1968.

Nelson, Norbert, *Selling Your Crafts,* Van Nostrand Reinhold Co., 1967.

Norman, Percival Edward, *Sculpture in Wood,* Transatlantic Arts, 1966.

Rood, John *Sculpture in Wood,* University of Minnesota Press, 1950.

Rottger, Ernst, *Creative Wood Design,* Reinhold Publishers Corp., 1961.

CHAPTER XXII—THE MUSICAL INSTRUMENT MAKER

Bate, Philip, *The Flute,* W. W. Norton, 1969.

Bessarotoff, Nicholas, *Ancient European Musical Instruments,* Harvard University Press, 1941.

Common, Alfred F., *How to Repair Violins and Other Musical Instruments,* W. Reeves, n.d.

Cooper, Robert S., *Lute Construction.* Savannah, Georgia, 1963 (privately printed).

Heron-Allen, E., *Violin Making As It Was and Is,* Ward Lock (pref. 1885).

Ridge, Eric V., *The Birth of a Guitar*, Pembridge House, The Park, Cheetenham (Gloucester), England, n.d.

Robinson, Trevor, *The Amateur Wind Instrument Maker*, University of Massachusetts Press, 1973.

Sharpe, A. P., *Make Your Own Guitar* (available through H. L. Wild, 510 East 11th Street, New York, New York 10009).

Sloane, Irving, *Classic Guitar Construction*, E. P. Dutton, 1966.

Sloane, Irving, *Guitar Repair*, E. P. Dutton, 1973.

Young, Thomas Campbell, *The Making of Musical Instruments*, Oxford University Press, 1939.

CHAPTER XXIII–THE CANDLEMAKER

Hart, Robert, *How to Sell Your Handicrafts*, David McKay Co., Inc., 1953.

Nelson, Norbert, *Selling Your Crafts*, Van Nostrand Reinhold Co., 1967.

Young, Jean, *The Woodstock Craftsman's Manual*, Praeger Publishers, New York, 1972.

CHAPTER XXIV–APPLYING THE ARTISTIC MIND TO NEW MATERIALS IN THE FUTURE

Borglund, Erland, *Working in Plastic, Bone, Amber and Horn*, Reinhold Book Corp., 1968.

Fisher, Edwin George, *Blow Moulding of Plastics*, Published for Plastics Institute by Lliffe, 1971.

Hart, Robert, *How to Sell Your Handicrafts*, David McKay Co., Inc., 1953.

Johnson, William Harding, *The Ceramic Arts*, The Macmillan Co., 1942.

Lappin, Alvin R., *Plastic Projects & Techniques*, McKnight & McKnight Publishing Co., 1965.

McLeod, James Harold, *New Materials in Sculpture for Church Furnishings*, University of Georgia Press, 1970.

Nelson, Norbert, *Selling Your Crafts*, Van Nostrand Reinhold Co., 1967.

Newman, Thelma R., *Plastics as an Art Form*, Chilton Books, 1964.

Newman, Thelma R., *Plastics as Design Form*, Chilton Book Co., 1972.

Roukes, Nicholas, *Crafts in Plastics*, Watson-Guptill Publications, 1970.

Smith, Lura, *Resin and Glass Artcraft for Flower Arrangers and Craftsmen*, M. Barrows, W. Morrow, 1966.

Index